SERMONS

PREACHED IN

MEMORIAL CHURCH, BALTIMORE,

BY

REV. OCTAVIUS PERINCHIEF.

EDITED BY

CHARLES LANMAN.

NEW YORK:
D. APPLETON & CO.
1870.

INTRODUCTORY CORRESPONDENCE.

BALTIMORE, *June* 15, 1870.

MY DEAR SIR:

It is known to you that the Rev. Octavius Perinchief became the Rector of "Memorial Church," of this city, last autumn. When he accepted the call, it was believed his health was permanently restored; but a few months of ardent devotion to his duties, developed too plainly the unwelcome truth, that he was physically unequal to the work involved in his charge. The congregation, which, under his brief ministry, had largely increased, would gladly have made any sacrifice to retain him, under an arrangement by which his preaching might alone have been enjoyed. But his sense of duty precluded the consummation of any such arrangement; hence, a separation became an inevitable result.

Only those who have enjoyed his ministry, can realize the loss sustained by the separation. Realizing this, there exists on the part of our congregation, an earnest desire to possess, in permanent form, the treasures of thought and feeling, which distinguish his pulpit discourses.

Knowing your intimate relations with Mr. Perinchief

as a literary friend, and the fact that you edited a volume of his Sermons, delivered in Georgetown, D. C., it has occurred to me, to solicit your aid in obtaining his consent to the publication of an edition of his Baltimore Sermons. By doing this, you will not only gratify a large number of his friends and admirers, but confer a lasting benefit upon all into whose hands they may chance to fall. I venture to hope that my suggestion may have your favorable consideration.

Your obt. servant,

JOHN S. REESE.

CHARLES LANMAN, ESQ.,

Etc., etc.

GEORGETOWN, D. C., *June* 25, 1870.

MY DEAR SIR :

I duly received your letter, and rejoice to inform you that I have corresponded with Mr. Perinchief, and he consents to the publication of another volume of his Sermons. He has placed a collection in my hands, and a portion of them will at once be given to the printer. As was the case when I looked over the Georgetown Sermons, it has puzzled me to select, where all were so full of soul-saving wisdom, but I have rather given preference to the more practical productions. As I recall the effect of his preaching, founded alone upon the life and death of the Infinite Redeemer, in the several parishes where he has labored, I can only the more deeply regret that, under a wise Providence, he could not have been blessed with an ample store of physical health.

In justice to Mr. Perinchief, I ought to add, that he will not be able to revise the Sermons, nor examine the proofs, on account of his removal to the country parish of Bridgeport, on the river Schuylkill, so that the responsibility of seeing them correctly printed will necessarily rest with me. But I shall do my best. I congratulate the good people of Memorial Church on the prospect of having a new volume of his Sermons; and I can assure you that their great kindness to Mr. Perinchief has taken a very firm hold upon his heart.

With high regard,

Yours very truly,

CHARLES LANMAN.

JOHN S. REESE, ESQ.,

Baltimore, Maryland.

CONTENTS.

SERMONS.

THE SPIRIT-ELEMENTS.

MATTHEW 22: 37, 38.—Jesus said unto him, Thou shalt love the Lord thy God with all thy heart, and with all thy soul, and with all thy mind. This is the first and great commandment.

THE times in which the Saviour lived, were times very similar to our own. Perhaps this is the same thing as saying that all times are very much alike. Still, there are times in which the world reaches certain special crises, and these crises bring into clearer view prominent resemblances. That age, like ours, was an age of great *mental* activity, and that means *universal* activity. It was an age of earnest inquiry, except where it was thought there was no need of inquiry, and that was where the power of a wise inquiry was lost—where everything was settled, as among the Jewish doctors.

Our text occurs in a chapter which brings before us one of those battle-days of Christ—those fearful encounters in which all darkness ran point-blank against all light. No sooner is one charge repulsed than another begins. "When the Pharisees heard that the

Sadducees were put to silence, *they* were gathered together," entrenched behind a narrow, one-sided creed—confident of their own strength—trusting in the power of a cold, dim, misguided reason—a lawyer, a man versed in the letter of Scripture, asks Christ which is the "great commandment in the law?" The Saviour, quoting partly from Deuteronomy, (the lawyer's own law-book,) replies: "Thou shalt love the Lord thy God with all thy heart, and with all thy soul, and with all thy mind. This is the first and great commandment."

I wish to take these words of our Master to-day and make them, by God's blessing, the occasion to us of a wider and deeper comprehension of our duty toward ourselves and toward God; or, in other words, of a better understanding and use of time and this present life, preparatory to eternity and eternal life.

It was no foolish question which the Jew asked, although he might have asked it foolishly: "What is the first and great commandment?"—What is the grand essential of religion? Fully to answer that is to answer—What is God? what is man? what is life? The Saviour does so respond as in His wonderful wisdom to answer all these. The wonderfulness of the answer will appear only to those of us who have reflected much upon the poverty of human language in expressing any soul-verities. In the presence of great soul-experience we are struck dumb. Language is for the earth; for gross and outward things. When we come to apply it to soul-vision, we have to use the same word for many different things. The thoughtless cannot get beyond the outward, and so the letter often killeth. The thoughtful only understand, because they *are* thoughtful; because they are *in the spirit*, which giveth life.

We are all familiar with this creature we call man; but perhaps, if *we* were asked what man is, no two of us would give precisely the same definition. If a being from another world, who knew not man, were here to-day seeking information, under all our answers he would grow confused, and perhaps conclude we did not ourselves know what man is. In some senses *man* means the race—then it means man and *woman*. Again, it means a human being of the male sex only. Then man means an animal; he is a biped; erect; he laughs. Again, he is an intellectual, social animal—he is a neighbor, an artizan, a tradesman, a scholar. Again, man has a soul; he knows there is such a thing as right and wrong. In short, a book could not exhaust all that is contained under that term "*man*." So with the term *soul*. What is soul? Five thousand years have been trying to tell us, and we do not yet know. You perceive, anything we look upon is not a simple existence, but a *complex* existence. Any term we use expresses, according to the grasp of the mind that employs it. All terms at first come from things outward. It is only as man advances he is able to attach deeper and spiritual meanings. Now in religious matters and for religious purposes, we speak of man as *body and soul;* or spirit as mortal and immortal.

But the *spirit* of man like everything else is complex. The Saviour, in the text, gives us the three constituent elements of the spirit—the three-fold function or power called spirit—the *trinity*, which makes the spirit-unity. These three—"*the heart, the soul, the mind*"—embrace the perfect spirit. They are the spirit—not any *one* merely, but all together—and these, under equal and harmonious development, will lead us to, or produce in us, a true service of God, this very love which is life.

You perceive, first of all, these three things constitute or characterize *man.* Man is an animal; that is true, but not merely that, nor mainly that; he has a nature in addition to that—something which lifts him out of the animal level into the plane of intellect, *or spirit.* Man is a *loving* being, or a being with heart. He is a being distinguishing *right from wrong,* or a being with soul. He is a reasoning being, or a being with mind. Now, unfortunately, we separate these elements—we divide the spirit, and view one part as the whole; we aim at developing one part without the other; we act with extreme unreason, and therefore come to disappointment. Suppose the growth of the *body* were left to an ignorant parent. The body is also a complexity. There is leg and arm—there is eye and ear—there are heart and lungs. One or other of these would appear supremely important, according to the view of the parent. Imagine the arm brought to its full development on the body of a babe. *What would it be good for?* Imagine a head of full size, to be supplied with blood from an infant's lungs. Do you see how every unity must be indeed a unity—how a failure in one part is a failure in every part? How there must be uniform growth; or partial growth, but little better than none at all? *This is what we forget in religion.* The spirit also is a unit—one part dependent upon all the rest. We, however, in speaking of *love,* connect it exclusively with *the heart,* supposing if a man exercise some sort of an affection toward God, he is religious, forgetting that the heart can only be safely and fully active, as it responds in its proportions to soul and mind.

The term "heart" is used to express certain facts which are matters of experience. We have an affectional, emotional element within us, something that yearns, and clings, and endures—something which feels relieved in the simple exercise of feeling. In the original language, I think, the term is often used for *consciousness*—the inner self. The child *feels* it toward the parent; the parent *feels* it toward the child; it is instinctive, involuntary. Under the influences of the Holy Ghost, who dwells with every man, through the atonement of Christ, men feel this toward God, and God exercises it toward men. It is this which makes a religion a fact in all lands. In the order of nature heart everywhere comes first. We find it in *birds* toward their young, and in lower animals where there is no higher instinct. We find it in uncivilized man, as in the Indians; they have a sense of God and of his goodness, but no moral code. It is as we come up to half-civilized, Pagan and heathen nations we get to moral codes, and last of all we come to real mind in what is called *civilization*. So in each individual. The little child *loves;* it afterwards begins to discover between right and wrong, and finally to think. If you say belief comes first, inasmuch as every nation has a belief or creed, the offspring of mind, I should say, *no*, not so much belief or creed as just this unquestioning acceptance of fact: *there is a God*. Just as the child accepts the parent and loves, asking nothing about it, or so far as it asks, asking only according to its general development. It is this heart-element out of which men feel there is a God; feel He is pure and holy; feel He ought to be worshiped; feel *they should* be pure and holy, and through this in development reach the perception that they are impure and unholy. You observe, it does not teach a man what is right nor what is wrong. The Indian indulges revenge, and as men always do, projects his own being upon God, and judges Him by that, or ascribes that being to Him—not having mind-culture enough to see, that revenge in God would be impossible. Hence creeds are always changing, and *feeling* is modified according to *general* culture. Heart is *simply feeling*. Left to this alone, the mother gives her child just what it should never have, and keeps from it just what it ought to have. Left to this alone, the devotee will throw himself beneath the wheels of a Juggernaut, with as much devotion as a martyr will go to the stake. Left to this alone, all sorts of absurdities and extravagancies are indulged in the name of religion; all sorts of creeds are sustained. Sometimes in viewing life under these manifestations, men tell you "see what belief will do;" "what men believe;" but you perceive these things are *not out of* ANY BELIEF. They are out of all real unbelief. It is abandonment of two-thirds of their being. It is a long arm swinging upon an infant body. It is a heart over which presides no brain. Still it is an element—it is the first element—an essential element of spirit. *Wherever it is certainly dormant, the man is certainly dead.* It must be awakened. It is the first part of the spirit to awake, but when once it is awakened, we should not rest content with simply that. Thus the object of the Gospel is not simply *to convert*—a thing we often forget, but to build man up, build the race up, in true God-likeness—into the full restoration of the God-image, once obliterated by sin.

We must go on to the development of *soul*. This word soul, while often used as a synonym for the whole spirit—*heart and soul and mind*—is here used as expressive of only one part, what we often distinctively call, the *moral* part of man. This function of the spirit it is which *wills*, which makes the *you* or the *me*, which determines what we call character, fixes our place as honorable or dishonorable, useful or useless—in short, moral or immoral. You see the spirit is a three-sided prism; you never turn it round and look at the second side. You see, you come now to where, when a man claims to be religious, other men hold him up and ask whether his religion makes him honest. *Soul* is that faculty by which we grasp moral obligation. We sometimes call it the "*moral sense.*" It distinguishes for us the right or the wrong. Because this is part of the spirit, its existence is co-extensive with heart and mind, but it is later in development. For the want of its proper culture we have so many *wrong* things in religious history. It was out of the absence of this the Jews asked Christ, why He cured a sick woman on the Sabbath day. It was the absence of *mind* which made it true, that hearing they did not understand. It was absence of this soul which made it true, "that seeing they did not perceive." It is the absence of this which makes our religion so often more of a fear than of a joy. People are very often afraid to do things, the right or wrong of which they have no conception. A Romanist will not eat a piece of meat on Friday. A Jew would starve, and so virtually commit suicide, before he would eat a piece of pork, attaching right and wrong when right and wrong do not adhere, at the same time doing many wicked and cruel things, without ever reflecting that they are wicked or cruel. It is the absence of this which turns religion into superstition; which makes us so constantly demand that everybody shall feel as we do, act as we act. It is absence of this which accounts for the fact, that under religious feeling or fervor we have inquisitions and dungeons for the best men that live, in our *heart* limiting *soul* and *mind.* It is the absence of this which turns enthusiasm into fanaticism. Fanaticism is feeling without soul or mind, a ship without rudder or freight, a delusive and dangerous thing. This soul, or will, or moral sense is the second in the order of development. You can teach your child to love you without much teaching, but you must labor diligently to enable him to distinguish between right and wrong. But in proportion as you teach him *that,* his love, his affection, all his emotional being will be refined, deepened, so that the love wherewith you love your aged parent is transcendently deeper and holier than the love wherewith your little child loves you.

But to cultivate this you must have the culture of a higher element still: you must bring in the *mind. Now* you know what the mind is. We sometimes call it reason; sometimes intellect. It is that faculty which produces thought, reflection, cogitation. It is that faculty which goes out and asks questions of all things that are: *Why* they are? *What* they are? What their mutual relations? What their specific forces? It is this in your child which so often puzzles you. It is this which in religion, upon the principle of dividing what God has not divided, religious people and Christians as well, have been in the habit of *ignoring, denouncing.* In reality it is the *grandest,* if we *could compare* things essential, *the* grandest faculty man has. It is the controlling faculty. It lifts man above the child, above the savage, above uncivilization and half civilization. It is this, in Jesus Christ,—I will not say more than anything else, but co-equal with all the rest in Him,—against which the gates of darkness have not been able to prevail. It is this which gives us science, knowledge, all that lifts human life above brute life—that makes society, which alone is human, a blessing, and which abounds most, only where Jesus is; a fact which is very natural, for a true cultivation of one part is a corresponding cultivation of every other part. Wherever this is *not*, uncultured man is barbarous. Men are barbarous in proportion as it is uncultured. No religion of any high degree can exist without it. The Christian religion is the best religion, because it appeals to this—gives it its highest and freest exercise—demands its development. Our Protestant religion is the purest and best of all things called religion—brings all blessing, all culture—the highest civilization, because it gives this mind the greatest scope—opportunity for untrammeled action. *I know Christians have resisted it.* We can none of us forget the struggle all light has had. The Printing Press, Chemistry, Astronomy, Geology—what a struggle! But you see it was the *misfortune* of the religion which resisted it, that it was not better. Do you see how we are unblessed, in proportion as *any* part of the spirit is asleep? "Oh," we say, "those days have gone by. They were days of darkness." Are we in the full light? The ages which resisted, while doing it in the very name of religion, we can now see were neither truly *affectional* nor truly *moral.* Zeal was without knowledge and morals were everywhere debased—a clear illustration in itself that we are well off only in proportion as the spirit is evenly and co-extensively developed. It must then begin to appear to you, why Jesus lays such emphasis here. This love—such love—is the first and great commandment.

Now we have spoken of these faculties as separate—as having an order. This is merely by accommodation. The lines which limit the zones upon our earth, do not divide the earth. They are only imaginary. So with these distinctions we have made this morning. Most men put mind-culture as the lowest thing in religion. I put it as the absolutely highest thing in religion; or rather, it is folly to put it highest or lowest. It is co-equal. Neglect heart and you have *atheism.* Neglect soul and you have wrong and vice. Neglect mind and you have Rome. Neglect one or the other, and you lose so much of Christ. I know the illiterate believer is better off than the gifted unbeliever. And what a blessing it is that the child and the peasant can come to Christ. But is it better to be *all* children and *all* peasants, or *always* children and *always* peasants? This *mind* is the last to reach a high development. It is only now that this race is learning truly to think. It is not the boy, but the mature man who knows how to think. But I say we err in making these distinctions. Our part can only grow as every other part grows, and wherever you find a highly developed religious character—I mean a character which stands the analysis of time—you find all three of them together. Take Moses, a man of profound *feeling*, the author of a *moral* code which has challenged the admiration of the ages—a man of stupendous intellect. Take David, and Daniel, and Elijah—all the prophets and seers. These three things must stand combined, and do stand combined and co-equal. Then an intellect, without morals and a warm, emotional, affectional nature,—in other words, a *mind* without soul and heart, is a cold, repulsive thing, with two-thirds of itself paralyzed. A *moral man,* without affection, gratitude, humility, and without *brains,* is the most disgusting and helpless being in the universe. A *heart,* without soul and mind, is a ranting, and tearing, and destructive engine, beating the air—narrow in all its aims and thoughts—re-acting, perhaps more than any thing else, upon the merely moral man and the merely intellectual man, and so producing what we call *infidelity.* Heart and soul and mind *must go together,* and then you get a being noble, exalted; a creature such as God loves and a creature who will love God. You get from any one only as it is aided by all the rest. It is the even activity of all three of these spirit-elements which alone makes *Wisdom,* a word often used, especially in the Bible, for *religion.* These three things will give us true belief, true worship, and true life. We shall be happy because wise, and happy and wise because truly religious. We shall discharge our duty toward God and toward man, and that is the sum of the law and the prophets. It is these rallying around God, striving for the good, that make love, and these three, loving, that make religion. In them is no end of all true blessing.

Now, I shall not say that a man who has only religious fervor is not better off than he who is indifferent to all religion. I shall not say that a moral man is worse than an immoral man. I shall not say that a man with mind-culture is worse than an ignorant man. Not at all. I thank God when I find a man cultured in either, and I feel ashamed when I find a man more cultured in either than I am myself. But I say this: if man can be a good Christian, with little or no mind-culture, he can be a great deal better Christian *with* mind-culture. A ship saved without her rudder is a good deal better than a ship sunk; but a ship saved with her rudder is not only saved, but she is a ship. A man of much heart, but of low morals and no mind-culture, may and will enjoy God. He will find much he can appropriate in God's blessed word. But there will be a thousand precious things in that word he cannot see. "With what measure ye mete *it* shall be measured to you again." All I contend for is *the three together.* As they are mutually dependent, so they are mutually helpful. The man with religious fervor will have higher morals and more mind than he would have had without religious fervor; but let him have all three, and he is truly a Christian.

I bring these thoughts to you to-day, brethren, because I feel, after much observation and deliberation, that the Church is making now substantially the same mistake she has so constantly made, in spite of all Christ was, of all He did, of all He said. We are making the mistake of dealing with, and cultivating *only* the heart, stimulating mere feeling, creating only *emotion,* which may be as often unwise as wise, from the simple fact that we do aim only at that. This mistake has *two general* consequences—consequences extremely disastrous—first, of placing religion in apparent antagonism to science and all pure thought, which is a sin, and committed with the same feeling that inaugurated and sustained the Inquisition,—men sincere enough, but as unwise as they were sincere; and second, of considering morals a matter of secondary importance. Two lines of absolute facts grew out of these consequences—first, that many moral and mind-cultured men are over upon the side of infidelity—*i. e.*, so far as they are not upon the side of the Church; and second, the general tone of morals even in the Christian Church—if not extremely low—is far from being as high as it should be. The pauper and vicious classes of society are increasing, giving rise to problems we know not how to solve. Yes! this mistake has other consequences. By aiming at the heart, as the *whole spirit* of man, much of our effort is thrown away, being too high for the apprecia- tion of the masses, they needing help like that the Saviour gave the Samaritan leper, before they can come back and drink in the deeper and diviner things of God. This mistake shuts us out from many fields of labor— many questions of moral and social science—in isolated, technically religious exertion, where wide and united benevolent and truly Christian enterprise would produce wider and happier results. Another consequence still is, that by aiming at what we call the heart, exclusively, Christian preaching is reduced almost exclusively to what we call exhortation, to what appears to many, a doleful monotony of thought, or want of thought, often an invitation of feeling, rather than feeling itself--an *artificial* sentiment, if a sentiment at all. A wide range of grand and highly useful subjects is kept from our pulpits, and multitudes of cultivated men and women are kept from our churches, giving rise to all sorts of ecclesiastic *questions*, because to extreme ecclesiastic *practices*, ritualism itself being only an attempt of anx- ious and otherwise good men to bring people to what they call the worship of God, forgetting that while they do it they may be crushing out two-thirds of their being.

But I bring these thoughts to you to-day because I

believe the Christian Church is now entering upon a struggle, harder than any she has ever encountered. The struggle will be fierce to the Church, not so much from the strength outside as from the apathy and weakness inside. The battles of God have never been fought with mere feeling. Excitement produced the crusades, but the crusades were mere excitement. The Christians, in the first battles of Christianity, had merely *the assertion of facts* for their work. It is true, they were amazing facts—facts that created morals and mind—facts of which morals and mind were the great defences. The struggles since, have been each after its kind, till we come now to where the facts themselves are to be explained, not merely asserted—where they are to be applied, not to mere individuals, but to man in the mass, to the multitudes for whom God intended them. The struggle is outside the Church, not so much against old truths as against old dead forms, against ceremony, the make-believe truth. Indeed, the world is rather asking for more truth—a livelier application of all truth. Because so many in the Church rest upon their forms, they think if the forms go, religion is gone, and when the forms do go, many lose the faith they thought they had. From them that had not is taken away what they seemed to have. In England the struggle at present is worse than it is with us. But here it is already thickening. Unhappily we stand so divided, each with some little ism of his own, no part of the real faith, and really a trifle at last. So occupied are we with this, that light passes us by, or if it is arrested by us at all, it is arrested by us in complaint. We often resist what we ought to attract, and attract what ought to be repelled. Thus we are defeating our own object, and the Church hinders what the Church was designed to promote. We do not need anything new, except it be a renewed understanding of all that is old. There is our weakness. We want a stronger grasp of the truths of Christ, and when I speak to you about mind-culture, as I do, I do not mean a power of hair-splitting argument—a knowledge of all the philosophies—an elaboration of tiresome doctrine—an assertion of dogma. Not at all. That is not the tendency of our times, nor would it be desirable even if it were. As I have shown you, a religion which is *only* philosophical is not religion; but so also a religion which is *un*philosophical is not religion. What I mean by mind-culture is *power to think*—meditation—cogitation—power to combine, eliminate, and harmonize—power to harmonize one part of Scripture with another—power to separate small and trivial things from eternal and essential things—power to receive a new thought. What I contend for, is just this that Christ tells us, the loving God with all the *heart* and all *the soul* and *all the mind*. What I complain of is, that with a great deal of Christian fervor, the world forces its morals upon the Church rather than that the Church imposes high Christian morals upon the world; with a great deal of religious fervor there is a great deal of mind-unculture—a great deal of wasted time—of wasted talent—of dwarfed manhood. The Bible is rich in precious thought—Jesus is infinite in far-reaching truth, which is hidden from our eyes.

We live upon the surface. Christians support more trifles than any *class* of people. What I would impress upon you is, that your spirit is a unit. It is *heart* and soul and mind, and if you are dwarfed in one you are dwarfed in all. You may have no time for thinking—

you may have neglected it so long as not to know how to think—then I would say to you, as Jesus says to us all, "What shall it profit a man, if he gain the whole world and lose his own soul." You think that applies to sinners—oh, my brother, it applies to you—it applies to me. You cannot waste one hour, nor one day, nor one faculty God has given you, except as you are to answer for it at the bar of the eternal. You think I make salvation hard; but did any wise man ever make it otherwise? Do I not make it just what Jesus made it? Let me exhort you, brethren, to dwell more with Jesus. There is our fault, we do not live enough with Him. You that are young—you that are old, especially—think of these words: "Thou shalt love the Lord thy God with all thy heart, and with all thy soul, and with all thy mind." Ask what they mean? They are the first and great commandment. Around it all truth revolves—upon it depends all safety. Study it and practice it as you would be an heir of God and a joint heir with Christ—as you would comprehend with all saints what is the breadth and depth and length and height—as you would know the love of Christ which passeth knowledge—as you would be filled with all the fullness of God.

SELF-CONTROL.

ROMANS 12: 18.—If it be possible, as much as lieth in you, live peaceably with all men.

OUTSIDE the Sermon upon the Mount, it would be difficult to find a collection of wiser, practical precepts than those contained within this part of St. Paul's Epistle to the Romans. To combine them in one character would be to create a character of exalted excellence—to make a noble Christian manifestation. It is a chapter worthy of its place—running through these Sundays of the Epiphany. In all Paul's reasoning he never forgets that we are creatures who have to deal with common life in an ugly world. Man is not more an individual than he is a being for society. Indeed, the value of a man's individuality is determined by his social relations. The man in the combinations of family, neighborhood, commerce, expresses his manhood. Domestic, social, and civil relations are the tests of his courage, his honor, his humanity. But for these relations the nobler qualities could hardly find expression—the finer qualities of mercy, sympathy, benevolence, could not exist. But for them *wisdom* could not exist, for wisdom is not what a man knows, nor what he thinks, but what he does, and what he is. The hermit who never speaks, nor is spoken to, does not know whether he has a good disposition or a bad one. The man who never had a trust committed to him does not know whether he is honest or not. The shoulder that never carried a burden is very likely, for that simple reason, to be a weak one. It is a true saying that nobody knows what he will do till he is tried. That we may all have some knowledge of ourselves, God has set us down in a world where trial is inevitable. This is the meaning of life. We may talk as we please about crosses and sorrows and troubles; it would be impossible to attain to the very idea of the thing we call virtue without them. In their absence, virtue itself would be unattainable. If there were no storms and no fogs and icebergs, a boy could take a Cunarder across the ocean. If there were no sickness, the science of medicine and the skill of the physician would be unknown. If houses never burnt down, and robbers never came, and all men were honest and honorable, some of us could be more successful in business. If all men were purely patriotic—if there were no such thing as faction, no men who preyed upon the vitals of the community, municipal and civil government would be easy. If there were no such things as cold and hunger and ignorance, we should want no houses and clothes and food and fuel and books. But, then, it would be difficult to tell what would be left of life, or what that life which was left would be worth. Idleness would be as good as industry, and ignorance as knowledge. The truth is, nature is built upon paradoxes. *Order* is the resultant of resisting forces. Any fixed point is the center of antagonisms. There may be a preference of agencies, but God puts all agencies to some use.

As a social and moral being, in a world of antagonisms, there is a sense in which man *cannot*, and *ought* not, if he could, live peaceably with all men. There is such a thing as ignorance. There is such a thing as error. There is such a thing as vice and wickedness. They each have their high priests—their sleepless advocates. They are aggressive. Their aggression is worse than a pestilence. To give over a struggle against them is to give over self-existence. Moral life is granted only on condition that we struggle for it. We can make no treaty with ignorance and error. Vice and wickedness in reality do not expect it of us. They instinctively know and bow to the supremacy of right and virtue. The devils that confronted the Saviour always instantly recognized *Him*, and His authority. The evil spirits will always make great outcry: "Why art Thou come hither to torment us?" But they never expect compromise or toleration; they *know* they ought to be tormented. Wherever we stop to parley with them they are themselves surprised. But once stop, and they are insatiable as death. They lay hold of every advantage and become clamorous. There are vices in our cities—wickednesses organized, which are amazed that they can exist; and yet, because we have allowed them to exist, they actually get to talking of their rights--think they have a right to be.

But possibly all vice and wickedness are only extreme degrees of ignorance and error. It is ignorance and error which are forever craving indulgence. They are determined not to be dispossessed. To point a finger at them, to raise even a flaw of suspicion against them, is to create enmity and strife. If you wish to get an enemy, you have only to strive nobly to do a man a moral good. If you wish to get an enemy try to do your duty. If you wish to raise a cry try to pull errors out of people. Men dwell in ignorance and error, like the Barons of the middle ages in their castles.

They have their host of retainers. If they sally forth it is to war. But they are in the way of civilization. Their existence is disintegration, decay, the paralysis of all good. They *must* be resisted. The serpent-head must be *bruised*. But, then, he who bruises it will be bitten. Only nobleness and piety and all virtue will undertake it. But that is the test of nobleness and virtue and piety that it should—that it does. The fact that a man has enemies is therefore no evidence that he is a bad man. It is presumptive evidence sometimes of the very reverse. The noblest men have fallen victims to mortal rage. Wicked and cruel hands crucified the Son of God. It was impossible that He should live peaceably with such men. His conflict He left behind Him, and this is what He meant when He said He had come to send not *peace* but a sword. Plainly, therefore, in the nature of things it is impossible to live peaceably with all men. The only thing to be sure of, is, on which side you are. You can always tell which side you are on, by ascertaining whether you are acting like Christ, and being treated as He was—or whether you are being treated like the Jews, and acting as they did.

My impression is, however, this is not exactly the ground the Apostle meant to cover in this text. When he says, "If it be possible, as much as lieth in you," I think he means that we should look *in*wardly rather than *out*wardly—more to ourselves than to others—that more is possible than we are apt to imagine. Even admitting that there are cross and ill-natured people—for beyond all doubt there are—there are people who seem to have been created for no other purpose than to create strife—people whose constituent elements seem to be wormwood, and pepper and vinegar, whose eye and ear are eager for deformity and discord—whose tongue is sharper than a two-edged sword. There are persons so selfish they exact absolute deference to their whims and ill tempers—people who never consider either the comforts or the rights of others—people to whom modesty and generosity and self-denial are unknown. They spoil all they touch—people saddled upon you. They will neither leave nor reform. The fly in all your ointment. They make any association or organization uncomfortable. The smaller the orbit in which they move the more fearfully they burn. They make village life anything but the poetic and elysian thing we read of. They make the family circle, sometimes, anything but a reflection of Heaven. But even admitting this, it does not follow that they are unmitigated evils. Within the sphere of social and domestic life—within the domain of feeling and disposition, the sour and morbid and selfish are not unfrequently extremely useful. They do a great many things nobody else would do, and things that need to be done. They are like burrs, the rough exterior of desirable things. In our common every day life there are things superlatively precious—things like order and decorum and morality—things embraced under the head of *proprieties*, relative to which we can make no law, except so far as society is a law to itself. In village life, in all our communities in fact, there are persons who constitute themselves the censors and guardians of public morals, and it is a great blessing that they do. There is such a thing as reputation for old and young. There is a sensitiveness and solicitude relative to our reputation divinely implanted within us. There is and ought to be a moral standard for all society, and that standard should be high and rigid, and the man or woman indifferent to it is from that fact unfit for a pure society. Society is always greater than any man or any woman. It has its interests, its rights, and it is the duty of every man who would be protected by society to see that society is protected. It is a great mistake to imagine that what our neighbor does, or allows to be done, is none of our business. Example is fearfully contagious, and its virus is fearfully fatal. Youth and inexperience cannot reason, and what is liberty to your child is license to mine—and a decay of manners is not unfrequently a decay of life. It is well enough for people, and they are generally young people who do it, to boast of independence, and shout defiance to public sentiment, but public sentiment is always bigger than any man or woman at last. It is not to be resisted. To defy it is like defying the yellow fever, or a miasma. It has us in spite of all defiance. Many a young man and many a young woman has suddenly waked up to the idea that their *reputation* was gone. What a strange thing that thing *reputation* is, a nothing, and yet a fortune cannot buy it, rather to be chosen than great riches, a stain, a flaw destroys it. Once gone, the victim is like the leper, branded, avoided, expelled from the haunts of rectitude and virtue. Fearful is the vengeance of society. It is all well enough to talk of the inhumanity of man toward man, and especially of the cruelty of woman toward woman, but it would be hard to tell how it can be helped. It is not so much a voluntary action as one of the vital forces of society. It is instinctive, inevitable. It is the instinct of self-preservation—better than any enactment of the civil code. Very valuable things are all its *police* agencies—

the eye that detects the first erring steps—the tongue that sounds out the note of alarm. Such eyes and such tongues are incorruptible. They are susceptible of no bribe. It is true, their office is not to be coveted. I do not say they are the wisest or the best people in the world, but they are not to be despised. The thing is to live above them in the true sense of the word—to live so they cannot reach you, and have no occasion to reach you. If they get hold of you it is your own fault. If you are honest and sober and keep good hours you have no dread of the police. They are a terror only to evil doers.

The thought then, is, that the sources of disturbance are not necessarily in others—not always where they seem to us to be. Thus, the reason why people hear unpleasant things said of them, is, very often, because the things are true. Our *friends* generally are very considerate, altogether too considerate—they do not wound our feelings by harsh announcements. Our enemies are not always blind—not always very bad, either. The worst thing about them sometimes is their unpleasant way of telling the truth, and then it is not always that *they* are *unpleasant*, so much as *the truth* they tell. If you have a deformity anywhere it is the first thing they see—the first thing they talk about. But then, if you do have a deformity anywhere, nobody is more interested in finding it out than you are yourself. They take your photograph, and I think that *photographs* are, generally, very unsatisfactory and disappointing things. But the *moral effect* of a photograph is good. It makes us feel humble. We cannot quarrel with it. There it is—there is no disputing it—it is ours. It is true, we never get two alike. We cannot appear always *all* we are. There is ever a crushing possibility left us, that we have something better in reserve—something that never can be taken—something that nobody ever sees. But our enemies are often only so many *camera obscuras*, to show us how, at least, it is possible for others to see us. You recollect the prayer of the poet Burns:

> "O wad some Power the giftie gie us,
> To see oursels as others see us:"

I think our enemies are that power. We are very unwise in keeping away from them, or at any rate in not reflecting on what they say. We cannot improve our faces, but we can improve our characters, and a wise man learns as much from his enemies as from his friends. But it takes a *wise* man to do it—a strong, brave man—and so St. Paul says, "as much as lieth in *you*." Yes, that is always the measure of your peace and of your peaceableness—"as much as lieth in *you*." Society is unhappy, never in our strength, but always in our weaknesses. Some men are never at peace, and never will be. There is no peace-culture in them. Their notions of honor, their ideas, or want of ideas, respecting a true manliness, will keep them in a perpetual broil. They have neither the courage nor the strength, under provocation, to keep their tongue still. It requires a great deal more courage not to strike a man, than it does to strike him. Only a real and true man knows he cannot possibly be insulted. Once, in debating a matter of vital importance to the State, Aristides, I think it was, was smitten by his opponent in the face. Without anger, his instant and only reply was: "Smite me, but hear me." All ages have said that man *was* a man. What could *he* have been who could smite such a man as Aristides? Who but such a man could think that violence was argument? Most of us allow other men to be the measure of our manliness. We *go down* to their level. Perhaps that is only apparent. That is the point. No man does *go down*. If you quarrel with anybody, you are both alike. If a man is on any level, he is on none but *his*. It is the emergency which defines the level to which he belongs. At any point a man will always do his best. I do not mean to say, that in the heat of excitement, or under embarrassment, a man will not do a thing his judgment condemns. But if he does, even that will not long disturb the peace, for such a man will know how to undo his act, and he is not *afraid* to undo it. It takes a brave man to make an apology, especially to a man he would disdain to set with the dogs of his flock, but a brave man *will do* it. You see, "as much as lieth in *you*" is all the peace possible for you. If *it be possible*, be strong enough for *all men*. You will be wonderfully strong if you are. But I think the thing is possible. I think there is an attainable point from which we can look upon the very meanest man as a natural phenomenon, and it is very interesting to do it. There is a point from which one man can study another, even under provocation, as dispassionately as a botanist would study a new plant, or an entomologist a rare bug. If some men knew the complacency with which they were regarded, that very complacency, more than any other thing would make them rare. It requires great self-possession to do it. But if you betray the complacency, in any degree, either in word or deed, you spoil it all. The moment it is betrayed it is not complacency—it is only anger. Steam in a boiler is as transparent as air; you cannot see it; it is strength. Let it out; then you see it, but it is no longer steam—it is only fog. The complacency which is heavenly, merges into pity; it begets the desire to bless, and turns hatred into love.

I take it that the whole object of this life is to make us wise. Everything in this economy has its mission. For this reason, while we are not to be heedless of all our enemies say, we are not to suppose their judgment infallible. No. We have a wonderful way of misunderstanding each other, even where we are not enemies. If you say one thing, somebody will say you said another. We are sent on many fruitless errands every day from the simple incapacity of men to understand us. If you are sincere and say only what you feel, somebody will say you are reserved and cold and unsocial. If you are firm in your character, somebody will say you are obstinate. If you are honest, somebody will say you are mean. The object of this life is to make you thoughtful; to make you define life; to lift you up to whatever is truly strong and pure and divine; to self-consciousness. See to it that all contingencies produce that effect.

Then your nobleness, if you can attain to it, is one way, not only to *prevent,* but to *cure* strife. The best way always is, at any cost, to yield to exaction. Of course business must be governed by business laws, but in the social circle, in any circle of mere association or organization, let the mean have their own way. Show them how mean they are. Refer to them. Consult them. Take off your hat to them. Let them see that everything yields to their selfishness. If they are human they will sooner or later feel the emotions of shame. The sunshine will melt the ice if there is only enough of it. You will sooner or later reach the heart. There may be very little of it to reach, but that is the only way to reach what there is, and to make it more. That, too, is the Christian law. If he hunger feed him—feed him according to his craving. By and by, he will despise himself more than you despise him.

One of the most touching features in the life of Christ is the fact, He *let* men treat Him as they pleased. He resisted not, nor reviled. "As a sheep before her shearers was dumb, so He opened not His mouth." The effect was two-fold. It showed the dignity and strength that were in Him, and the meanness that was in us. Yes, it was three-fold. It *ended the strife.* You observe—to retaliate in kind, is to put fuel in a fire. Not to retaliate at all, is to let the fire go out forever. It takes two always to make a quarrel. Christ's quarrel with this world was the only one that was wholly one-sided. It was no quarrel. *We* demonstrated our sin. *He,* His divine, exhaustless love. He showed us how to end all strife—by standing like a rock, around which beat the waves as they will. They must eventually, exhausted, subside. This I take to be the law of Heaven. We read that there is no strife there, no sighs, nor tears, nor any more woe. You see the reason why. There is nobody to make strife; and if there should be, each soul is strong enough to end it.

Thus the text is an exhortation to us—to self-culture. But if it exhort us to so much self-culture as shall turn the enmities of life into streams of blessing—to so much self-culture as shall enable us profitably to resist—what shall we say of it as an exhortation to that self-culture which shall make us agencies that nobody wants to resist? those positive agents which shall dispense everywhere only peace? There is no time to dwell upon that. But there comes before me those possibilities in life, in which, without intention to offend, offences spring from ignorance and inexperience—grave offences in which sometimes our whole lives seem wrecked, which bring shadows across our hopes, acts never to be obliterated; but when, after all, forgiveness can mitigate and heal—where if the *garden* cannot be again, there need not be a *desert*—where a heart, big with Christian generosity, cannot only half redeem, but turn apparent evil into sources of eternal good. Then come before me those spirits we sometimes have in our homes—patient, noiseless, thoughtful. Those saints not down in the calendar, but the only real saints in which we believe. Then come before me those men and women—whose feet are always plodding—whose hands are always working—whose hearts are always throbbing in labors of love; those *peace-makers*, who shall be called the children of God. These and others—but we must put them off for another time. Only let us so live, that we shall not only pull out the thorns from life, but smooth the road and make it broader and easier for all who journey with us, following Him, whose disciples we are, and whose very name, so full of promise for earth, and so full of hope for Heaven, we cherish and revere as "the Prince of Peace."

TRAINING CHILDREN.

PROVERBS 22: 6.—Train up a child in the way he should go, and when he is old he will not depart from it.

SOMETIMES these proverbs of Solomon appear detached and isolated. Sometimes again they gather in clusters around a particular thought. In this immediate locality, the wise man is making observations upon life in certain of its social aspects. He notices a line of facts and he condenses, to a single expression, the principle which produces those facts. This is to be a prophet, or teacher, to see the original principle of things and reveal it to others. This is wisdom, to accept the principle and weave it into the fabric of real life. The great hope for man is, that he will one day see all principles and put them into practice. The millenium will come when the race is wise, and not before. The more truly wise any man becomes, by so much he is truly a benefactor to himself and his race. He helps us on to the day of promised peace and rest.

The evils and misfortunes which afflict mankind are the resultants of unlawful action—*i. e.*, action in ignorance of, and in violation of natural principles. This assertion of Solomon's has a great fact and law underlying it, which perhaps more than any other we have ignored. It suggests the attestation which God set to all His works in the beginning. "Behold it was very good." In the very nature of things it must be that

God *could* not make a mistake in His creation. If He made all things else to subserve a purpose and meet its destiny, most certainly *would* he not have made man, the highest of all, to defeat all purpose, and be alone a curse for all time. In his original organism—in the fundamental laws of his being—it must be that man is as good as all things else. He needs only wise development.

But in point of actual fact, when we turn to our observations and experiences, we find man, we might almost say, *alone*, but certainly more than any other creature, at variance with highest good. This also is the resultant of a law. To all other creatures attached only what we might call a mechanical being. To man alone attached a moral being—*i. e.*, a being not only capable of knowledge and wisdom, but a being whose real life was in proportion to his knowledge and wisdom. Man alone had the power of combining laws, not creating or changing, but *combining*, or of setting laws to acting and re-acting upon each other *artificially*, so to speak. It was a fearful power. It was like placing a child in a magazine with a lighted match in his hand. The very first thing he would do, would be very likely to be a wrong one. And yet only by such a process could there be such a thing as moral force, merit, moral glory—the highest glory known to us. Only by such a process could there have been the brighter and higher half of the universe. We have the pledge of this, in the very nature of God. If there had been any other way, or if it had been better that this way should not be, infinite wisdom would have known it, and infinite love would have done that which was best. *Infinite love did do what was best,* AND MAN WAS. All questions for the truth, how simple it seems, when at last it comes to him. If we had truly reasoned, we would have seen that wrath, anger, hatred, or any unlove, were really a weakness, and therefore impossible in God. They are merely the absence of mercy, patience and love. If they had looked into the divine dealings with our race, they would have seen mercy, restraining and guiding love, in them all, an attempt to prevent evil consequences, and so to redeem and bless mankind. They would have seen that every element in man and every element in nature, under the direction of wisdom, under the influence of *reason*, of love, were burdened with divinest ministration. All that nature wanted, all that God asked, was that man should not be a brute, that he should mount up to a recognition of his soul-nature, his true man-being. The very point contemplated in his being was his recognition of his moral being, his realization of soul. It was only as he got away from his fears, his passions, his grosser self, that he could find God. What he needed was not facts, but *the power of seeing them*, not truth, but the power of perceiving truth. He and all other things were *so* made, that he should find his soul level, his moral or spiritual existence. *The essence of moral being is that the* SOUL *find it and accept it.* Divine love and wisdom, God Himself, could not frame any other uuiverse or make another moral being. You perceive, individual volition creates moral being. Take that out and there is no moral being. To have finite spirit existence at all, it was *needful* to have it just as it was. There was no unlove whatever in making the world as it was and in creating man as he is. It *must* so be, or *never* be. That lies in the very fact that God is God. There is a conception of God—*i. e.*, to say, a

God is the being having most knowledge of divine things, and most obedient thereto. The being furthest from God is the being who thinks any way in which he pleases to live is as good as God's way—the being in greatest transgression. Now, this way of God, this way of right, is a way of study, of tuition, a way to be learned, and, thank God, a way once learned, capable of being taught. There is at once the duty and the destiny of the race, *growth*, not a way that our theologies or dogmas can make right, but a way that is right, a way to be learned. The original basis of our nature, the laws as God made them being good, reason would teach us that real instruction and wise training would result in good. As matter of observation and experience, we know that much sin is the result of ignorance, and much more sin the result of habit. From observation and experience we deduce the law, that the goodness or badness in us is the use or abuse of nature's endowments. We deduce also the fact, that nature once trained or left untrained is hard to change. Hence Solomon derived the thought, and we are able to see its force. "Train up a child in the way he should go, and when he is old he will not depart from it."

And this is neither new in Solomon, nor peculiar to our religion. The Romans had a maxim: "The child is father of the man." Given the conditions and belongings of childhood, and you can forecast the capacities and destinies of manhood. Every mature life is simply a resultant. Every man and every woman is simply the net product of educational forces. The degree to which this fact is ignored is one of the most astonishing things in life. We bewail human infirmity and degradation, but we nowhere seem to be in earnest about preventing it. *Our religious doctrines have made us blind to some of God's most palpable laws.* A colt we know must be trained, and his future value depends upon his training. We have laws even for the protection and multiplication of the fishes in our rivers; but children, the most precious freightage our world carries, are left to partial and sporadic endeavors, multitudes of them being worth not so much as the calves of the stall, or the sheep for the shambles.

Hence the fearful dilution of all our civilizing agencies; for every community is simply the net product of all its educational forces put together. Since every community or nationality is a unit in itself, in spite of ourselves, members one of another, the diseased parts are but a discount, or tax upon the healthy parts. Every diseased globule of blood in your body is only so much tax upon the globules not diseased—multiply them, and the question of health, and even of life, for you is easily solved. Educational forces are of two kinds, positive and negative; or, a better expression would be, that there is everywhere either a proper force or the absence of a proper force; but where a wise force is not applied to give direction to development, it is not simply that a mere inertia or quiescent condition remains, but the life-force in the subject acts, assimilates whatever is within its reach, and takes its direction according to the preponderance of its surroundings. A remarkable organization, strong moral and mental development, may guide or give a bias toward a wise selection of auxiliaries; but an ordinary or defective organization may guide toward an unwise selection, and thus it is,—the absence of a direct training, becomes a training force itself. So that a child not trained is a being uncultured, and that means a being demoralized, and a source of demoralization to others. You will sometimes see men with peculiar endowments, but with nothing else of what might be called advantages, still attaining to great virtue and usefulness—but because men are generally only ordinary, and because vice and ignorance tend to demoralize and weaken, in the absence of training, you will oftener find men sinking into vice and degradation, till it might be said, multitudes are trained in error and iniquity—in the way they ought not to go. And so true it is, that when trained in it they do not depart from it, it is felt that the task of converting them is almost hopeless, and because of our neglect it is, that the world is filled with so much that is hopeless. We are intent upon the task of converting, when we ought to be busy with the God-given work of building. This thought, it seems to me, should be at the very head and front of all our exertions for human good.

Nor must we imagine that they who, without positive training, attain to virtue and usefulness, attain to the same degree they would reach under a wise training. If great benefactors have risen up to our race whom we did not deserve, how much greater had they been, and how many more of them, had we been worthy of them! Providence contemplates a direct training force. Nature nowhere imagines that a human being shall at any stage of its progress, but especially in its youth, be left without guidance. Guidance is God's prime provision for humanity. *The Family, the Church, and the State, are the three ordained Educators*, and they do educate or train, right or wrong. The duty of educating wisely, is inherent and imperative in all three, and thus every man, by virtue of his relations to one or other of these, owes it as a duty to God to bless the young. The teacher's work is the most sacred of all works. But nature's sovereign preceptor is the parent. In the order of time, and as a matter of fact, our mothers impart to us our first lessons in being. There is a keen and hidden force in that Bible record, which makes Eve the *occasion of the fall in Adam.* When women are studying their rights, what a pity it is they will not study in the right direction. In all time, it would seem as though God had put all well-being in a holy, sensible womanhood. No GREAT MAN has been so great as his mother. The mother's eye, her smile, her tones, convey to the infant spirit life or death. There is a singular force in another expression of Solomon's—"A child left to himself bringeth his mother to shame;" he does not say "*his father,*" but "*his mother,*" as if he had seen the apparent law that, beyond a mother's fidelity, there was no greater force upon earth. And yet her sovereignty remains but for a time—her problem soon becomes complicated. The rest of the family—friends, associates, neighbors—gradually assert their influence, till Church and State, or, what would be here an equivalent expression for both,—*society,*—exerts as great an influence as parentage itself.

Hence, the question arises, whence is parental wisdom itself to come? The aggregation of families is but society, and society but the aggregation of families. We at once make society and are made by it. This is a wonderful circle on which we live. Life is everywhere reacting upon itself—society cannot rise higher than itself. We impart only what we have received. A child born in China takes its language, its thought, its habits of life from its surroundings—it becomes Chinese.

A child born in Ireland, takes its language, its religion, its being from the Irish. There is, as it were, a plane of being fixed for it, beyond which it cannot rise. The parent itself has received a certain amount of being, *more than which it cannot impart.* Parentage is fettered by prejudice and prestige. Its facilities are only those which have been inherited from antecedent generations. Still it remains that the family is the great integer of human society, the first fact, the organic basis of human life. *The prime duty of parentage, therefore, is* SELF-CULTURE. Here is the fact that lies at the basis of this subject. No matter what the forces of society are—no matter what the facilities or hindrances which have been handed down—all well-being for humanity concentrates at the one point of parental wisdom and diligence. Without thought, without reading, especially of God's Word—without prayer, without constant circumspection—neither the unconscious influence of example, nor the positive employment of means, can be in any high degree salutary. Without a wise independence of social dixit; without individual character; without a Christian plan and purpose, the family will only drift with the common tide. In the slavishness of society, in the dominance of conventionality over all true wisdom, lies one of our greatest hindrances. Viewed in some of its aspects, it is wonderful that we have as much promise in our youth as we have. We are told sometimes that we have no longer that reverence for parental authority which is traditional in our race. The great wonder would be if we had. We have forgotten that the fifth commandment is just as much a commandment to the parent *to be honorable,* as it is to the child to honor the parent. The very first law in this matter of training is in this filial honor and affection. The very hook on which all hope of success depends is filial obedience. If there is nothing to honor and nothing to obey, the discharge of duty in the child is impossible. In the very large majority of instances, the order of God is inverted. *It is the child that trains the parent. It is the parent that* OBEYS *the child.* It is here, in the want of parental authority, in the want of home discipline and culture, that our hopes are staggered—our exertions towards high and wise development neutralized. It is here that instruction and advice about training children become useless. It is in vain for an artist to tell a clown how to be an artist. There is no receptivity, no skill; nothing to appropriate the advice. Rules for households are of no use to those who are above all rules—*i. e.*, *below* all rules; so that the one essential of all human progress is thoughtful Christian parentage. With that we have all blessing. Nothing upon earth can transcend in responsibility the office of a parent. It is no use to talk about the care, or the wrong, or the burden, or any other name by which we choose to call it, woe is unto us, if we betray our trust —woe in this world—woe in all worlds. We may delegate our work to nurses, to the streets, to society, but for it God will bring us into judgment. How many cups of woe are pressed home every day to unwilling parental lips. How many wrecks tell of parental infidelity! How many souls are waiting in that other world till their children, blighted and cursed, their own work, shall follow them there to condemn them. We can bow down to society. We can teach our children to bow down to society. We can make respectability and fashion and ease and other people's opinions, our Gods and their Gods, but it had been better for both of us if we had never been born. Life is very solemn. God will not have us assume an office, except as we assume the responsibility. We must teach by example as by precept—unconsciously, as well as consciously. We must show that life means something, by ourselves attaching a meaning to it. If we do that, and I believe, thank God, that many of us are trying to do that—if we do that, we must study *first of all the children.* It is no use to say children differ, and it is so hard to tell what to do. That is true enough; children do differ, and God meant they should differ. A sorry world it would be, if we were all alike. Sometimes we say, this child has such a bad disposition—such an evil trait; but, if there be anything *evil* or *bad* about it, it may be our fault—*i. e.*, it may be a good trait perverted, indulged or pampered into badness. Sometimes people tell us how hard they have striven and how much they have failed. Both may be very true, and yet it may be equally true that they mistook the case in the beginning. Beyond a doubt, there are *inherited tendencies.* There are lusts and cravings and things that go to make up character, which come down from other generations. Intemperance and vice send their blight upon children's children. There is a law of nature by which the sins of the father goes down to the third or fourth generation—a law in itself enough to alarm us and make us wise. But in the child itself it is not sin. It is a tendency. It may be a weakness, a defect, a tax upon exertion, a discount upon our endeavors, because it is a discount upon all the rest of its being. Still, it can be watched; it can be fought against; it can be overcome. Of course it intensifies the problem, but it also pays. That child saved is a gem for the skies—a work to follow us and call us blessed. But very often the dispositions of which we complain are the very best things a child could have. Sometimes we complain that a child has a very strong will. I know of no greater blessing the child could have. Most of us have no *will* of our own; we will as other people will. No farmer complains that a colt has very great strength; he takes care it shall be properly applied; *he trains it.*

Toward a child with a strong will, our danger is either of crushing it altogether, or of turning it into *wilfulness*, and both are fatal to the child. Some parents themselves have a will that is stronger and heavier than iron—*i. e.*, a strong *wilfulness* that they mistake for a strong will. It has no elasticity. It is not tempered with affection. It has forgotten its own childhood. It teaches the child no self-control. It brings into play none of those finer sensibilities and agencies, which God gave it for the very purposes of self-government. There is perhaps not a single faculty which dominates, or characterizes any child, which is not itself a great blessing *if we only knew what to do with it.* And the way to know what to do with it, is not to isolate it—not to separate it from all the rest of the child, but to put it in the combination in which God put it—turn it to harmony with all the rest of the child. The dominating faculty itself will then be the richer, a blessing to itself and to thousands. How many characters there are in history; how many men we see every day, whom we feel have one great faculty, but which itself is not as great as it had been, if only the other half of them could have been developed. If, however, we enter upon illustration here, the subject would be endless. But I say study the children. Work up the elements God has created, no matter what it costs. The prayers, the trials, the struggles, the self-denials, why, they shall build a mansion of glory for you. They cannot fail. Create the cause, you establish the effect. God neither sleeps nor forgets. There is an element above you and above it,—the Holy Ghost—*God.* Train your child, and then as long as you live, it will react in blessing upon you, and if you are taken away, you can leave it no heritage which will compare in value with the recollection of your fidelity and example.

I had intended, and would like very much, if there were time, to extend these thoughts into the duty of the State to *educate.* What is the State? There are many senses in which that word is used. If you use it in the sense of government, then government is but representation. It may be used in the sense of an aggregation of families—society. Then, in society, there are always unfortunate people, who, as I have said, know not how to train their children, or who, knowing how, are unable to command the needful facilities. They know not much to impart and therefore are unable to impart much. Since we are members one of another, or since, as I have otherwise expressed it, every untrained child is necessarily so much disease to the body politic, no State *can afford* to have one ignorant, or untrained child. Every man is better off, in proportion as his neighbor's children are better off. As a matter of policy, to say nothing of benevolence, *it is wise to educate.* We often have it said, that schools are cheaper than jails, and teachers better than policemen. *We do not yet believe that.* The level of the higher stratum of humanity is always dependent upon the level of the lower. The top of the church spire depends upon the elevation of the tower. The nobility of Ireland would have been vastly happier to-day, if they had taken care of themselves, *by taking care of the Irish.* If Christian civilization is the highest upon earth, it is because Christianity sends men out of themselves to take care of themselves—not as a matter of selfishness, but as a matter of love. That is Christianity—that is the law of sacrifice, giving life to find life. Mind and heart are the jewels of God. The more of these the State has, the more we all have—the richer we all are. Those of us who have of these, owe it to God to impart it to those who have it not. You are only a steward. That is the law of society, the law of accountability, the law of stewardship. In our religious zeal and sectarian wisdom, which is very often only *ir*religious zeal and sectarian *unwisdom,* we deny the right to impart one, when, what we take to be the other, cannot go with it. No greater mistake was ever made. If twice two are four, if a knowledge of it is invaluable in human intercourse, and a man is that much better off for having it, then we are bound to teach him, and we can and ought to appoint a teacher for the purpose. If it be universally accepted that a man should be honest, then the teacher who should teach that it were better to be dishonest, would be in conflict with all our instincts, and not only should be, but would be, dismissed. If it is a questionable thing whether a Bishop, or immersion, are essential to religion, then that they are, should not be taught in any school. Wisdom is to teach us things that are certainly known, that we may be better able to judge respecting things that are so far unknown, and hence it is, that the average of civilization is higher where such a course is pursued than where it is neglected. There is no question, in my mind, whether Prussia is better off than Italy, and I cannot believe that we as a people are going to be long entangled in the snare that has been laid for us in the question about the Bible in the schools. That is not the question at all. The real question is, schools or no schools. It is a question, too, which has come in its time. If we are alive, there is life in it for us. We must realize that while there is a law which tends to simplicity, it often so tends through, what appears to us, complexity. Two women in ancient times could grind at a mill, and do all the work contemplated in flour, perhaps from the planting of the grain to the eating of the bread. But many agencies, each with a specific work, are needful in our times, and we have more flour and better bread. Time was, when society was patriarchal, and all that is now embraced in Church and State, was embraced in the family. Church and State have too long been complicated, and God is now eliminating the one from the other, and writing out in characters too legible to be mistaken, the duty of every Christian. Time was, when the State—and there are still such States—gave all the religion there is—and how much is it?—what is it worth? Time is, when God is saying to every family, your work is *there*, and to every Christian your work is *there*. Time is, when God is saying to every Christian man and woman, whether you have a child or not, of your own—there is a child for whom God has made you responsible, and whom He will look that you bring with you, when you come up in glory. The gain was immense when the Church broke away from the State, and the gain will be immense when duty is defined before every Christian, and we have a life power in every man and woman that belong to the Church. I look upon it that out of the agitations through which we are passing is coming a renewed life to the Church. Parental duty will be better defined, and parental energy will be quickened—social duty will be better defined, and social energy will be quickened. The Church herself will turn back again from profitless theories to high practical themes—from dogma to religion—from Paul and Apolos to Christ. One good begins, I think, already to appear, and that is a higher life in our Sunday Schools. The inauguration of the Sunday School was a great step in advance, but up to this time it has been more of a sentiment than of a work—our Sunday Schools have needed system and talent. Our Sunday School libraries have aimed at amusing, rather than at instructing. They greatly need weeding. Any foolish thing, will no longer do for a Sunday School book. *Anybody*, will no longer do for a teacher. To bridge over an hour on Sunday will no longer be sufficient. An immense importance attaches to the work.

It is the recurrence of our Sunday School anniversary to-day, which has been the occasion of my bringing these thoughts before you. I had intended to speak more of our work here, but there is no time. I must defer it to this afternoon. But I may say we have much here over which to rejoice, and much to encourage us. Our work has prospered. We have a band of indefatigable laborers—many instances have come within my observation of good accomplished. From the Superintendent to the Infant class, there is life; so much, we need more room, and one fact I must mention, which is, that before long we must increase our capacity for this work.

In closing—as I must close—let me ask you, dear brethren, if we cannot catch from what has been said, some higher glimpses, at least, of the solemnity of life—of our duties as parents, as citizens, and as Christians? Can we not attach a somewhat higher estimate to childhood, and realize the influence which we, through them, can exert upon generations to come after us. We do not love children enough. We love *our children*. We need to love childhood—innocent, helpless childhood—poor, dirty, neglected childhood—the stray lambs without a shepherd. If we could *love* them for Jesus' sake—love them as God loves them, enough to make some sacrifice for them, enough to stand up in our lot and demand of our legislature better laws for them, we should be blessed in our love, and make them a blessing to thousands.

I have not said anything about the promises of God, the influences of divine grace, the power of the Holy Ghost. I have dwelt upon *our* work. God will take care of His side, if we can only take care of ours. If we can sow the seed upon a broad and cultured ground, the elements of God's great providence will do the rest, whether we live or die. There are laws we can reach and ought to reach—then there are laws which work, and which nobody can reach. Thank God for that. When I look upon my little ones, and feel I must shortly leave them with no father-hand to guide them, and no father-heart to shield them, it is unspeakable comfort to know that God will not leave them nor forsake them. Blessed is he—blessed is she—who, when called to leave their little ones behind them, can feel, that they have themselves beaten the path and trained their little feet to the blessedness of that road which leads to the Kingdom of God. Blessed is he who, over and above his own, can feel that some child shall follow him to that kingdom and call him blessed! May your children and mine be blessed! May God's spirit be outpoured upon all our work, and by and by, may you and I, and all who have sown and all who have reaped, through Jesus Christ rejoice together!

THE UPLIFTING OF CHRIST.

JOHN 12: 32.—And I, if I be lifted up from the earth, will draw all men unto me.

THIS is part of a discourse, perhaps the last, our Lord delivered upon Mount Moriah. He had just ridden into Jerusalem amid the hosannas of the multitude. There was great excitement everywhere concerning Him. His mission was drawing to its close. Three years of such a life had brought a crisis. Even Gentiles crave the privilege of seeing Him. Certain Greeks which had come up to worship, come to the disciples with the request: "*Sirs, we would see Jesus.*" The disciples make the request known to the Master, and it becomes the occasion of His discourse.

The simple fact of being desired by Gentiles, seems to suggest itself to Christ as a pledge to those around Him of the eventual fulfillment of His entire mission. These Greeks belonged to a people remarkable for their *powers and habits* of inquiry. They looked thoughtfully into everything, and this request rises like a grand response from this human nature of ours, to that sacred mission of Christ. The first words of His answer were: "The hour is come that the son of man should be glorified." To all appearance He was about to die, but in reality He was about to begin to live. A grain of wheat cast into the ground seems to be lost. In reality it casts off only an outward form, and springs into a grander and richer and *reproductive* life. All true life is attainable only through such a process. The gross, outward form, must pass away. Whoever lives only in that, lives not at all.

There, in that hour, were drawing to a focus the plans of the ages past, and the hopes of the ages to come. The Saviour feels its solemnity and exclaims: "*Now* is my soul troubled. I know not what to say. Father, save me from this hour, and yet for the purpose of meeting this very hour have I come. I would not therefore turn from it: Only, Father, glorify thy name." (Contemplate Christ as you will, conscious of a mission committed to Him—conscious of having fulfilled it—beholding a future depending upon it, in the very hour of its consummation, from the very depths of His sincerity appealing to God; did ever any man so speak before?) A voice from heaven answers: "I have glorified it and will glorify it again." Jesus explained that this voice was not for Him, but for them that stood around Him. It was God's response to these Greeks. Deep responds to deep, truth to truth. The divine things in Christ had been perceived. It was this the nations had been longing for. Christ was truly "the desire of all nations." In the nature of things, all that was in Christ should become clearer and clearer to men. The old, sensual, carnal life, men had been living, was now to be condemned. The prince of darkness was to be exposed as indeed a *prince of darkness*, and be deposed. The Prince of Peace was to be reached as indeed a Prince of Peace, and be enthroned, and real life begin to reign. "Now is the judgment of this world—now is the prince of this world to be cast out, and I, if I be lifted up from the earth, will draw all men unto me."

It is abundantly evident, that in this discourse and in this verse, Jesus Christ is speaking of Himself as the means by which God will reconcile all men to himself. The whole plan and process of salvation is not by Christ logically, consecutively—if you please—*philosophically* expressed. It never is, for man hath no word-forms to which that plan and process can be reduced. We should have been worse off with a philosophical expression than without it. Heaven's logic is love. Love knows nothing of syllogism; love simply *sees*. Place redemption in an earth-created form, and you only increase the materialism which has already crushed mankind. Language is not thought; thought everywhere overlaps language; compress the thought to language, and "*the letter killeth*." It always must, because thought is continually outgrowing language, or ought to do it, and this is why those who have the most creed have the least life.

Perhaps this plan of God's salvation is, not so much a plan, as it is an essence, which is to pervade all plans—not so much a thing, as an element of all things—not *directly* and immediately to produce a desired result, but to make things already existing produce it. If man were in a garden of dying and fruitless trees, and wanted fruit, he would make a new tree to produce it; he would tear up and destroy and start anew, and repeat his old failure. But God's plan is, not a new root, or new trunk, or new branch, but a *new life* sent through root and trunk and branch, spreading out into leaf and bloom and fruit. It is redemptory—it is quickening. As such, it is as incapable of philosophical form as the life of vegetation is beyond our touch or any of our senses. A thing admitting of endless manifestations, a thing to be perceived and realized only in its effects. Such this plan of God's salvation would seem to be. It was incarnate in Christ, and yet it could only *outcrop*, so to speak, in word, in act, in life,—sometimes dimly, sometimes clearly, and yet not so you can grasp it, till you take all Christ was from Bethlehem to Calvary, inclusive, and not then—till you take Christ as He stands upon all time, in the *promises* of the ages antecedent, in the *fruition* of the ages subsequent, and not then, till you have Him in your heart and soul and mind—not by logic or creed, but by the life-force which you know experimentally to be in Him. The scales must fall from your eyes, the inner vision must be opened, if you would see Christ. It is *needful* for us to do just what these Greeks wanted to do—*see Christ*—not a second-hand ideal—not a mere report of Him—not one of His disciples, but what *He* is, what constitutes divine life, and even then, you do not comprehend this plan of salvation. You only feel it in you, and see it round you, and perceive it reaching out over all time, and stretching into far eternity. You cannot express it. At every one of its outcroppings, men have undertaken to give it expression, but their best attempts have been only approximations. They have talked of atonement, of sacrifice, of imputed righteousness, of election, of justification, of sanctification, of faith, of works—looping, analyzing, questioning, till those who saw only their own position, and not much of that, have denied the position of others, and thus have given rise to contradiction and confusion. They have dissected it, and given us here and there a lifeless limb, when what we wanted was a living, loving, present Christ—a talking, sympathizing, shielding God—an imparting, radiating, quickening life. But, what is a grand and consoling fact, amid all confusion, each comes back to Christ at last, and says, my central thought is *there*. And it *is* there. All central thought is there. Each word-form is in part expression of that life which is beyond expression—that which is, alone, the full expression of eternal life for man. What is in Him is wisdom and righteousness and sanctification and redemption. We are to see that, to feed upon it. That is the power of God to salvation, of necessity only to him that believeth. But that is the precious thought, men shall go on believing. The nations shall enlarge their vision. It shall be lifted up, and the craving shall keep increasing, *till all men shall be drawn to Him.* The prince of this world shall be cast out, and Christ, not only lifted up, but enthroned.

Thus, this life is directly and always connected with Christ, and He, again, directly and always connected with this "lifting up." This "lifting up" was literally His crucifixion. The very next verse tells us this. The crucifixion was the ripening, the culmination of the whole scheme of divine redemption. It was, in the nature of things, the only process by which the life of Christ could be indelibly fixed upon the mind of man; *the* process by which it should be kept from the whirlpool of oblivion—by which, through all time, it should stand out in bold and unmistakable relief. It is, and will always stand, *the wonderful thing* of all wonders, that have occurred in human history. It was to finish, to make perfect, the work of ages. For this hour Christ had come, but He had come for every other hour of His life which had preceded it. At the manger—in the temple at twelve years old—at the well-side—at the grave of Lazarus—in pleading with Scribes and Pharisees—in the Sermon upon the Mount—in divine instruction to the disciples—everywhere—He was but going to Calvary. That hour was the sum of all His hours. That "lifting up," was but the fullness of three and thirty years—that three and thirty years but the fullness of all time. It is through this we are to look at that cross. Christ is there, the prophet of all time, the Priest of all people, the king of all ages. Two eternities, the everlasting past and the everlasting future, met there. Two worlds, the earthy and the heavenly, met there. Two beings, the divine and the human, met there. That crucifixion was sacrifice, was atonement for human sin, reconciliation between God and man, not in its bare, simple self, not in the isolated act or fact, but in the *Christ* that was there, in the incarnation that closed there, and in the spiritual life to man that began there, in the *divine being* that was there that day so uplifted, that it never again should be hidden from mankind. That *uplifting* was needful, not only to make the atonement complete, but so to complete it as to bring out its force, to make it effective, that man might not be drawn to Christ merely in theory, but in fact—not merely in desire, but in actual attainment.

It seems to me, if we fail to get this thought, we fail to penetrate very far into this scheme of divine redemption—we fail to perceive the consoling force, the inevitable necessity of the truth in this promise of Christ, if He be lifted up, He will draw all men to Him. I do not wonder that they who do not see it, become despondent, and forget that Christ ever made such a promise. And what a promise it is! Christ will draw all men, all nations, every family of this race to Him—not all at once, but slowly, as the sun draws out the harvest. And if we could see that this promise is based upon the nature of things, in the infallibility of God, what a support and encouragement is there for all work and all faith!

For us to tell *in all respects* how Christ is atonement, or expiation for human sin, is impossible. In my judgment we have seen but the beginning of Christ's Gospel. But in that beginning there is very much we can see. We can see this atonement has two sides—first, God's reconciliation to us, and second, our reconciliation to God. The first we cannot penetrate; the second we not only can but ought to understand. The first involves such questions as, whether God needed anything to appease Him, whether there were any justice to be satisfied—involves questions theological and, at best, speculative—questions in which we are wise overmuch, in that we attempt to pronounce where Christ was pleased to be silent—questions with respect to which, if we knew more, we should find to be no questions at all. If the atonement were because God needed anything to appease Him, either as an angry God or as a just God, then the atonement is made, once and forever, full, perfect and sufficient. If the atonement were merely declaratory—merely an act expressive of the fact that God already loved us and wanted us to love

Him, that he was reconciled to us and only wanted us to be reconciled to Him—then that atonement is also made, full, perfect and sufficient. This part of the atonement is eminently practical, a part that we can understand and need to understand. The atonement is so made that it proclaims to us what the reconciliation is that God wants—so made, that it *entreats* us to be reconciled to God.

In viewing it from this position, that it is a declaration of God's reconciliation toward us, and an entreaty that we become reconciled to Him, we can see, to begin with, the need of a sacrifice, and what the sacrifice was that Christ made, and how natural it was God should make it. That God is love, there can be no disputing. If we need it in authoritative statement, we have it in the declaration of Christ Himself: "*God so loved the world that He gave His only-begotten Son.*"

The atonement is thus, not a cause of God's love, but itself a resultant, made *because* God loved. If you analyze the idea of God, you will see it embraces everything of strength, of mercy, of *help*. That which is the most useful thing in the universe—that without which nothing could live--is God. That which is most helpful to the thing most needful—that which helps where nothing else could, or would ever think of helping—that is God. If man lay at the very opposite extreme of being, how *the very idea of God implies that* He *should go there to help him!* What sort of a mother would that be, who could do nothing for her child? How rich would he be, who could only take care of himself? What would that philanthrophy be worth, which could only come and look upon the stricken sinner and pass by on the other side? If man were ever to be helped it must be by a higher being, and that help of necessity must involve suffering, or sacrifice to that being; and oh! what God would that be, who could afford nothing of help or comfort to His helpless children? You must perceive, it seems to me, the idea of sacrifice in the very idea of God. Men tell you they cannot conceive of God suffering. I ask you whether you can get a conception of God without that idea? It is of the very essence of the idea of goodness. It is there you begin to get a pledge of the promise made by Christ in the text. If you can get men to see that, you start, in man himself, a force which is in its very nature redemptory. The one idea grows upon the other as naturally as a rose upon its stem. It is a declaration or manifestation of God. And in addition you perceive, not only sacrifice, but vicarious sacrifice. One being suffering for another, not undergoing the same suffering, for that is imposible, but suffering in a way to remove suffering, in a way to prevent the cause of suffering. Nor is this alone in Christ, it is a law that pervades existence, and has its perfection in Christ only as all laws have their perfection in Him. The mother does suffer for her child, the soldier for his countrymen—in a thousand ways we suffer for each other, and the more and more voluntarily, in proportion as we are godly, or God-like. I say there is a law about it—a law which *demands* of you the higher you are the more help you shall be. Yes, I would put it stronger than that: a law which determines, that the extent to which you do help and bless another is the exact measure of your own elevation, or goodness. Out of that law grows the fact, that if you can get one man truly elevated, you get a seed, as it were, which will eventually get the race elevated, therefore the fact, that Christ *being lifted* will draw all men unto Him. Only God knew this law—only God could make such a sacrifice, and blessed be God, He *did do it.* It seems like a paradox, but it is one of those divine paradoxes on which the foundations of the universe are laid.

Now, what was the sacrifice Christ made? It was man to be lifted. You look out upon your city, and see whole classes vulgar, ignorant, degraded. You see little children neglected, squallid and wretched. You *wish* them better off. Will that help them? Must you not go to them, or send to them, or in some way *reach* them? Must you not in some way beget self-action in them? If you go there to teach them, can they treat you any better than they know how, and must you not of necessity encounter all the evils their condition involves, in order to impart to them the blessings of the condition to which you wish to lift them? We read of a Missionary who went to the West Indies to preach to the slaves. In order to do it, he had actually to become a slave—to work with them, and expose himself to all their hardships. He did it. "A very good man," you say. Yes, I have shown you that; but can you see his sacrifice? Because he was exalted, he was capable of the sacrifice; he showed them the good-will of Christians toward them, and what it was to be a Christian. So Christ became a man, *for man's sake.* In this prison-house with us He showed us that God had now no enmity toward us. He wanted us to love Him, and *so become loveable.* We knew not what the loveable thing was that God wanted, nor how to become that thing. Christ became that thing for us, and showed us how to reach it. This simple fact was so constituted as to make two demonstrations—one of what God was, one of what man was. We needed to see both. What was our condition? One of infirmity first of all. There was nothing of ignorance, of misfortune; nothing of poverty; nothing of prejudice; nothing of social disadvantage; nothing of pride, of civil or religious intolerance, He did not encounter. *He literally "bore our infirmities."* He bore our griefs and carried our sorrows. Then hypocrisy, ingratitude, injustice, falsehood, error, love of evil, envy, hatred, malice—these were our sins, our prison-house. These Christ took upon him. *He literally bore our transgressions.* Insult, buffetings, sicknesses, want, everything down to murder—these were consequences of our sin, these were incident to our condition. These, Christ encountered. "He was wounded for our transgressions and bruised for our iniquities." "He was a man of sorrow and acquainted with grief." He did not heedlessly aggravate wickedness. He did not strive to stir it up and make it worse than it was. Nay, you know it is a law that you have only to accuse error or wrong—*i. e.*, merely to point out error and wrong to make them at once active—active according to their own instincts. He let them have their way. He literally exhausted them. He resisted not, nor complained. "As a sheep before the shearer is dumb, He opened not his mouth." He let our evil nature have, what to it was victory. Our wickedness could not measure His goodness. Our hatred could not subdue His love. He would have been only a man if it had been otherwise, but his love was divine. You can see there a divine being, a being that was divine. Do not mix it up with the question whether Christ was God. I say we see there what all our instincts tell us to be of God, *tell us to be divine.* It was quenchless. The struggle was fearful and to the last extremity. His very innocence exasperated us. We made a cross and nailed Him to it. We lifted Him up in cruelty and derision. *From His lips fell only the accents of love.* The elements sought to hide our shame in darkness. The earth put on sackcloth. The human race had conspired. God had triumphed. That crucifixion was the demonstration of our vileness and weakness on the one side, and of God's love and goodness on the other. There was what we are. There in that Christ was what God wanted us to be. The light that struck down from that cross floated back over that life, over it all was written God, and every letter of that word was *love.* The light that struck down from that cross penetrated the darkened recesses of our fallen being, and revealed to us what sin and Satan had made us—revealed our unnaturalness, our deformity. It had this effect, by the spirit of God, to make us condemn ourselves and desire God. "Now was the prince of this world judged"—now was God in Christ glorified! To create that fact, itself so near to impossibility, was to create this other fact, of which Christ speaks. If the work could have a beginning, it should accomplish that whereunto God intended it. If a handful could be drawn to Him before His work were completed, then, when he was lifted up and the whole mission were fulfilled, all men should be drawn to Him. There was much yet to be revealed. That Christ, passing through a crucifixion, passed really to a resurrection. That fact opened a future of eternal truth. That Christ-life leads to glory, to a kingship, to power and dominion which can know no limit in time, or degree. Plant that thought upon earth and, though it be but a grain of mustard seed, it shall grow into the grandest of all trees, and the nations of the earth shall take refuge in its branches. If Christ be lifted up all men shall be brought unto Him. Oh what a future opens there! and how God calls us to it, not in the thunder-tones of Sinai, but in the still small voice of endearing and consoling love.

You cannot help seeing, then, redemption. If you can make every man what Christ was, you take him out from his old nature and make him a heavenly being. If you can fill this world with such beings, you make a heaven. There would be a new earth wherein would dwell righteousness. I would like to take you along the Christian centuries, and show you that this work has been really going on. You say this world is very wicked, and truly it is; but do you know how wicked this world was when Christ came to it? If all the evils that then existed could be concentrated in your lot under your present advancement, you would rather die than live. But is it nothing to know this world is a wicked world? Does that fact in itself set none of us to standing guard over principle and honor and truth? And if we are wicked, have justice, law, liberty, gained no ground? Are none of those life-forces, which were in Christ, directly acting in us and upon us? Are none living unto Him who died and gave Himself for us—living in that same self-sacrifice He marked for us in His own footsteps—and if there are any, *do we know that there are not many?* If *we* are influenced by that life and death of Christ, is there not a pledge in that, that by and by even all shall be drawn to Him?

But a question far more vital to us than this, is, what effect has that life of Christ, that cross of Christ, had upon us? What think ye of Christ? What think you of His atonement? Has it taken away your sin? Do you feel you are reconciled to God? If not, then of what avail has time been to you?—what avail that cross? In those out-stretched arms there is mercy—in those wounds there is life, but what if you pass them heedlessly by? That is a solemn question, my dear hearer. That was a solemn day when Christ uttered the words of our text—His hour had come! There is a time when our *hour*, too, shall come. That hour may very soon come. The flight of seasons tells us life is very short. When we lie upon our back and feel the life-tide ebbing away—when we realize we are to come before the presence of God, we want something strong and something in which to trust—we want to feel we have had Christ, God's own Son, for our guide and our strong salvation. But suppose, in looking back, the testimony of our days be, that we have not followed Christ at all—that His life and His death were alike matters of no consequence to you. How can you die? And if you cannot die without this Christ formed within you, your hope of glory, how can you live without Him? You do not know the extent to which you are a sinner. And yet God does not know you as a particular sinner; he only knows you as a particular soul that needs salvation. You are to be reconciled to Him, not He to you. You need no oblation to bring, but the simple oblation of a believing heart—that is all. God asks only with respect to your sins, that you leave them behind; He asks only that you take Him at His word, and hunger and thirst after Him. If you can forgive yourself, He can forgive. If you can forsake, He can forget. God loves you: that is what the Cross says to you. If you would know how God loves you, begin to love God.

God loves you! this is the voice that greets you in the solemn vigils of this Passion week. This is the voice that rises from the whole incarnation—from the manger to sad Gethsemene—from every footprint of that sacred life—from the hungry and thirsty wilderness to His buffetings amid the contradiction of sinners—from His noonday journeys and His midnight watchings—from the Judgment Hall and the Uplifted Cross,—God loves you! *Will you love Him?* This is the question pressed by every need of your soul. This is the question the Spirit of God yearns for you to answer. The very airs that breathe this week—the very fact of Good-Friday—the bells that toll—all speak to us of Christ and the Cross. They tell us how God loved us; that the Son of God was "lifted up," and they all ask us whether *we* have been drawn to Him. May the Spirit of the living God be with you and me, that we may be able to feel, that in Christ Jesus we have found life everlasting!

WHAT IS PRAYER?

Mark 6: 31—And He said unto them, Come ye yourselves apart into a desert place and rest awhile, for there were many coming and going, and they had no leisure so much as to eat.

Christ had sent his disciples out to preach the Word. Having fulfilled that special mission, they gather themselves home to Him again, and tell Him all things, both what they had done and what they had taught, and he said unto them, "Come ye yourselves apart into a desert place and rest awhile, for there were many coming and going, and they had no leisure so much as to eat." Having departed, however, the multitude follows them, and in the wilderness Christ performs the miracle of feeding five thousand with five loaves and two fishes. He dismissed His disciples to cross over to the other side of the sea. He sends away the multitudes and betakes himself to a mountain *to pray*. In the midst of the night, while His disciples are toiling—contending with winds and waves—He appears to them, and entering into the ship with them, He stills the elements and goes with them safely to the shore.

This whole passage is impressive and peculiarly instructive. Man is an active, restless being; he has of necessity much work to do, but he makes by far the larger portion of his work for himself. He forgets he has a soul as well as a body; he absorbs his time and energy in the affairs of the flesh; he leaves his soul pinched and starved. In this forgetfulness he creates for himself his severest conflict—makes the elements of his being antagonistic. When he has made a paradise for his body, that becomes a desert for his soul, and what is a desert for his body, is often the paradise of his spirit. One of the offices of religion through all ages has been to equalize the claims of body and soul—to place man in harmony with his true being, and put an end to our strifes by putting an end to their causes.

Even in its religious matters the world has often been a little super-religious. In its blindness it has laid upon itself many a necessity God would willingly have spared it. Because of our lame and helpless condition, religion which would otherwise have been the life of all work, has been only itself an additional work in life. The absence of religion in many men, and the absolute need of it in all, makes it the duty of some to find out what religion is, to keep it alive, to extend it—makes the Church a necessity—introduces an agency, the responsible duties of which, are as arduous as any that can be laid upon frail humanity. The Apostles had no leisure. They pressed their mission with ardor. Christ saw they had need of a resting place. He said to them: "Come ye yourselves apart into a desert place and rest awhile." The Master had to tell them to do it. Though they were engaged in a religious work, there was danger of their making it just as much a work—of running through it—absorbed in it—neglecting the wise and proper culture of their souls, as the men did for whom they were laboring. This has always been man's danger, of secularizing even religion. It was needful their souls should be fed, their spirits should drink in, the rich and deep things of God. He had something precious to impart to them when they were in the desert, something no city could give, the precious knowledge, that to be with Him was to have all they could desire—to have God for their friend. They wanted the still, small voice—not the whirlwind nor the storm.

What those Apostles needed is just what the whole Church has needed, what all men need, the turning aside from the heavy, pressing cares of life—the self-imposed and time-imposed burdens—the jostlings, vexations, strivings of the world, to be alone with God; to lift the soul up to higher altitudes and clearer revealings; to let the soul define herself, her capacities, and her longings. Like those Apostles, the Church of God needs it for a two-fold end—needs it for personal edification and for universal benefit. How can the blind lead the blind? How can the Church tell men of God and heaven, if she knows not God nor heavenly things? It was not simply to rest their bodies, that Christ took the disciples aside. It was rest, as all rest should be, improvement. It was rest, as rest in heaven will be, learning of God. Come ye *yourselves* apart; I have something to tell *you;* I have food for *you,* and food for you to give others. Amid the din and excitements of life, this is the one thing we need. Perhaps it is because we are so little and so seldom apart with ourselves and Christ, that life presses upon us so heavily. It is, after all, the strength from within, with which we bear up the burdens from without, and if that strength from any cause be wanting, life is only bewilderment and unrest. God has mercifully appointed Sabbath-days, one-seventh of our time, in which specially to feed on divine and eternal things. Christ calls us apart, to be with Him and with God and ourselves. Great blessings are these Sabbaths, if we so spend them, not letting the *work of religion* infringe upon this real purpose of soul communion. And yet, God would not limit us in this purpose to Sabbath days. He would have us *often* apart by ourselves, and perhaps one reason why the Church in her aggregate, with all her machinery and doctrines, is not more efficient, is that the Church, in her individuals, is not more frequently and closely in direct and far-reaching communion with God. I wish, therefore, this morning to direct your attention to a few thoughts upon the subject of prayer.

For the edification of our souls, for that is the true meaning of rest to our bodies, God has mercifully appointed *Sabbath* days, one-seventh of our time, in which to feed on divine and eternal things. Christ calls us apart. But "the Holy Church throughout all the world," at this Lenten season, pauses to turn aside with Christ to go up with Him to rest awhile—rest in holy contemplation—in meditation upon the great human struggle—in attuning the soul to heavenly things. Lent is called a *fast,* an abstinence not merely from meats and drinks, but a foregoing of many of those pleasures and indulgencies, the giddy, frivolous things of life, from which, it were better for man, would he declare an eternal separation. Being here in the *retired place,* the Master shows us the proper privileges of the time and place, works of benevolence and prayer.

But more especially of prayer, and yet I do not know that I ought to say "more especially of prayer," for this is the season in which we should particularly count up the mercies of God to us, and ask ourselves whether, according to our ability and opportunity, we are sustaining those heavenly instrumentalities, which have for their object, the giving of bread to human bodies, and the meat which endureth to eternal life to human souls. But it is of prayer I wish more particularly this morning to speak. The question which naturally and first presents itself is, What is prayer? And it is a question much more easy to ask than to answer. If there be up to this hour of mortal progress, one thing more clearly defined by human inquiries into the constitution of things than another, it is, that man everywhere stands upon the shores of a great unknown. The universe is an infinite circle. At any point of the circle on which man rests, on each side of him, stretches an infinity. Gaze in whatever direction he may, he beholds the wonderful. The most that mortal thought can do, is to promote *science*—*i. e.,* knowledge of what is—but no science can ever reach perfection, because no science can ever measure all there is to be known. The telescope reveals an infinity above us, and the microscope an infinity below us, or rather, neither is above us nor below us, but we live, everywhere, with an infinity all around us. Man is the center of creation, and yet, what we anywhere know, is as nothing to what we do not know. In us and around us are forces and agencies more subtle than our keenest perceptions. By these forces and agencies, men and all things to which they apply, have their being. As electricity kept the pole to her center, and made the world revolve in blessing for man before he knew there was such a thing as electricity; so, there are agencies more vital and powerful than that, doing their work for us, of which we still are ignorant. Effects of electricity were in the world as long as there has been a world, only we could not explain them. Effects, endless, are all around us: we cannot explain them: we call them mysteries. "What we know not now we shall know hereafter!"

What is prayer? First of all, it is a something for which man finds in him a special and peculiar need. There is a law in our human being, there is a relation between the moral intelligence *creating*, and the moral intelligence created, which absolutely demands between those two communication. *Prayer is the outgrowth of a law in moral being.* Go back in the past as far as we may, take as wide a range as our investigation can, we find no age and no people to whom prayer has been unknown. Whether you call the nation, Pagan, Jewish, or Christian—whether you call the spirit of that people, idolatrous, religious, superstitious or philosophic, the fact of prayer remains the same. It may be that in many people and for many ages together, the idea of the fact is but dimly defined, or more than that, the manifestations may be, rather the perversion of the fact than the fact itself—still, the perversion proves there must have been a great original, and wherever there has been cultivation, there has been prayer, pure, comprehensive, intelligible; and the purer, more reasonable, and intelligible, the philosophy or religion of a man has been, so much the more pure, comprehensive and intelligible, have been his prayers, until, to select the purest, noblest men of our race, the men in advance of their kind, in all usefulness, goodness and moral grandeur, is to select the very men who have resorted most to prayer, to what is otherwise called, "communion with God."

They who have not been true, nor great, nor useful, have not been men of prayer, and so far have proved that with whatever they communed, they lacked a communion with goodness, and consequently with God. The purest religious systems, and so far as I know, all religious systems, enjoin the exercise of prayer. Nor is prayer the result of the written commandment, but the written commandment is the result of the original, natural law. Like all true commands, it is but the transcript of divinely ordained nature. So that whatever prayer might be, many reasonable considerations conspire to show, that he who employs it is wiser than he who neglects it; he who employs it, is in unison with one of the highest laws of his being. He who neglects it, neglects his own soul. He who will not pray, or cannot pray, or does not pray, is out of tune with highest being. There is a blank in his spirit. There is the best territory of his soul to him locked up, unknown, utterly lost. That is part of what it is to be lost, not that we are lost to something, but that something is lost to us. There is a joy transcendent, perhaps the highest joy known to man, of which he is utterly ignorant, and whether he be wholly lost or not, in that kind of being, and to that degree he is unfortunate, because he is in darkness. If there be one here who thinks prayer is useless, who from any cause is not in the habit of praying, let not this thought escape you. The absence of prayer, or of desire to pray, is a blank in your highest and noblest being.

Because prayer is an office of our higher being, and because it is responsive to a law, it cannot be that prayer will soon cease, to a true child of God. It is common for us to talk of our prayers being eventually turned into praises, but I think that is taking a very narrow view of prayer; for, take away prayer from the saints, and you take away the sweetest privilege they have—it is heaven, it is presence with God; it was, hence, that Jesus prayed—He, though upon earth, in prayer was with the Father. The same moral need which is in all men was also in Him. That is the reason He prayed; archangels pray; all holy beings pray; they must commune with God. Prayer is not always asking for something, not always praising; prayer is communion; your little child communes with you even when it has no petitions to present.

Whatever it is, if it be as it would appear to be, by God's own ordering—in His wisdom, which framed all things—if it be, as it certainly is, the injunction of God in His holy word, then it must be that God will have respect to him who prays. If you establish the cause, you of necessity establish the effect. It is here you strike the certainty of all God's promises—heaven and earth may pass away, but God's word cannot pass away.

God's word is based upon eternal law; its foundations stand fast forever.

Strange it seems to be—this very consideration, which is the sinner's great encouragement, his almost only plea—God's fidelity—has been brought sometimes as the very reason why prayer was unreasonable. We are told if God works by laws, then of necessity nature must hold her course; causes must go on producing their effects; things must be as they are decreed to be. How can we in our misconceptions—asking for things which are perhaps impossible—change the will of God? How can we, when we know that He doeth all things well, ever desire that his will should be changed? But we do not desire God's will to be changed. What if this *law* of prayer be one of God's fixed laws? We do not ask *impossible* things. What if prayer itself be part of the warp or the woof of the fabric which constitutes His providence? If it be, and I think you have some reason to believe that it is, even nature herself yields us what we persistently in another way ask her for, but if it be, is it unnatural or unreasonable that it, like all law, should effect its purpose? Is there not only an additional reason then why we should pray? But look again. Does prayer necessarily presuppose a change in God? Is there nothing else to change? Suppose, instead of God's being turned into a likeness of our minds, our minds should be turned into a likeness of God. What then? Would that be no desirable effect, no blessing, no profit in prayer? May it not be, God instituted it for this very purpose? In our blindness we know not God—we know not what is for our good. The blessing, the crowning glory of the creature, is to be like God. To see Him in His wisdom, His beauty,

His perfection—that is the creature's well-being. The creature must change out of darkness into light, out of weakness into strength, out of nothingness into real being—man, and no doubt all creature-being, begins at a germinal point. Man is to work his way from that point upward; he is to learn of God—that is being. He is to learn the laws of trust, of affection, of all well-being. A man finds a barrier across his path; he entreats God to take it away. But suppose God does not want it away; suppose he is upon the wrong road; suppose by prayer he finds it out, and comes back again to where God does want him, and where there is no barrier? Is prayer of no use? Suppose he has a burden upon his shoulders and he entreats God to take it away. You know if you do not use your arm, how weak it gets; if you do not train yourself to great achievements, how incapable you become. Suppose God sees how weak his shoulders are, and for that very reason put the burden there—not that he might have something to carry, but be able to carry something—not that the burden is with the carrying, but that the shoulders should get stronger. You all know how the burden of ten years ago, would now seem to you no burden at all. You have grown. Suppose God has some great work for him to do, and is preparing that man to do it, and suppose, by and by, he comes to see it, and does not ask any more to have it removed, but prays God to go on and make him all the stronger. Is there no profit in prayer, and do you not see how it is God lays his heaviest burdens upon his strongest children? Is there then no profit in prayer? *May* it not be—is it not *certain*, God always answers, whether he gives us what we ask for, or not? Is there no glory in the thought, that though the thorn be not removed, the sinner can stand at last and say, God's grace is sufficient, and he can now do all things through Christ strengthening him? Did He who came from heaven make a mistake when He prayed Himself, and taught all men to pray, and showed us how to hope and endure, and be patient; how in waiting we were still serving, and how out of all serving came at last a reward?

And what a short-sighted view of God is it, to contemplate Him only as a combination of laws known to us! Do we know all there is of God? All His ways of working? Has He no resources, no ministering agencies but those which have reported to us? Do we know all there is of ourselves? Are there no forces within us which our philosophies have not discovered? What is that longing, man feels in his spirit? There is a part of God's being, the broadest, grandest, highest, of which, we as yet know almost nothing, with respect to which, man is yet slow of heart to believe, a part not without law, a part the climax and perfection of law, an essence that, like gravity to material being, underlies and pervades all moral being, that part called love. Who yet has measured even *human* affection? What line or plummet ever sounded the depths of a mother's love? What dictionary can define for us that word "*Father?*" What within the limits of possibility has not been wrought by the quenchless impulses of a devoted heart? There is no relation in which God delights more to be viewed, no thought of Himself which He delights oftener to present to us, than that He is the "Father," not simply, as we will persist in thinking, that He is the creator, the source of being, but that He is a sympathizer, a being of feeling—feeling *for* us, feeling *with* us, absolutely interested in everything which wisely interests us, a being who knows our whole nature, our present wants, our future need, a being absolutely more ready to give than we are to ask. "Like as a Father pitieth his children, so the Lord pitieth them that fear him." This is the injunction of Him who came from the Father, God's Son—came that we too might be sons—that we might, when we pray, say "Our Father." Come nestling home, come believingly, come as a child.

Is there no danger of presuming? Yes, very great danger; all folly or pride is presuming. But where there is humility and love, and submission, and faith, and childlikeness, not child*ish*ness, but child*like*ness—then, there can be no presumption. Presumption is possible. When you come with some craving out of a carnal heart, when you petition for something worldly, something to keep up your pride and vanity, something you have lost, but which you ought never to have had, something you never had, and which you ought never to have, then you presume. Because God is a Father, it does not follow we should be foolish children, making our prayers an abomination. You ask again, are we to bring none of our worldly affairs before Him? Oh yes, all *our* worldly affairs. Blessed is he who has no affairs which he cannot bring before God. You know in this world how many of our affairs there are, which are not what God has laid on us at all, but which we have laid upon ourselves. Look at Martha, anxious about many things. Carest thou not that my sister come and help me? Yes; "but why have so much to do?" You ask again: Are we to be indifferent to our affairs? Never, never. Would that nine out of ten of us were more earnest and diligent than we are? What a blessed world it would be if there was more fidelity for God's glory? Are there then any of our affairs which press upon us, to which God can be indifferent? Not one. That is it. If they are thine affairs, then they are God's affairs too. Bring them to Him. But in all our asking we should always add: "Not my will, but thine be done." I do not say it is easy to do. I do not think it is, and this shows us, prayer is intended to lift us up to God, rather than to bring God down to us. If we are in trouble, does God not know it? Is He not there with us? "When thou passest through the waters I will be with thee." It is a blessed thing for some men and women to get into real trouble. There is many a one of us, absolutely not a man or woman at all, until we get into trouble. There is a varnish over our manhood, a tinsel outside our real gold. God brings trouble sometimes to wear it off, to make us seem what we really are. There is a wide chasm between some of us, till a great trouble falls into, and makes us accessible to each other. It will be found in God's kingdom, that out of our apparent misfortunes sprung our greatest blessings.

In all our troubles, it is always the faith and submission and love of God we need more than the thing we pray for. We do presume when we dictate too much to God. Israel asked a king, and God gave a king, not because he wished to give it, but because it was the best that poor, faithless Israel could receive—Balaam. God may give us many things we ask for, and yet bring leanness into our soul. Is not that contrary to his law of love? Nay, what He gives may be the best we can receive. It might only prevent us from being worse off. It might delay our destruction and give one chance to avert it. We are the measure of our gifts, not God's love. In a proscribing spirit, we may indeed be worse off for our prayers. When we pray God to convert the world, we may mean convert it to our particular way of thinking. We may not think that we ourselves need to be converted to the right. We may pray God to reward our enemies, or we may ask Him to bless them in such a spirit, that God sees we really mean that He will do to them as they have done to us, and then our prayer is turned into sin. When Christ says, ask what you will and it shall be given you, He presupposes it is Christian asking. If it is a child you long to see converted—if it is a heart you wish to win—if it be some act of mercy and love, you wish to accomplish, you cannot be too importunate. If some great sorrow is at your heart, if some longing beats there, you cannot tell to another, bring it to God. If some temptation is in your path, some fear darkens your way, be not afraid—temptation is not itself a sin—bring it to God. If some sin lies upon your conscience, some denial of Him or His cause—if you are out of the way, so that the heavens look like brass, that you even cannot pray, bring it to God; He is your best friend, and prayer is your highest hope. If you look within you and see there a worldly heart; if you look upon the Church, as most plainly you may, and see there worldliness; if you look out upon the world, and see there darkness and cruelty and wrong and bitter woe; if you desire to be a child of God, and wish many to share your heritage with you; if you wish to see love and peace upon earth; if you wish to see grace and piety and all that is lovely upon earth; if you wish to see God's will done here as it is in heaven, then pray. You cannot be presumptive, you cannot be too importunate. What saith He who wanted us all to be with Him the true children of God: "Knock, and it shall be opened." Knock where? "I am the door. My very being here, is pledge to you of a Father's love." Knock when? At morning, and at noonday, and at night—in the closet, at the family altar, with thy children around thee. Knock for what? "In everything, by prayer and supplication make request unto God." Knock how? Humbly, submissively, earnestly, perseveringly. Feel that God is there; feel that He will not turn you away. Come as a child to a Father, with a big heart and a high hope, because you are needy, and sinful and weary, and long for a new life. So coming, then, what though we be in this wilderness? there is bread enough and to spare. So coming, then, what though we be toiling in the darkness, buffeted by the elements? the Master does not forget us, He is not only interceding for us, but will soon appear, to take us to our rest. So coming, then, Sabbath days and all seasons of communion with God, will have lifted us further from this world, nearer to the Saviour. So coming, we shall feed ourselves on things divine, be better guides to others, and glorify our Father which is in heaven, and lay up for ourselves treasures that are eternal.

THE FRUITS OF RIGHTEOUSNESS.

PHILIPPIANS 1: 9, 10, 11.—And this I pray, that your love may abound yet more and more in knowledge and in all judgment; that ye may approve things that are excellent; that ye may be sincere and without offence till the day of Christ; being filled with the fruits of righteousness, which are by Jesus Christ unto the glory and praise of God.

PHILIPPI is supposed to have been the first place in Europe in which St. Paul preached the Gospel. From some things in this Epistle, it would appear, that the Philippians were a people of a somewhat higher culture than was usual in those times. Paul was a great fault-finder. His vision was so penetrating, he discovered all the blemishes, all the omissions and commissions. He was so much in earnest, he never failed to point out evils, warn the people against them, and exhort them to wisdom. This Epistle of his, to the Philippians, differs from all the rest of his Epistles, in this respect, that he utters no complaint. The relations existing between him and them, were of the most endearing nature. There was something in the people, which had caused them deeply to appreciate the Apostle. Their souls responded to the simple richness of his spirit. This very Epistle was occasioned by an act of kindness. They had heard that he was a prisoner. Fearing lest he should suffer from want of something their means could afford, they sent a messenger with money to administer to his necessities. This act of theirs was the occasion of his writing. It may be supposed, their kindness toward *him* had made him partial toward *them*, but the probability is, their kindness toward him was a proof of their superior nature, so that Paul was not blinded by their gift, but only made more sensible of the graces and virtues, without which the gift itself had not been possible. He could say respecting them, I thank my God upon every remembrance of you, always in every prayer of mine, for you all, making request with joy: "And this is my prayer: that your love may abound yet more and more in knowledge and in all judgment; that ye may approve things that are excellent; that ye may be sincere and without offence, till the day of Christ; being filled with the fruits of righteousness, which are by Jesus Christ unto the glory and praise of God."

This is a very comprehensive prayer; it is worthy of such a heart as Paul's. It was not that he cared more for them, than he did for his other Churches; he did not reflect so much upon the fact that they cared more for him, only, there are souls whose sympathies go out toward us, and souls toward whom our sympathies go up, and to whom our hearts can make a clearer revelation of their yearnings. The Apostle wanted to see this rich and appreciative nature in them, still richer. He desired it to be developed: "I desire that your love may abound," *i. e.*, be constantly increasing "your love." He must have meant their loving disposition—the spirit of love that was in them—the affectionate nature. It is surprising how a given spirit will sometimes pervade a whole community—a whole church. Towns and congregations just as much have their dispositions, their characters, as individuals. Unhappily it is not always a spirit, the essence of which is love. If you run through Paul's Epistles to his different churches, you will find his tone varying, so as to bear with effect upon their respective peculiarities. The Romans were a proud people. The Corinthians, a worldly-minded, skeptical people; the Galatians, a fitful, irresolute people, and so all the way through. Each had its characteristic, and so it is still. Some congregations are sociable and friendly; some are humble and affectionate; some are receptive and charitable; some are worldly and trifling; some are proud and seclusive; some are talkative and gossipy; some are suspicious and cold; some are captious—never satisfied; some are enthusiastic, running into ecstacies over nothing; some are not much of anything. Blessed is the people that find the man who suits them, and blessed is the man who finds the people that suits him, *provided* they both be of the right kind. There can be no suiting, unless both are assimilated. If they are both wrong—if a worldly man gets into a worldly congregation—there will be woe to them and to their children, here and hereafter. Where they are both right, there will be mutual joy, full, free and deep. To a minister of the Gospel, the recollection of the righteous among any congregation he has left, is full of peculiar joy, even long years after he has left them. Paul said of these people, "I long after you." He found in them a people to his mind; they loved him and he loved them, only he desired that this loving disposition of theirs, should not be a negative one.

This is the peculiar danger of such dispositions: to be timid and easy; to run into routine; to take things for granted; to verge upon the sentimental; not to realize duty, in its stearner aspect; not to be very aggressive. When we sometimes meet what is called a loving disposition, we feel, if the world were full of such spirits, it would be a very sorry world. We should all only drift.

There is no fire in them, nothing for grand or glorious deeds. There is no depth, nor height, nor length, nor breadth. If the world went to the bottom, they would sigh and think, after all, it were best it should. If the whole world were asleep, they would think it better not to disturb it. Paul had no desire that the Philippians should settle down into this. Christianity was not intended for that. Activity and truth are not antagonistic to love. Put vigor into the love, and you have what Paul was himself, and it was very natural he should desire these Christians to be like him. He had been striving to realize his own ideal. His Master before him, was his model. A loving disposition, was the very best kind of a disposition, if it lighted, and warmed a whole Christian manhood. Take a loving disposition abounding in positive qualities, and there is nothing nobler. It is the beginning of an archangel. "I pray that your love may abound more and more," but I desire that its increase shall be in knowledge and in all judgment. In St. Peter we have this passage: "Add to your faith, virtue, or manliness, and to manliness, knowledge."

You observe how both these Apostles agree in this, how they contemplated Christianity, as going down to the foundations of our being, pervading and quickening our whole nature. Peter says: "Add to your faith knowledge." Paul says: let your love increase in *knowledge*—knowledge of God, knowledge of ourselves, of nature, of this humanity in its capabilities and wants, of art, of science, of all that God hath done. What worlds would open to many of us, if we could spend our time in learning something. How we should cease to want amusement. How we should no longer be clothed in levity and folly, but in truth and wisdom.

The Savionr said, we should love God not only with all our heart and all our soul, but with all our *mind.* Paul says, let your love increase in knowledge. To this he adds, "and in all judgment." The word he uses here for judgment, is peculiar, and expresses rather what we express by our phrase, "*common sense,*" understanding. It is a word which conveys a very important idea, perhaps more important to us to-day than to those to whom Paul immediately wrote it. You will find in your margin, for the word, sense. I desire that your love increase in knowledge and sense. They are far from being the same thing. Many a man knows a great deal, who has not sense enough to know, whether, what he knows, is worth knowing, As a general thing, our Christian knowledge runs in single veins. Owing to the peculiar condition of our Christianity at this moment, we are not educated, which means that our powers be developed, so that we shall be able to think and know something for ourselves—so much as we are *in*ducated, if I might use the word. Something is crowded into us. When we are full, we are supposed to have knowledge, but we do not pause to consider of what kind it is, what it all amounts to, what it is worth, what it enables us to do. This word of Paul's embraces the whole idea of the practical—of that which is *wise, discreet,* available. A doctor may know by heart the *materia medica,* and yet not be able to write a proper prescription. A lawyer may know all the codes, and yet not be able to manage a case in court. A minister of the Gospel may know all the fathers and the history of the Church, the decrees of councils and the work of the Middle Ages, and yet be all the worse for his knowledge; he may have nothing to apply to his times—

nothing that is religion--nothing that anybody wants, or ought to have, even if they want it. This is, unhappily, too much our condition. We accept without inquiry, that to which, by our birth or other accidents, we become accustomed. A Romanist follows the teachings of the Church; he administers his holy water; counts his beads; runs through the requirements of his faith. Suppose he should pause to do as Paul bids us all do, exercise judgment, common sense—ask how it is possible for things to be as he is told they are—his common sense would break up his creed. If any of us should grow thoughtful, and exercise sense, and ask the meaning of much to which we are accustomed, it would work a revolution in our religion—*e. g.*, why so many divisions of Christianity? When millions know nothing of the Gospel at all, why so many men, each preaching a peculiar doctrine? What is the use of our peculiarities, even if they have foundation in some reality? What do we gain thereby? What does man gain by them? Where is their wisdom? Why do we build so many churches, to be occupied only a few hours out of every week, when, if we would worship at different hours, one church would do for all. Why do we do it, especially when so many poor are in want of bread? When a town wants schools, and libraries, and lyceums, and lecture rooms—when so many agencies are crying to us for help, and we always complain that money is so scarce? How, with all our religion and churches, we still work against each other! Suppose we ask ourselves, What though the world be covered with beautiful churches, if man be vile, if God be not worshiped in spirit and truth? What though we have infinite creeds, if nobody really believes, if mammon govern us, if passion and pride and folly be the rule of our lives. If where piety and humility—brotherly love and rich heart-culture and every virtue ought to be, there is only vanity and show, what is the use of so much religious machinery? If we should stop to define real religion, and then define what passes for religion, the definition would bring us to our senses. We should have some sense in our religion. If we should exercise our senses, that would bring us to make definitions, and we should get much nearer to a *unity* than we are.

That this is embraced in Paul's meaning, is evident from the next clause. I desire that you abound in knowledge and judgment, for this reason, "that you may approve things that are excellent," literally, "that you may try things that differ," that you may find out the elements amid which you live, and assimilate the best. Who of us could do that? I verily believe, brethren, that notwithstanding our attachment to our respective churches, our devotion is rather negative than positive—more out of our ignorance than out of our knowledge. First of all, a very large proportion of our religion is mere attachment to church organization. Then we know very little about that, about our real doctrines, the reasons we have for things. Very few Episcopalians can give a good reason for bowing the head in the creed. You will very often be amazed at the absence of anything like large information upon very simple and common subjects. There are few of us that could not be argued out of what we have thought we believed for years, if a stronger and better informed mind encountered ours. That is the reason why men change their creeds. They knew nothing of their old creed. They know nothing of their new one. They will soon be ready for a new change. We do not try things that differ. It would not be safe for some of us to try. Cut us loose from where we are, and we would be adrift, unballasted, blown about by every wind of doctrine. We have no mind-force to move us toward any real haven. We are not weaned from our senses—from mere habit. I do not wonder people guard their pulpits the way they do, that they so jealously watch the lips of their appointed teachers and raise a cry the moment a new idea comes in. Methodist, Puritan, Quaker. Why, we will not let our teachers teach. We go fast enough, where knowledge and sense do not lead; no extravagance, no absurdity gives us pause. With all our religion and churches, we have no time to devote to real subjects of the rich and deep things of God. We have no reason for any hope that is in us. I sometimes try to conceive what the general idea of heaven is. I conclude there is no idea. If there be, it excludes mind and common sense, it robs eternity of all dignity and worth, for there is nothing to do. It will be impossible to tie the kingdom above, down to our limitations, as we try to do here—down to mere bodily sense; and so some of us will lose our heaven for we shall leave it behind us. "I desire that your love may abound in knowledge and sense that ye may try things that differ," in other words, that ye may know something, and that you may inquire and select and get the best, dwell in such love and intercourse that you may compare notes one with another and so aid each other. But the Apostle goes on: "*That ye may be sincere and without offence.*" Both these words are very forcible and peculiar. The word translated sincere, is compounded of two words, one meaning sunlight, and the other discrimination; literally, to be put in the sunlight and found pure and bright. It goes down into the very recesses of being. It drags up motive. It demands transparency. I do not think transparency of character and action is considered a Christian grace. We, at any rate, assert that we do not practice it, by always inferring a motive in others, other than that avowed.

I do not know that all do it, but I think you will all agree, that there is too much suspicion—too much fear that we have an underhanded motive. And this might arise from our practice, which is wrong and unchristian, of concealing our motives, even in things themselves perfectly right and lawful. We do not wish people to know our business, and yet they do know it, too much of it—take pains to find it out. We give ourselves too much trouble as to what others think about us. We are not aware how much we are slaves to other people's notions, and that must be why they have so many notions of us, because they know we mind them. We have nothing to do with what anybody thinks of us. We are only to know that we are pure and right. Let people think what they please. "That ye may be sincere," viewed in the sunlight and found pure. What a blessing would absolute manliness, Christian courage, true independence be! How free is such a man! How loved of God! *Sincere.* Suppose we examine ourselves. Why have we been to church to-day? Was it custom? Was it curiosity? Was it amusement? Was it fear of what others would say if we staid home? Was it love of God, to worship Him. Whatever it was, when we were here, did we worship? Did He who seeth the heart, know that you prayed? Was there no formality? This word sincere, even in our English has a peculiar meaning because a peculiar origin. It is composed of two Latin words, "*Sine*," without; "*cere*," wax—*without wax*. In old times, people used to write notes to each other, and tie a string around them, and seal the ends of the string with wax. When friends were intimate, and open-hearted toward each other, they folded the letter, and, leaving off the string and wax simply wrote the word "sincere." Without formality, without any make believe, my heart to your heart. I heartily wish there were no string and wax in religion, or society, or anywhere else. There ought not to be among Christians. Instead of adding more to our religion and to our intercourse with each other, we ought to strip it of much that is. Christian purity, pure Christianity, will of necessity tend to simplicity, not to ceremony, and formality. Ceremony eats the core out of soul. There can be no soul where there is ceremony. At any rate, soul and ceremony are in inverse proportions. Our world is dead of ceremony. It goes to church with us; it abides in our homes. It carries us to our graves. It mourns for us afterwards. There cannot be anything of it in heaven. If there is, heaven is not heaven. Oh! to be rid of it; to be free! We *can* be, we ought to be. Paul wished the Philippians to be. Jesus had no ceremony. What a figure that is—that Son of God standing in the majesty of a matchless simplicity! Oh! to be like Him.

Christians, you cannot be "*harmless*" or "without offence" if you are not sincere. This phrase, without offence, is also a compound word in the original. It means "*not a stumblingblock*." It does not mean that you simply pass through the world not being yourself offended. It recognizes the duty—the very object of a

Christian—to be a light, a guide, a helper of souls towards heaven. It implies something to do—a life-work. There are two kinds of lights—true beacons and wreckers lights : sometimes, when wicked men wish to destroy a ship, they build a fire on the strand; a false light shines as well as a true one; the unskilled mariner is lured to his destruction. Such a light is a ceremonious, half-hearted Christian; and oh, brethren, how many of us, by ignorance, by thoughtlessness, by neglect, by worldliness, by insincerity, by endless mistakes, are luring others into danger. God would not have it so. It does not grow out of your religion, but out of your want of religion. The Saviour wants you close to him, in thought, in discretion, in sincerity. What a richness there is in all true being! What a glorified condition must that be in which every soul is full of knowledge, full of wisdom, full of love unfeigned. What a condition must that be when all is real. Such is heaven. God wants you and me to be such souls, that we may enter that heaven. Oh, what a God is our God, and oh, what a glory it must be to be His child. Christ came to show us what such a child is; he set us an example that we may follow His steps. God wants us to be such here below; that ye may be sincere and without offence *till the day of Christ.* This expression, "till the day of Christ," might just as well be "*to the day of Christ,*" or even "*in the day of Christ,*" *i. e.*, in this your Christian day, through this day in which our Christian work is all to be done. The idea, however, at last is the same; clear this life, up to the day in which life will be closed, and Christ will come to take you to the land of reward—the home for glorified souls—till He shall come to pronounce upon our work—the degree in which it has been done to Him, "to the glory and praise of God." This is the summing up of Paul's prayer—this its fullness—that we may be filled with the fruits of righteousness—rather *laden*—as a tree with fruits—laden with righteous fruit—which are "*by Jesus Christ*," by faith in His name, by trust in His redeeming love, by imitation of His example, by love and devotion to Him, by longing to be with Him, to enter into His rest, by the power of His spirit, for we can do nothing of ourselves—by the efficacy of His intercession, by His divine grace, "to the praise and glory of God." This is the consummation of it all—this is what we are created for—God's glory, God's praise. This is why we are left here to work, to chasten ourselves, and mould our hearts; that by our works, this world, this whole race, may be brought to salvation, to know the true God and Jesus Christ, whom He hath sent—this whole race be lifted to the privileges we enjoy ourselves, and all be made sons of God. This, then, is my message to you to-day—*a higher life*—"nearer, my God, to thee—nearer to thee." We are called from darkness to light—called to the power of spiritual resurrection. Oh, brethren, it *is* worth striving for, and the day is very short; the reckoning will soon come. Let us then strive and strive *lawfully*—strive according to God's own plan. If we keep the faith we shall have the crown of righteousness, which the Lord, the righteous Judge, shall give us at that day, and not to us only, but unto all them that love his appearing.

THE VICTORY OVER SIN.

1 CORINTHIANS 15 : 56, 57.—The sting of death is sin, and the strength of sin is the law. But thanks be to God, which giveth us the victory *through* our Lord Jesus Christ.

THIS fifteenth chapter of St. Paul's Epistle to the Corinthians is too well known to Christians generally, to render any minute explanation necessary. The Apostle begins with a partial expression of the Gospel, with evidences of facts relating to Christ, and particularly with those respecting the resurrection. From this he seeks to establish the fact of our resurrection, and closes, in the glowing exultation of a soul already alive in the blissful hope of immortality.

The great fact of the resurrection of Christ from the dead, is, throughout the civilized world, to-day, the one absorbing thought and theme. In all languages, among all tribes, there is to-day the throb of a higher life. Spirits, strangers to each other, are quickened by similar emotions, and participate in the same universal joy.

It is a pleasant thought, that amid all the vocations, ambitions, and struggles of life, *religion*, the idea of a future, never dies. Wherever man inhabits, under all that is outward, above all that is transient, swells the thought of an endless existence. Men instill the thought into their children. They give life to keep it alive.

But in four hundred millions of our race to-day the same thought, upon a loftier level, is connected with this one being, Jesus Christ. Patiently, as the year revolves, we contemplate *Him*, in His wonderful incarnation. We follow Him in His instruction, His life, His connection with all time, His grasp of all being. We stand humiliated, in the face of our meanness, as compared with the majesty of His greatness. From the depths of the contrast, spring the foundations of hope. *Though so unworthy, we are still worth saving.* There is death in us, but there is life in Him. We see this lower nature smite Him, and trample on Him, and bury Him. Over us, over what we call nature, over death itself, there comes a triumph. Through the gloom of mortal ignorance, sin and wrong, across all doubt and uncertainty, away beyond the grave, from the shores of the "better land," comes the *assurance* of an endless life. Christ is risen from the dead. As in Adam all die, even so in Him, shall all be made alive.

This is the thought the Apostle would impress: "Christ is risen" and become the "*first fruits*" of them that slept. *The rifled tomb* proclaims, *there is no death in any such sense as annihilation, or ceasing to exist.* Whatever truly *is*, forever *is*. To prove this *absolutely*, by human logic, is impossible. We have not the elements of an absolute proof, or if we have we are incapable of so combining them. But resurrection is written in universal nature. Preservation of all things that are, is as wonderful as original creation, itself. To everything there is an essence that never dies. It changes its form, but preserves its identity. The spring-time with its flowers; the ages with their myriad reproductions, combine with the beatings of the human heart, and tell us of immortality. Before Christ came, from periods very remote, men believed in a human resurrection.

To stop to prove the fact of Christ's resurrection

would now be a work of supererogation. We do not need it. But that fact *in itself*, does not absolutely *prove our* resurrection. It would if we knew all the connections, but those are just the items unknown to us. We cannot say, because He rose, *therefore* we shall rise. We can say this, as Paul says: "If Christ be preached that He rose from the dead, how say some among you that there *is no resurrection* of the dead." "If there be no resurrection of the dead, then is Christ not risen." But if Christ be risen, then we can certainly say, resurrection *is not impossible.* There is such a thing as resurrection, whether we are to have part and lot in it or not. Now when we combine the utterances of nature, the voice of the ages, the longings of the heart, *the teachings of Jesus,* with the *fact* of the resurrection,—then we can say: "As in Adam all die, even so in Him shall all be made alive." Here is the point of the resurrection—it proves that Christ was true. The evidence is cumulative. The *proof*, to the eye of faith, is *conclusive.* The value of the resurrection of Christ is, it is an example, a practical illustration. It sets at rest conjecture. It crowns all evidence with a fact. It never-more can be rationally said, that there is no resurrection of the dead. If Christ said there would be a resurrection, and proved Himself true by His resurrection, then there will be a resurrection. Let us hold fast this idea, for it is the clearest *certainty* to us of immortality.

But to what extent is this fact, when established, a consolation to us? *All* are to rise—the just and the unjust—they that have been wise, to a resurrection of life, and they that have been unwise, to a resurrection of condemnation. You see there, hanging over that fact, other and greater facts. What is the value of the assurance of an undying future, if that future, by any possibility to any of us, should be an undying remorse? Is existence so precious in itself, that it can be coveted, even though its continuance were a misfortune? You see, the death and resurrection of Christ must have a force and significance, over and above the mere letter. If we confine ourselves to that, there is as much there still to consume us, as there is to comfort us. Myriads of beings would be delighted to know just the reverse, of all this fact proves—would be delighted to *know* there were no future, no hereafter.

From the *crucifixion and grave* of Christ, you learn, that *dying and burial* are not death. From the *resurrection and ascension* of Christ, you learn, that *mere existence is not* life. Over all that God has done, still swells the great truth that man's responsibility is forever the same. If we are to exist forever, it is of infinite importance to us that we should know it. If that future is to be what we make it, it is of eternal importance to us that we make it as wisdom would have it, and that we be taught what wisdom is. There is the goodness of God in sending His Son *to save* us *from* our sins. That is the voice of the incarnation, the whole of it, with all it included. God would reveal to us the real life everlasting. There is the universal fact of death. We cannot resist it, or by any possibility escape it. There is the eternal fact of future existence. We cannot by any possibility escape that. The one is as fixed as the other. When we lie down in the grave ourselves—*when we lay our beloved ones there, we can be as certain of another world, as we are of this.* But what of that world? That is the question. What *are* we? Are we walking in light as God is in the light, with the sons of God, or moving in the outer darkness, where there is but unrest and bitterness? God is reconciled to us. Are we reconciled to Him? If not, we are in our sin. There is a "*sting*" to death. "That sting of death is still sin." You see *that*. Take the wickedest man in the world. When he comes down to die, he still believes he cannot altogether die. He wishes too to live, and knows that whether he wishes it or not *he must*. Nature, *being*, as God has made it, asserts itself. Man not only clings to existence, but *feels* it will cling to him. Not only is there a sense of continued existence, but at the same time also, a sense of guilt. The one is as natural as the other, a feeling, a consciousness, not under our control, a part of our nature. There may be degrees of sin, as when a man dieth, as the brute dieth, "without bands in their death"—asking nothing of the past or of the future, insensible alike to life or death, but that is, if possible, the most hopeless of all death. It is an insensibility hardly human, and fortunately for us, seldom reached. But the most of us have a conscience, a foreboding of judgment, a feeling in us of shame, of fear. We have *no friend*. We go alone. The essence of guilt, guilt itself, if you analyze it, is not something in which God mercilessly wraps us. It is an instant consequence of transgression. Nature is her own police force. Adam disobeyed God. What then? He instantly slunk away and hid himself. He placed himself under arrest. Your child transgresses. What then? It is instantly afraid of *you*, the best friend it has. The instant effect of sin is, it makes us *feel, God is our enemy*. It asserts a lie, a cloud rises, a feeling that we call guilt, a worm and *fire in us*. But

God has not changed at all. He is just the same. What then is the matter? Why, we have transgressed, disobeyed. Transgressed what and disobeyed what? Why, a law, the law, an arrangement of God, *the constitution of nature, the right thing.* You see how guilt at once asserts a righteousness, a law of right. You see how the Gospel, in speaking of *the law*, does not mean the Mosaic law, but all law, this law of right. That law is still there. It hangs over you. It cannot be broken, or annihilated, or removed. Endless worlds hang upon it. *It has strength.* No conspiracy, no ingenuity, no power can destroy it. There it stands. It does nothing, only to try to resist it, is to be instantly stricken with a feeling of unworthiness, of shame, of fear, to have that grim law, between the transgressor and God. Violate the law of noble manliness. It is a good law. Do a mean thing and then you feel mean. The law itself strikes you with condemnation. The sense of guilt is the voice of warning, the alarm of danger. Suppose God is love. Suppose He forgives all the time. What of it, if He is beyond that barrier, and the spirit feels He is its enemy? That is what guilt does for us, makes us misconceive God, blinds us. Tells us God is something which He is not. It surrounds Him with fires and thunderbolts and wrath. And when the soul looks down into the grave, and beyond that, into the fathomless darkness of death, it shrinks, and real death is there with its sting, goading the spirit into an unutterable wretchedness. "The sting of death is sin." A consciousness of sin, a God offended, no way of escape, that is it, which makes death so ghastly, the coffin and the grave so utterly repulsive. That it is which makes us shrink back from ourselves, from existence itself.

"The sting of death is sin," and "the *strength* of sin is the law." The law is good enough; the law is needful. What said the Saviour: Heaven and earth could pass away sooner than that a jot or tittle of the law could fail—and so it would, for if the law could fail, then heaven and earth would pass away. He had not come to destroy the law, nay, but to magnify and make it honorable. The law has strength; it is the cohesive force of the universe; take it away, and all is chaos. It is because it is needful, that it is strong, and because it is strong, it must hold its way, though a myriad souls are crushed by its power. Salvation, is to be in harmony with it. He who thinks that Christ rendered it inoperative, misunderstands Christ; he who thinks that faith in Christ can justify disobedience, has no faith. *Christ changed nothing; he brought a new law to our knowledge.* Obedience to the new law, changes our relations to the old law. The whole change effected by Christ, must be in the sinner, or else there is no change; hence it is, that while the Gospel is for every one, it is for him that believeth. "Whosoever will may partake of the waters of life," but, if he would have life, he must partake; he must be born from above. "Neither circumcision availeth anything, nor uncircumcision, but a new creature."

Christ does not save by any arbitrary efficacy, or divine feat. There is no such thing, for all divine action is by law. Christ saves, by putting into the sinner that which is in Him, or, otherwise to express it, the sinner is saved by putting on Christ; what Christ was; becoming a fulfiller of the law: "He that hath the Son of God, hath life." Faith is perceiving, accepting, applying. *Any one of us is saved only as—precisely to that ex-*

tent to which—we understand and obey Christ. If there were such a thing as an arbitrary efficacy in Christ, then all men would be saved, and then too *moral* nature would be gone. But because moral nature is still left, and there is no such thing as arbitrary efficacy, man is saved by faith, and faith is, rising into Christ, and being what Christ in His being showed us what to be. This is the victory through our Lord Jesus Christ. But faith is *victory*. We are victors—we must *overcome*. The law which Christ brought in was the law of *parental authority*, or, if you view it from the other end, the law of *filial obedience*. Sin is ignorance of law and hostility to it. Religion is, *knowledge of law and obedience to it*. Man in all ages has neglected to study, to learn. When by any means knowledge has come, he has preferred that which was pleasant, to that which was wise, that which was dogmatical, to that which was true. We Christians of to-day are making religion, custom and doctrine, not truth and life. Thus he has destroyed himself—he has considered the law a taskmaster, his enemy. But because it was fixed, his refusal to obey it, *made* it a taskmaster and turned it into his enemy. He ran point-blank against it; something had to yield; the law was strong, and he was crushed. Now the Saviour comes in and says—recognize the law, realize its strength, obey it, find it out—*learn of me*—and you at once invert all relations, and the law is henceforth your slave—you are master. Put my yoke on, and you find rest to your soul. Remember, God is your Father. *All* that is, is calculated for your good. Be His child and love Him, and then you instantly outstrip the law and anticipate all good. You swallow up the first in the power of the second. *The law of love in Christ, sets you free from the law of sin and death*, by taking you out of your antagonism to it. It has not changed nature, but it has changed you. There is a renovation in you—a new life. Before Christ, there stands the law with its code in one hand, and the rod of correction in the other; man grumbling, doing just as little as he could, and being chastised at every step. In Christ then is the code, but its enactments are anticipated—its will is done without its speaking. The rod is annihilated, because it is useless. In Christ, man is not a passive agent, acted upon; but a being, active, combining all law into a force, lifting him into the dignity of a son of God. Before Christ, the law is penalty, and prison-house, and death. In Christ, all law is school, and culture, and rich development; it is truth and freedom. In the family, the disobedient child requires rules and correction. The loving child, anticipates all rules, and the rod is unknown. In society, the criminal is the victim of the law. The honest citizen is set free from the law. The useful citizen is its guardian protector, and even its maker. The wisest people have the shortest code, not that they know the fewest laws, but that they *know* most laws. The law is written in their heart. You are not afraid of the police; you are so for above them, it even seems strange to you, anybody should so live as to make a police needful. Out of Christ, the sinner is destroying himself. In Christ, man, poor and frail as he seems, becomes a co-worker with God, and is making for himself a heritage with all that is eternally glorified. The divine law is written in his heart. Like the Saviour, he delights to do God's will. *Love* is the fulfilling of the law. The rod and the code grow useless and die; the soul grows stronger and lives. It has vanquished the law. A perfect love has cast out all fear. There is victory. Does this, then, throw any light upon these words: "The sting of death is sin, and the strength of sin is the law, but thanks be to God, which giveth us the victory *through* our Lord Jesus Christ." Suppose it should have to be said to you to-day: "Thou shalt not steal." What a reflection it would be upon your condition! What a thrill it sends through you, to even think of it. Suppose you should, practically, in earnest, *have* to say so to your child, how it would grieve you! How it must grieve God to have to say this to His own offspring! But when it was needful for Him to say it, how merciful in Him to step in and write it for our instruction! Do you see, how even Moses himself was only part of the eternal love of the everlasting Father? Do you see, how man hath been all along under only one dispensation, and that a dispensation of mercy? How Moses was a schoolmaster to bring us to Christ? Do you see, that if Moses is a hard taskmaster, it is because we were degraded slaves? The law says, "thou shalt not steal," "thou shalt not murder." Jesus says, "thou shalt *love* thine enemies and do good to them that hate you." "The *law* was given by Moses, but *grace and truth* came by Jesus Christ."

In Moses we were servants; in Jesus we are sons. In Moses, under a law which proclaimed our degradation. In Jesus, in a law which asserts our exaltation. Now, suppose it be needful for any voice from God to come in to-day and say to you, "my son, give me thy heart," are you born again? Have you any victory? What does that imply with respect to you? Suppose you are buried up, not under the old decalogue, but under worldliness and selfishness, under vanity, and earthly, and carnal indulgence, under idleness and uselessness, though you have escaped from Moses, have you entered into Christ. If you have escaped from the swine, have you got home to your Father's house? Do you see what the cross means, what the death of Christ means, that the old, carnal, earthly manhood must be crucified; that, to save a life, you must lose a life; that the old manhood must be buried, and the new manhood raised? Do you see what the resurrection means, that we must leave the oldness of the letter and enter upon the newness of the spirit? Do you see what Paul means, when he says: "Christ, our Passover, is sacrificed for us, therefore let us keep the feast—*not with the leaven of malice and wickedness, but with the unleavened bread of sincerity and truth?*" It was needful that Jesus should be crucified, that we might know the depth of the meanness there was in us—the meanness that placed him there. Think of a race that could crucify such a being. It was needful that we might know that no depth of meanness in us could exhaust the riches of His heavenly love. It behoved Him to be obedient even unto the death of the cross. It was needful that He should rise again that he might proclaim the fact and power of an endless life—that he who is obedient and loving and faithful and true, hath life, hath it abundantly, hath it eternally, is victor over all law, all death; that death has no more sting, and the grave no more victory, but that the child of God is glorified forever; that the service of God is perfect freedom. Do you see the victory which looms up through all time for this world, and through eternity in the world to come—victory over self, over wrong, over all evil, over ignorance, all that is negative and sensual and earthly; victory in knowledge, in virtue, in grace, in peace—in all that can truly elevate and glorify. Death hath no more dominion! Do you see how the fact of the incarnation, gives you a mission upon earth, and calls you out of darkness into light? Can you see how *resurrection* must be a fact—not merely for our day, but a fact perpetual through time and through eternity? A fact in you and in me, or else we cannot ascend to our Father in heaven? And can you to-day, in view of what you would have been without Jesus, and in view of what you might be by Him, exclaim as Paul did—"Thanks be to God?" If, out of the fullness of a rejoicing spirit, you can say that, to-day, then the grave may be there, and the law may be there, but you have already risen, you have entered into life. When you contemplate your dying hour, and think upon God, there is no shudder of fear, no thrill of condemnation—the forerunner is there, the advocate is there, the crown of life is ready. Yes, when we close the eyes of our loved ones, and lay them away in the dust, there is no death—"Thanks be to God." The dying hour is the messenger which God hath sent to welcome us to Himself—"Thanks be to God." We never can be thankful enough for that blessed life, that blessed death, that glorious resurrection. We have victory through Jesus Christ. Death is swallowed—Heaven is opened. We and our Father are one.

But there is the point, whether we have entered into this life. When we look around this world in its darkness, its selfishness and its sin, when we contemplate the quarrelling, the fraud, the envy, the vice and all wrong, under which our race groans, when we realize the loneliness and unrest, which broods upon life, we feel there has yet been in man, as a race, no true resurrection. The law is still the strength of sin, and sin is still the sting of death. The law is weak, because we can never compel a soul. The one want to the human heart, is this law of love. To that alone all good is possible. When we contemplate the Church, that universal body, made up of what we call believers; when we behold the vast machinery, the endless outward signs of respect and reverence for the name of Jesus; and then reflect that it is yet early, the day of life not yet dawned; we must feel that we are like that band of hearts which went on the first Easter to an empty grave, to "find a risen Christ." We cannot help feeling that somehow, with all our love, we have made a mistake. With all our affectionate preparations for embalming, what is it we would embalm but a dead body after all? And does this world want that? And no wonder as we go, we have misgivings, and endless problems start up before us, and we say to ourselves, "Who shall roll us away the stone from the door of the sepulchre?" Brethren, we are to-day, and long have been, looking back into the grave of the past and seeking our Christ from there. The great evil which afflicts the Church to-day, is the fact that she would have only an embalmed and historic Christ. We look back, and behold Christ is not where we have laid Him. It is not possible that He should be holden of death—a voice comes from the cave and says, He is not here. Go tell my disciples the Lord is risen, and bid them seek a living Christ. If we could lift our eyes and realize that thought, and it is a thought I would like to leave with you to-day, that ours is a living

Christ, a Christ that is with us always—then our eyes would be opened, and we should know *Him* and the power of his resurrection. The news would spread, unbelief would die, joy would thrill through our world, and Christ, risen and glorified, would once more go in and out among us, in sweet and peaceful communion—our whole manhood would be raised up into a new life, and then would be joy along all our world. This is the thought that we want to realize, that we must have Him to live with us, and live in us *here*, if *we* are to live with Him hereafter. To realize what it is for us to live in Him, and have Him live in us, is the one work that you and I have to do, upon earth. That we may, under the banner of His love, through all duties and trials of life, amid all its chances and changes, go on to do it, is the one prayer that wells up from my heart to-day. It is to this living Christ I have tried all along to lead you, to whom I believe I am trying myself to come, and in whom and with whom I trust, when all the chances and changes of this mortality are ended, we shall *all* stand together forever. May all our Lents and all our Easters, and all the experiences and vicissitudes of life, only build us up more and more into the likeness of Him who died and rose again, into that blessed likeness which shall make us heirs of God. And now, brethren, we are about to celebrate the death and passion of our Saviour Christ, in the memorial He hath commanded us to make. Our communion is the expression of our faith in Him, as an all-sufficient Saviour. It is an act of thankfullness for the love wherewith He loved us, and a promise of service and perseverance so long as life shall last. Is there one of you who has not some hope through that crucified Christ?

> "Was not for all, the victim slain?
> Is one forbid the children's bread?"

It has been our privilege to thread a few steps in our life-journey together. We look out to-day across a little span of time, upon a future which we trust will be ours together forever. Let us come together, then, in this expression of our common faith—our common purpose—our common hope. Let us come together in a prayer for each other, that we may be kept from the evil which is in the world—that we may be fed with the truth as it is in Jesus, and be built up as lively stones in the eternal temple—so that, whether life be long or short, one by one, we may be victors over sin and death, and stand with Christ in that kingdom which shall know no end.

All "who are religiously and devoutly disposed," I earnestly invite to come and be partakers with us in this communion.

TRUTH.

MARK 4: 24.—And He said unto them, Take heed what ye hear. With what measure ye mete, it shall be measured to you: and unto you that hear shall more be given.

OUR Lord had been uttering sublime truths in the shape of parables. He perceived that even His disciples did not understand Him. He then turns to speak concerning the nature and object of *truth;* He calls it *light.* Its nature is progressive and diffusive; its object is the benefit and convenience of man.

The word truth, whilst it expresses one thing, is used to express that thing under two different relations. Truth objectively expresses all that is, the laws and relations of things—the whole infinity of reality as God has made it. Truth subjectively expresses that portion of the whole, which we have acquired or received, our aggregate knowledge of the all-real. Nature expresses both the landscape, and the eye that sees the landscape. Wealth expresses the whole sea of riches, and also that portion we have individually secured. By means of the wealth we have, we acquire more. The eye most familiar with nature, sees most in nature. I do not mean, that the farmer who looks upon the landscape every day, sees most of the *landscape*. The farmer sees the *farm*. I mean, the mind most responsive to nature, sees farthest into nature. The soul that has most truth, will receive most truth. Truth, in the sense of our aggregate knowledge, is to be held up, set upon a candlestick, that it might give light to the whole household. Such a use of it will reveal the things, that around us open the whole domain of being to us. "*There is nothing hid which shall not be manifested*—neither was anything kept secret but that it should come abroad." This is the object God hath in the universe, that His children should know it, and be blessed in it.

The words following here, and immediately preceding the text, are those so often recurring in the discourses of the Master: "If any man have ears to hear, let him hear." Perhaps, as He gazed into those faces, He saw something which told Him, He was much beyond their depth, or some shade of incredulity, which as much as said He was mistaken. Ignorance always undertakes to pronounce in some way against wisdom. So, He virtually says, I know some of you do *not know* what I am talking about. Yet it is necessary that I try to instruct you. Some of you have an inkling of what I am saying; therefore receive as much as you can, that so you may be enabled to receive more. "Take heed what you hear." According to the culture within you, you will receive or reject my words. All will be measured to you in exactly the same measure you bring. To you that hear, will more be given.

These words, like all the utterances of the Master, contain a germinal thought. They express a root idea; they go down to the bottom of things—enter into the essence of cause and effect. Truth was made for man; man was made for truth. Light was made for the eye; the eye was made for light. The *glory* of the moral being is to develop into the full stature of perfect being. Man cannot create anything, nor change anything that is created. He can only go on to know that which is. His glory is in knowing that. *To know God is life eternal.* The progress upward, the adaptation of the finite to the infinite, that is the bliss of immortality—that is salvation. This progress and adaptation, must be a thing of personal and individual acquirement. Or, if you take the race as an aggregate, it must be a thing of race, acquisition. The millenium is the resultant of race, progress. We are so constituted that truth can in no case be arbitrarily given, but must in every case be voluntarily received. You may tell your child the highest formula of abstruse science, but you tell it nothing, if the thing be wholly beyond what we call the child's apprehension. Even the highest wisdom, the divine Word, Jesus Christ, could not make the Jews understand Him. He could furnish wisdom, but not the capacity to receive it. When you die, you can bequeath your houses and lands, but not your knowledge and wisdom and virtue. The true riches, each soul must obtain for itself. The true riches the human race must work out. The human race is rich only in proportion to the number of its individuals that are rich. *Who therefore becomes truly rich, to that extent enriches his race.* Whoever is poor and lean in spiritual things, is a burden for the race to carry. There is your work, and more, to obtain the true riches. There is the work of all mankind. Were it otherwise, intelligence could not be intelligence—we should be no more than the tree or the stone.

We ourselves alone set limits to our well-being. Nature, truth, will always respond to our highest comprehension. To him who truly loves her, truth is divinely communicative. On all sides are infinite treasures. They are absolutely free to all who have intelligence enough to know they are treasures. We trample on them sometimes like swine on jewels. God's delight is in them that find Him out, and His delight is in proportion to the nearness of our approach. We have however all the interval to traverse, that lies between nothingness and perfection. We begin at an infinite remove from God, and begin *to all appearance* under circumstances of greatest disadvantage. So the divine wisdom has ordered, therefore, it was not good, or possible, to have it otherwise. We know nothing. We have to learn to know.

The human mind at first is like the eye of a babe. It cannot bear the light. Then when it begins to know, nature is full of reflections of herself. We know not the reflection from the thing reflected. Human history, thus far, is hardly more than the record of human mistakes. It would appear that truly to know, involves that we know *what is not*, as well as *what is*. That is about the experience of each human life, for each of us is but the epitome of the race. It is well enough to say, as we say sometimes, if we had known as much ten years ago as we know now, we would not have made the mistakes we have, but if we had not made those mistakes we could not have known as much as we do. Our folly is, our sin is, we persist in following that which has been infinitely demonstrated to be nothing—to be wrong. The wise is he who, through all nothingness and wrong, has an eye to see the true and right. It is written, "Understanding is a well-spring of life *to him that hath it*."

But that is the point, *who hath it?* How are we to know the reflection from the thing reflected? How are we to know when we have the real truth? The Saviour intimates that it is extremely difficult to tell. The history of our race demonstrates the difficulty. "Take heed what you hear." For guiding us in the search for truth, man hath wrought out many devices. But even these devices, are only according to the resources in man up to his capacity. In early ages, when man was nearly all animal, the giant was supreme power. The strong man became a god, an ultimate authority. You have that fact embalmed in the fables which relate to Hercules. In later times, as man advanced toward a conquest over nature, to some knowledge of mechanical art, rude artistic power became salvation. The tower of Babel attests the fact. As man advanced to his higher being, to the regions of mind and spirit, he advanced toward what we might call doctrines and systems. Forgetting that truth must forever grow, because "all that was secret must be disclosed"—forgetting that the problem grew more intricate as it approached the regions of pure spirit, man fixed limits to what was illimitable, and grew dogmatic in proportion as he should have been humble and patient in inquiry. In spite, however, of all folly and error, truth kept on growing. Its branches spread; no dogma could cover them all. Philosophy secured her apostles; science secured hers; and all branches got to something like a natural living, except the religious branch. That, because highest of all, became more trammeled than any. Man undertook to take special care of it. Most of all needing inquiry, it was most of all hedged with dogma. Less capable than any, of being compressed to limits, man determined most of all to limit it. When the Saviour came to the race, He found it bowing down to glow-worms, supposing they were suns—found it in the night, supposing it was broadest day. There was not power of vision to endure a true light. There was ignorance enough to despise the very thing they wanted, as all ignorance does. They knew not what to hear.

Where the race was then, a very large proportion of the race is to-day, and the duty of taking heed—the question of *what* to hear, is just as imperative to us as to those whom Christ immediately addressed.

Now, what shall we hear? If the question were asked respecting science, we should know who to hear. I should go to the astronomers about astronomy, to the geologist about geology. What they agreed upon and could prove by experience and observation, I should accept as truth. What they could not agree upon, what was yet undecided, I should leave them to experiment upon, and leave each to his theory—knowing that none of them *knew* anything about it, but feeling that by their united inquiry truth would be disclosed, and that he who knew most would do most to disclose it. If the question were asked respecting religion, a similar course should be pursued, but here we are persistently unreasonable. We do not accept that, the substance of religion, in which all agree, and then leave those, who ought to know, to discuss the philosophy of things, that which is unknown, and proved to be unknown, from the very fact, that no agreement can be reached. But we undertake to discuss what we know nothing about, and quarrel over matters relative to which all that is *certain* is, that to some extent, we are *all certainly wrong.*

Some men would say, " Hear what the Church says." But then, who is to determine what the Church is, which is to have its say? There is, perhaps, no other word in the language which conveys a more indefinite idea than the word "*Church.*" Some men do not know enough to know that. Some men use it as if its meaning were patent at once to any ear, and set the man down as a fool who does not accept their definition of it. But take it in any of the senses, either as embracing all Christendom, or as confined to a mere sect, who is to determine *what* the *Church* says? Through all the ages, the Church has said different things. *Paul had occasion to resist Peter to the face.* If *opinions* of men are the voice of the Church, then opinions differ. If the decrees of councils are the voice of the Church, then we must believe that the world does not turn round. If the Church is infallible, then no utterance of hers can be wrong, and so no utterance can be changed, and therefore, if she says the world cannot turn round, we cannot believe that it does. If, as has been said, she undertakes to legislate in matters not within her province, then she is not infallible, and so how are we to know when she is right, and when she is wrong?

Some men would say, "take what the Bible says." But what does the Bible say? The Bible, in any language to-day, is a translation from ancient MSS. There might have been, doubtless were, many mistakes in the MSS. There might be, doubtless are, many mistakes in the translations. How can we arrive at the true original? Then, when we can agree upon the original word, how can we agree upon the exact word which shall represent that original in our language? *We* say "*repent*," our Romish brother says, "do penance," and that too, when there is no dispute whatever, as to the original word. Then, when we have settled the translation, who shall fix the meaning? Men take the propositions of Paul, and stir up darkness. Men grapple with questions which they are wholly incapable of comprehending, and hence the confusion even in many Christian pulpits.

Some men would say, "take what Jesus says." But what does He say? Even when there is no dispute as to His words, *the mind interpreting, can never give to those words a meaning higher than its own capacity.* "*With the measure we mete it, it is measured to us.*" Even under His immediate, simple, beautiful, loving words, with all their accents and intonations, men did not understand Him. He said relative to one of His disciples: "What if I will, that he tarry till I come," and they made Him say, that that disciple should not die, and so men are forever making you say what they say, and it is a fearful burden to carry other people's sayings. It has been the calamity of Christianity, to have to carry our interpretations rather than Christ's own words. He said "I am a king." They made Him say *Cœsar was no king.* He said nothing about Cæsar. When they cannot grasp His saying, or perceive that He refutes their saying, then they declare "He hath a devil." And so it ever is. *Unwisdom is always down to its own level.* There is need of saying: "Take heed what you hear." There is need of realizing that with what measure we mete, it is measured to us.

Still the question remains, what are we to hear? We talk about the "Rule of Faith." We often repeat the expression that "the Scripture is the *sole* rule of faith." *Then* we *reason* about the Scripture, and make reason at last the ultimate arbiter. The fact is, the Scripture is not the *sole* rule of faith, nor reason either, if you mean *that* by which the ultimate life-action is to be guided. The sole rule of faith, like all unities, is a trinity. *The Scripture, the reason, and the moral sense, these three combined make the unit that is to be our guide.* When I use the expression "moral sense," I mean an element which God has given to man—an element we can feel and do exercise, though we seldom define it. To use an illustration: A flower has a property by which it appropriates certain rays of the sun, which rays make that flower different from any other flower, protects and preserves its peculiar nature and character. The human eye has a power in gazing upon that flower of perceiving its beauty. You cannot tell a man what is beautiful, but he perceives what is beautiful. The stomach craves food, but it does not accept straw, or wood or sand; not from any education it has received, but from an innate, natural sense—a sense responsive to the fitness of things God has ordained. So the moral sense in man is the property which asserts to us the just or unjust—the right or wrong. If you encounter the highwayman, and he attempts to reason with you that his calling is honorable, you know his moral sense is perverted.

The moral sense is not exactly what we ordinarily call the conscience. It comes nearer to what the Quakers call the "Inner Light." It may be work of the Holy Ghost. Whatever it is, we have it. I believe it is the Holy Ghost, but then, that is only my belief, and I therefore do not bring it in as an element of the thought. Some men cannot read the Scriptures—some men cannot reason—some men have very little moral sense; so that neither the Scripture, nor reason, nor the moral sense alone, can be the rule of faith, but only the three combined, and their combination in any man is the stature of that man. Their *voice* is the "sole rule of faith." When we speak of *Scripture,* I mean Jesus Christ—what He said—what He was—the *divine Word.* All the rest is only reflection of Him. I can put nothing in His place, nor allow anything to take His place. And when we speak of *man's* reason, or *man's* moral sense, we do not mean *man,* as you or me. Man is not a fraction. I am *a man,* but not *man.* Man is the scholar, the sailor, the artisan, the philosopher, the tradesman, the hermit—everything, all put together—so, reason is not my reasoning, or your reasoning, but the aggregate reason of the race. The moral sense is not yours or mine, but the enlightened moral sense. The Scripture, the reason, and the moral sense, in their broad and comprehensive grasp, are a trinity, which, in their unity, make the sole rule of faith. *What any one of them contradicts cannot be true.* What they all agree upon, must be right. The *witness* of the three, not any one of them, is the sole rule of faith.

Now, we see what our Church says—this grand old Church—so sublime in her comprehensive utterances. In the VIth Article she says: "Holy Scripture containeth all things necessary to salvation, so that whatsoever is not read therein, *nor may be proved thereby*, is not to be required of any man, nor be thought requisite to salvation." Observe—"*nor may be proved thereby.*" *Proved by what?* The same act, which lays down the Scripture as the foundation, makes the reason and the moral sense, the judges to which that Scripture is to answer. Again, in the XXth Article, she says: "It is not lawful for the Church to ordain anything that is contrary to God's word written." Well, how are we to tell what is contrary? Not by any procurement of a clique, arbitrarily called a Church, but only as the reason and the moral sense witness—*the aggregate reason and moral sense*—so that, again, the sole rule of faith, is the resultant, the testimony of the Scripture, the reason, and the moral sense combined. Now, as the Scripture is not *absolutely* perfect, not from any deficiency in Christ Himself, but from deficiency growing out of our inability to secure the perfection—as the reason is not *absolutely* perfect, nor the moral sense *absolutely* perfect—so, it follows, that the sole rule of faith cannot be *absolutely* perfect. What, then? Is there nothing that we can hear? Not at all! Science is not absolutely perfect—is there, then, no science? The beautiful has not been absolutely expressed—is there, then, no beauty? Truth has not been all made known—is nothing known? The Saviour said

He had some things to tell us, which we could not bear—is there, then, no truth? Did He therefore tell us nothing? You see, the Scripture, and nature, and the beautiful, are infinite and fathomless—they are fixed. *Our reason and moral sense, are the measures which set limits to our supply.* A perverted reason and moral sense, will take the wrong thing—a Church, which ignores reason and the moral sense, will have an inquisition. Do you see any force, then, in the words: "Take heed what you hear, for with what measure ye mete, it shall be measured to you, and to him that heareth shall more be given?" I would give a great deal, if I had it in my power to make that plainer for you, but I believe I cannot. It opens for you all a view of life, and in that view a most solemn duty—the duty of so using time, that it shall develop intelligence and moral culture, till we are truly responsive to the eternal Word.

Such is this moral being in which God has placed us. The higher up we are, the more there is for us to do—the more solemn is this being.

These thoughts directly involve another thing of which we talk—the right of private judgment. And this is one of the lessons we draw from this subject. Do what you will, your salvation depends upon yourself. You cannot part with your responsibility. If you let a priest do your thinking for you, and tell you what your faith shall be, still it is *you* that do it. If you part with your private judgment, it is your private judgment that parts with it, and somehow, while parting with it, you still keep it. It is the thing from which you cannot part. Never was there a dogma more foolish than that which denies the right of private judgment. It, in the very act of denial, asserts the thing itself. It thinks private judgment should not be, and what is that thinking but private judgment itself? If you break your own arm, you suffer from it. If you let somebody else break it, you suffer from it. The best way is to take care of your own arms. For what you do, or for what you do not do, your soul must answer to God.

The next lesson, is the imperative duty of cultivating your reason and moral sense by all the means within your reach. Suppose you do not know how to answer? Then you may well be afraid of a thought, and shut yourself up in seclusion. Then draw your lines as narrow as you can. Only the truth can make you free, and if you are more afraid of losing what you have, than of gaining more, you will so contrive as to lose what you seemed to have. Without real reason and culture, you will think you will have to believe all you hear, and at last not know what you ought to hear. Only those in God's light see light. And here we reach one of the greatest evils now in the Church. I contend, that with all our so-called civilization, it is *man* at last that is not cultivated. With such a burden of earthiness to carry, as we have to carry, it is impossible that *man* should be cultivated. Very few men and women, even in the Cuurch, know how to think, and especially to think upon questions involved in moral philosophy. Thinking implies something more than conjecture or opinion. It implies knowledge, experience, and above all, habits of analyzing, weighing, comparing, in much diligence and patience. Even the Christian ministry is not given enough to thinking. Things are, first of all, prescribed to us in our seminaries, before we have had time to know how to think.

We are not taught so much to think, as to receive what we are told. We are not taught truth, broad and universal, so much as our ism—*our doctrine.* We go out never to question our tenets, nor to allow them to be questioned. We go out not to preach the Gospel, but to sustain, each man, his party, till we are not only divided, but antagonistic. Each is skilled in the use of his own arms, till even the Mormons can make as many proselytes as any of us, and the advocates of Sunday liquor laws, of gaming tables, and dens of all iniquity, make more than all of us put together. Proselytes, once gained, react upon the Church. They insist upon hearing that by which they have been captivated. Nothing new or unusual must be introduced. The teacher who follows the old formulas, and rumples nobody's feelings, who is in all respects safe, gets smoothly on. The man with a real thought, with a positive teaching, is set down, like the Master, as Beelzebub. We have no teachers any more. Everybody knows too much. The pews dictate to our pulpits, and the more imperatively, as they are the less capable. A few young misses can, *often do,* determine the theology for a whole parish, till—God being in all cases true to Himself, to His own laws—nothingness produces nothingness, worldliness produces worldliness, superstition produces superstition. The Church is everywhere grieving over the fact. Young men no longer seek the ministry. Men are driven out of our churches, and we are left exclaiming against the impiety of the age. Men start up elsewhere to preach God's truth, and we are left protesting against infidelity—calling those hard names, who, if they *are unfortunate,* are made *unfortunate,* in great part, by our *fault.* The reason abandoned, the Scripture unheeded, and they who, ostensibly, are the followers of wisdom, are most certainly and superlatively unwise; they who have sworn to renounce the world, with its pomps and vanities, are they by whom those pomps and vanities survive, till, instead of the Church being a teacher, we need to intercede with God for somebody to come to teach the Church. Then, as if to confirm us in any errors in which we might be, and to keep us confirmed, our pulpits are barred to any light from outside. In our immediate Church, particularly, no man can enter here, unless he has had laid upon him a so-called Apostolic hand—this we know to a certainty, that hand can convey no truth, nor power to perceive the truth, for whilst it prudently fears an error, it fatally assumes it knows all that can be known. A man who was yesterday made a deacon, may come here and preach, though, in the nature of things, it be not possible for him to *know* anything. While a man, whom the world counts a wise man, whose wisdom is the accumulation of years, cannot even set his foot within the railing. The Son of Man, wandering in his plebian simplicity, would be worse off with us, than He was with the Jews. He could enter into His temple of old and teach them that had ears to hear, but should He come to us, we could never hear Him, unless we heard Him in what we refuse to call a church, or outdoors in the streets. Is it *possible* that mental common sense can endorse such action as wisdom? It has been asked, "where will you draw the line?" I would ask, why draw any line? You have your family circle, and you keep it pure—but what line do you draw. Your judgment and object in social life are your guide, and your purity and culture your protection. Then, if we go into any other pulpit, we must never say a word about their follies or their errors—that would be rude and impolite, though our business is to save souls. That would be wrong, though we are seekers for truth, and we know that one side of a story is good, only till the other side is heard. What wonder is it, that men sit in churches for years, believing, as they think, all they hear, when, by some fortuitous circumstance, they hear another story, and find themselves converted to that? At this rate, do we Christians *believe* anything? Some skillful reasoner could reason multitudes out of their faith to-morrow. I believe that many of the evils around us, are because of evils existing within us. We talk about Christ rather than receive Christ ourselves—what He said, what He was. And, brethren, when I speak of Christians, I mean myself as well as you. I am not, and do not pretend to be any wiser than other people. But I feel the force of what Jesus said: "Take heed what you hear, for with what measure ye mete it shall be measured to you." I see it every day. I would always carry you to *Him*. If I may carry you anywhere else, I lead you astray. I may be at every step wrong. He can never be wrong. I would like you to have an ear to hear Him. Have I been able to show you any force in that utterance of His? Have I shown you any duty of culture in your study of Scripture, in your spiritual being, your reasoning power? Do you see, if you are to love God acceptably, you are to love Him with heart and soul and mind? Have I given you any reasons why you should let go the shadows, the follies and deceptions of the world, and cling more ardently to Christ? Apply your life more devotedly to things above. In all the confusion of tongues let us come back to Him. Let me remind you, with humble and affectionate earnestness, that life is no trifle, that you and I can never drift into well-being, that a *little* knowledge is a dangerous thing, and anything taken for granted is still more dangerous, that nature is full of parables. The wise speak always in parables, even the blessed Jesus. No power on earth can make you see what you have no power to see. If you live in the accidents of life, you will take only more accident. If you live in the essentials, you will crave more essentials, for you will live always in your highest being. If you cannot hear the voice of Jesus, you will hear the voice of the High Priest, and the more you hear that, the more foolish you will become, only the more persistent you will be in believing you are truly wise. *Read, mark, learn, and inwardly digest.* In listening to opinions, consider their source. Be much in prayer and meditation with Jesus. He knoweth His sheep, however the world may treat them. His sheep hear his voice, and follow him. In other words, those who hear his voice and follow Him are His sheep. Them he will bring to the green pastures and the still waters of eternal life, to the everlasting fold where there is everlasting safety. "Take heed what ye hear, for with what measure ye mete, it shall be measured to you; and unto you that have, shall more be given."

PERCEPTION OF TRUTH.

JOHN 8: 46–48.—Which of you convinceth me of sin? And if I say the truth, why do ye not believe me? He that is of God heareth God's words. Ye therefore hear them not, because ye are not of God. Then answered the Jews and said unto Him, Say we not well, that thou art a Samaritan and hast a devil?

THIS whole chapter presents us with one of those marvellous scenes, to me among the most remarkable connected with the life of Christ. The wise and gentle Saviour is contending against the contradictions of the foolish and cruel Jews. He came to His *own* people, but His own people fight against Him. Except the crucifixion, there is nothing in history more humiliating to our humanity than these attempts of the Jews to reason with Christ. Perhaps we should hardly except the crucifixion, for that is but the culmination of rage. These debates on their part, are the patient delineation of ignorance and utter impotency. They could not resist the force of Christ's wisdom, and yet they could not admit it to be wisdom. They undertake to answer His arguments, and yet had no perception of the truth He imparted. They could not account for His miracles, and yet could not admit His power. In the case of an unhappy woman, low cunning of their nature had made Him the arbiter. His innate modesty and mercy, combined in a justice so simple and impressive, drove them self-accused and self-condemned from the judgment hall, and yet they knew all things better than He. No evidence of the divine nature of Christ is strong enough to reach them. They insist upon asking Him,

"Who art thou?" and yet persist in refusing to receive His answer. It was not that He was confronting the illiterate and uncultured. On the contrary "the common people" heard Him gladly. *They* believed He was a prophet. Those who undertook as they thought *to reason* with Him, were the learned, the *guardians* of the nation, set up to be the Church. The High-Priest himself, on the night of the final arrest, said to Christ: "I adjure thee by the living God, that thou tell us whether thou be the Christ, the Son of God?" How could Christ tell Him, except as His whole life proclaimed it? What answer did he want, except that Christ should deny his own nature?

Now, these thoughts are worth inquiring into. These facts are worth explaining. They indicate certain conditions of mind, *possible* to all men, because they existed in these men, dangerous to any men, because they were death to these Jews. We might discover *that truth for any man, or any age, does not depend so mach upon the vividness of the truth itself, as upon our power to perceive it.* We might find that there are conditions of mind, things assumed, results of defective or erroneous education, which preclude the possibility of perception, which make a man the victim of superstition and delusion. It might be, if we understood all the laws of the case, that it would be more wonderful for some men to see the truth, than it now appears to be that they do not see it. We might find many of the elements, the tendency of which is to blind, mingling more extensively in us all, than we are aware, making it imperative that we use more diligence, more down-right, thorough honesty with ourselves to attain that freedom which real truth alone can give us.

One element presented to us in this chapter is of special importance, the element not of an actual Christ, but of *such a Christ*. This thought indeed attaches in relation to the whole incarnation. Man never can complain with respect to Christ, that he had no chance to do himself justice, to do his best, that we were taken at a disadvantage, that anything was appealed to, except our reason, our understanding, our humanity—in short, the best of everything there was in us. Turn the picture over and think. Had Christ been a monarch, as men are monarchs, we could not have reached Him. Had He been a High Priest, invested with the trappings of a false dignity—had He been a philosopher, robed in the forms of profession—had he been anything that was conventional, we could not have done ourselves full and exact justice, because we should have lacked the freedom of an action absolutely unrestrained. He could not have had just His own individual influence and no more, rather we had better say, *and no less.*

We must all have observed, how much more powerful, temporarily, office, position, wealth, family, and the extensive accidents of life always are, than mind, reason, real justice, or any other actual good or personal worth, and that is one reason why there is so much more of the one in the world than there is of the other. Few of us are aware to what extent a man's belongings are more powerful than the man. We are not convinced by mind, by virtue, by real moral forces, so much as by policy, by etiquette, by deference, by conventional habit and prejudice. In other words, we are not convinced at all. In the presence of outward dignity and authority, we only do not express *ourselves.* We yield, and think we accept. In the absence of outward assumption, we hold to our opinions still, if we had any that were really ours, whether wise or unwise, good or bad. We have done many a thing to a man not knowing him, which we would not have done if we had known him; but what we *did*, was an expression of ourselves. Your unconscious action is often much more yourself, than your most studied behaviour. The bowing and scraping a man pays to my dignity or wealth, is not respect for me; it is only the outcropping of his own selfishness. *The respect we pay to the humblest man we know, is the measure of our respect for humanity.* All the rest is respect for ourselves. He who would not know wisdom in a scavenger, would not know it at all; he who despises it in rags, in the very act of despising, simply expresses his own ignorance and distance from God.

This test, the incarnation of Christ, applied to our humanity. We did what we pleased, and what a pleasure it was! There was no restraint and no depth to our degradation. The treatment the Son of God received, was an exact photograph of our moral condition. There were you; there was I. Verily, "for judgment Christ came into this world"—for discrimination—for defining who and what we were—"that they who saw not, might see"—that the humble and the pure in heart might find the truth and God—learn the way to heaven—that they who saw, might be made blind"—*i. e.*, demonstrate that they were blind; not that they themselves would know they were blind, or ever perceive it, for that never happens, but that others, they who can see, might know it—that it might be palpable to all generations that they were blind—that they did not see things that were true and divine.

This was one prime reason why those Jews could

not see. They were buried in deference to externals, to that which was established, to all that was formal, ceremonial, etiquettical, conventional, historic. It was no part of their practice to inquire into anything, *to reason about* things, human or divine. It was not then the custom of the world. It never had been. In a few nations there had been here and there a thinker. The thinkers in those ancient nations, are the most wonderful things those nations ever produced. They stood alone; the multitudes thought they were mad. It is not the custom of the nations to think now. The real thinkers are still considered beside themselves. The Jews lived in assumption—in what we call "*taking for granted*"—in a sort of artificial life—in an atmosphere they created. Or, perhaps it were better to say, they received certain historic facts, accepted them, said they believed them, without inquiring what those facts implied; they actually knew nothing about them. The facts were not fed on and digested; they were kept to be looked at, and, as is always the case, were least understood by those who laid most stress upon them. In the absence of inquiry, they made them imply things that were impossible. "We have Abraham to our Father." Certainly, but that did not make them true children of God. This was one of their mistakes. They said, "God was with Abraham; therefore God is with us." The *therefore* did not by any means follow. "We never were in bondage to any *man; therefore* we are free." Here was another "*non sequiter*." They were in the most galling bondage, only were too insensible to know it. All that they held was not wrong, but it might just as well have been, for all the good it did them. Ignorance, prejudice, error, transgression—that is bondage. Knowledge, virtue, wisdom, usefulness, all grace and excellence, real power to see the truth--that alone is freedom. I do not think we all quite understand that.

Then another fact rises up here. Ignorance and error arm themselves against light and truth. The first assumption of narrowness, of wrongheadedness, and wrongheartedness is, that whatever differs with it, is not only necessarily wrong, but its enemy and the enemy of the race. *Assumption, hereditary creed, forever claims universal guardianship.* It then denies the one grand tenet, that truth must stand forever, in its exhibition of fear that truth can be overthrown. Its assumption, is an assertion of a falsehood, *that truth needs to be guarded.* Think of guarding the sunlight, or gravitation! or the tidal wave!

All that any truth wants, is full and absolute ventilation, circulation, analysis, sifting. There is much more of it, and much, nearer to us than we know for. All we want is an eye to see it. For some men to say they do not see certain truths is simply ridiculous. It would be a miracle if they did. Truth can never grow except as men have power to discuss it. *Wherever truth is perfectly guarded, truth is perfectly dead.* In the city of Rome you can buy no Bibles, and if there was but one Church, no matter which one it was, if that stood alone, there would not be a Bible at all. The spirit of the Jews—" We have Abraham to our Father," is the spirit of all sect, and practically, because human nature is the same all the world over—the difference between sects, is merely accidental. Sectarianism demands not the truth, *but only repetition and confirmation of what it already holds,* and that is most sectarian, which most persistently refuses to hear anything but itself. To change the expression a little, that is narrowest which claims alone to be catholic; that is most sectarian which assumes that it alone is true, and to assume that, is to lose the power of perceiving the truth. We see this in the Jews. There was certainly truth enough in Jesus, but what the Jews wanted was an eye to see it. You must observe this, for it is the very point of this Scripture, "If I say the truth, why do ye not believe me?" Those people whom Christ said were not of God, were the very people claiming to be exclusively God's. If they had been of God, they would gladly have received Christ; but they were mistaken, and, with all their pretensions, were Christ's enemies. That spirit—desire to make something true, rather than to find out whether it is true, deference to anything but the truth itself, is the enemy of Christ to-day, as much as those Jews were on that day to which our text takes us back. Like seeks like. The blind love the blind. If you are buried in any ism, and I come to you to confirm that ism, you receive me gladly. If I attempt to tear away your error, you attack me as an enemy. My truth may be as plain as was that of Christ—but, you see, a soul full of error crowds out the truth, blunts the perception. Whoever is unwilling to have discussed what he holds to be truth, has lost the truth. In what church or sect would Christ have a better chance to day, than He had there that day? You and I, if He were here, should be first, perhaps, to say, "we cannot sanction that—that is not what we have been taught." We should have no power to set quietly down and say, "*is this true.*" Oh, yes, if we knew it was Christ! That would be another matter! But God does not wish you to know, except as you perceive. As I have been showing you, that would be to constrain you; you would yield to authority, not to conviction. The thought would not be your's. It would only be, that you assent to it. You would not know anything about it. Truth bears with it, its own authority. In God's light we see light. To *tell* you it was Christ, would not make you know it was Christ. Oh! what a blessing it was that Christ came, then, *as* He did; that He could not be bought up by the Jews, nor by any influence. Do you not see what it was that crucified Christ? They felt toward him all that we would feel toward a man who does what we call outraging the general religious sentiment. We think that to persecute such a man, is good enough for him. Christ did outrage all common religious sentiment, but it was not His fault. It was their fault. What a blessing that He did go on and say all He did say. Because He did do it, other men have done it. "Because He lives, we shall live also." He has shown men how divine it is to be true to their convictions. They ought to have listened—if possible, to learn. That is our want, thought that is ours, perception of truth out of powers, vital and inherent in us. If we cannot receive a thing, we ought not to say it is not true. We ought to say we cannot see it. Nor ought we to receive a thing, because somebody tells us so. No—it is not the food a man puts in him that keeps him alive, but the food he assimilates. It is not the truth we accept, which does us any good, but the truth we understand. Whoever accepts any truth, into which he is afraid to inquire, puts a millstone round his neck. It is because we receive so little, and understand so little, that we are mentally and morally so lean. This is why, with all our churches, and sects, and preaching, and what we call means of grace, our world is so graceless. We have too much contrivance, too much that is establishment, and not enough truth. The influence of Christ, at least, was infinite, because every atom of it was real. We have so much that is artificial, we have so little that is effective. We wonder we do not accomplish more. The greater wonder would be if we did. The world is as well off as it can be. All things considered, it is more hopeful than we have any right to expect. Nine-tenths of us have little truth to give it—only our ism, that which is of the fathers. We are not living trees, yielding fresh fruits for living men, but only stalls, laden with last year's fruits, and but the remnant of that—black and wilted. Now, another thought. Truth alone can receive truth. Truth alone stands confident that all things help her. There is a majesty in that expression of St. Paul's, where he says, some preached Christ to help him, and some to thwart him. Still, it matters not any way—Christ was preached, and it all helped him. This, also, is included in truth. Not only is it a tenet to be held, it is sincerity in holding it. Truth comes to the true. Christ hath no fellowship with Belial. Truth is life. Who is not quickened by truth, holds no truth. Truth alone passes by the accident, the husk, the occasion, the circumstance, and inquires diligently, turns it over, looks through it. How hard that is to do, none knows but he who earnestly tries it. It requires a discipline so great, that Solomon made no mistake when he said, he that ruleth his own spirit is greater than he who taketh a city. Error says, as the Jews said, unbelievingly, "who are you?" Truth says, as the boy whom Christ had cured of his blindness, said, "who is he, Lord, that

I might believe on him?" Error, in its pride, would stop the truth, and in its impatience, smites it. Truth, in the energy of its quenchless life, courts the truth, even though it may he smitten by it. If we could all go up to our churches to discuss, to hear, to try to understand, not to be stuffed with what we have taken for granted, what we think we already know, what our sect teaches; how broad, and strong, and noble, and useful we should become. A new vigor would pervade the Church. A grand worship in spirit and in truth, would swell upward as incense before God. Our world would recover of its leprosy.

It seems to me, now, you can get some insight into these words of Christ—" which of you convinceth me of sin?" There stood Christ, a pillar of all virtue, benevolence, and excellence. He virtually said, what is religion for? Is not the very idea and essence of it this, to make us wiser, to help us to lead a godly life? If I were seeking to overthrow any good, if I practiced upon your credulity, if I fattened myself at your expense, you would have cause to suspect me, and complain of me. But my life testifies of me. Let the fruit bear witness of the tree.

If, then, my life is true, and I speak the truth—if you can find no wickedness in me, and are not able to refute my teaching, why do ye not believe me? Plainly, there must be some cause in *you*. It is greatly to your interest that you discover that cause. I tell it to you plainly: He that is of God, heareth God's words; he that is true, perceiveth the truth; to him that hath, more is given. All things seek according to their nature. Vice loves vice; folly indulges in folly; error craves error; the iceberg seeks the iceberg; purity loves purity; wisdom inquires into wisdom. All real truth is of God; *you hear not, because you are not of God.* Your eye penetrates not into things divine. You are not in earnest with yourself—with your soul; you are not dealing with the real, but with the fanciful; the fabric you have built, much as you feel interested in it, is not that with which God has anything to do, or cares anything about; you are living for self, for time; you are not living at all. It may seem strange to you that truth should be so near, and you not be able to see it, but it is more strange that you should not be able to see how deluded you are. If you were of God, you would hear God's words; you therefore hear them not because you are not of God. And let me ask you, brethren, if the reasoning of Christ is not plain? But, if any proof were wanted of the truth as the Saviour expressed it, and as I have been endeavoring to show it to you, their answer furnished it—"Say we not well, thou art a Samaritan and hast a devil?" How true to themselves! What had that to do with it? Abuse is no argument—hard names prove nothing. They are only the resort of weakness—the revenge of littleness. But what an exhibition then, of the fact that we can never rise above our real selves. How that which is brutal resorts to brute force, and that which is ignorant to weakness, and that which is malicious to malice. We may always safely leave people to their own convictions, tenets and creeds. A dire necessity is over us all, to make us tell evermore what we are. Strange paradoxes are in nature. We cannot express our experiences, nor can another tell us what we are, but life-action is forever writing us out and telling us to the world. If any of those Jews have ever become wise, what would they not give to be able to go back there, and wipe out that record forever! But if they have never become wise, they do not wish to blot it out. They think it is glorious. This is the reason why the foolish glory in their folly.

Well, brethren, this is the question, if we are not wise, who shall make us wise?—if we know not the truth, who shall teach us truth?—how shall we know it when we hear it? If the angels are weeping over us, what angel shall make us feel we ought to weep for ourselves? Is our life, our earthiness, our treatment of the Bible, of Christ, of all sound wisdom—is the barrenness of our world, the inefficiency of our Churches, the prevalence of sin—is it all telling what we are and how much we are worth? And, oh God! is all going up before thee, going upon the record of those books that are to be opened—to consign us to a place with those Jews that despised thee? Do we wish to blot it out to-day, and put another record in its place? Well, no Lazarus will come from the dead—no angel with a lash will stand over us—no constraint will come even from heaven. There is Jesus, Son of God, better than Moses and the prophets—better than angels or man. Every word, every line, every incident, is full of truth, if we only have ears to hear, and eyes to see. In the commotions of our world, in the churches and sects, and isms, in the successions, ordinances, and conventionalities, everywhere there is truth enough, if you can distinguish truth from churches and isms, from successions and ordinances. Whatever is of sect, of ism, of ordinance, of mere tradition, is *sin*. There is death in it. Let those Jews be a warning to you. Let this Scripture teach us whatever is not of sin is of God.

Our Father would have us so live. You see the solemnity of life and eternity, so demands, that we walk as wise men, in much thought, meditation, prayer, in patient hearing, sifting, testing—that we take heed how we hear, how we stand; that we be able to bear the truth. He who rends our creed into tatters, may be a better friend to us, than he who mends the rents already in it. Blessed is he who, when he sees it going, can feel it is not his all, but that he has that in him, in Christ, in God and heaven, against which time nor eternity can ever prevail. Not only that he hath hold of God, but that God hath hold of him. He is a true friend to us, who shows us that with our creed, even though it may never be torn, or in any way destroyed, we have very little—that over and beyond it, in the deep things of God, are things richer than that—who shows us, that forgetting the things which are behind, and reaching on toward those which are before, we press toward the mark of our high calling, of God in Christ Jesus; that, leaving the rudiments of Christian doctrine, we go on to perfection. This is our calling, that we be enriched in all knowledge and spiritual understanding, that we come behind in no gift; that we be strengthened with might by the Holy Ghost, in the inner man; that Christ, in all He was, in all He said, may dwell in our hearts by faith; that being rooted and grounded in *love* we may be able to comprehend, with all saints, with the true and pure, and the wise of all ages, what is the breadth, and length, and depth, and height, and to *know* by experience, by perception, the love of Christ, which passeth knowledge. In short, to be filled with all the fullness of God. This is our calling. He that is of God, heareth God's words. This is our life-work, to believe in Him whom God hath sent. Let me entreat you all, young and old, draw nearer to Christ—of all things you do, sit at His feet, learn of Him. Take His yoke. There, in all He was, is virtue and grace for you, truth and wisdom for you, life in earth and in heaven, peace, and joy, and rest, forever and ever.

THE TRINITY.

MATTHEW 28: 19, 20.—Go ye therefore and teach all nations, baptizing them in the name of *the* Father, and of the Son, and of the Holy Ghost; teaching them to observe all things whatsoever I have commanded you.

THESE were among the last words Christ uttered upon earth. They were spoken after His resurrection, just as He was about to ascend to His Father in heaven. He had given His disciples notice of the time and place whence He would take His departure. At the time and place appointed many of them were gathered. When they saw Him, they worshiped Him. But some doubted—*i. e.*, doubted perhaps whether it were He, whether it were a reality they beheld. So He came and spake unto them. He would dissolve all doubt. Among the things He said was this: "All power is given unto me in heaven and earth." *I* have overcome. *I* am King. *All* power is given to *me;* to *me* whom you recognize, to *me* who called you all, to *me* in whom you believe, to *me* whose disciples you all are; all *power* is given. "*Therefore* go ye," go to all nations. You see how the "*therefore*" evolves out of these facts. "*Therefore* go ye." And this is the way you are to go: teaching—teaching in two ways; by word of mouth, everything *I* have commanded you; and by overt act, baptizing, in the name of the Father and of the Son and of the Holy Ghost. You are not to teach any doctrine of your own, any more theories, or temporal systems; and you are not to teach anything which *I* have not commanded you. You are to baptize, but you are not to baptize in my name only; nor in any name, except this one which I tell you: Father, Son and Holy Ghost. "You are to teach men to observe all things whatsoever I have commanded you." Here you have the power commissioning, and also the commission given.

Baptism, in the Christian dispensation, took the place of circumcision in the Abrahamic. There are reasons for believing, that baptism had begun to supercede circumcision, among the Jews, anterior to the coming of Christ. Converts to the Jewish faith, instead of being circumcised, were baptized. Perhaps, John the Baptist accepted what had already begun to be a custom, and made it the specific sign of adherence to his teaching. Christ endorsed John's decision, or adoption, and made baptism the first rite of the new dispensation. The connection of baptism, however, with the idea of the Trinity, in the New Testament, is very remarkable. Christ's own baptism was made the occasion of a miraculous manifestation of the Trinity.

Circumcision had been the sign of the covenant made between God, on the one hand, and Abraham, on the other. It was the condition of Jewish nationality, and assured to every descendant of Abraham the promise of the Messiah. It was one element of a perfect proof that God, the one true God, had made such a covenant with Abraham. The elements of a *perfect* proof of any historic fact, are three: the written record, the visible, material monument, and the stated rite, or ceremony, or sacrament—as we call it, specially referring to it. Of the Abrahamic covenant, these three elements combined in the proof. There was the written word, then the tabernacle, or afterwards, the temple, and circumcision. A historic fact may be believed without these three elements in its record; but where these three elements are, *the fact cannot be doubted.* All sacraments have this historic value. That which has not such a value is not a sacrament. The word *sacrament* means an oath. The essential idea is that of testimony. In Jesus Christ the Abrahamic covenant passed from promise into fulfillment. Baptism took the place of circumcision. Circumcision bore testimony, that the covenant was made between men and the *one God,* the Lord Jehovah, the God of Abraham, Isaac and Jacob. That, you know, was one specific characteristic of Judaism, its assertion of the oneness of God. Baptism bears testimony that the covenant is complete between man, and the one God; but, that this one God is Father, Son, and Holy Ghost, as revealed by the Messiah, or Revealer, whom circumcision pledged. Where there is water, without this form, or this form without water, there is no baptism. Baptism is as monumental as the Lord's Supper. The Lord's Supper commemorates the fact that Jesus Christ lived and died; was instituted for that purpose—"*do this in remembrance of me.*" Baptism commemorates the fact that Jesus Christ revealed God to be the Father, Son, and Holy Ghost. All power is given unto me in heaven and earth; still, do not baptize exclusively in my name, but in the name of Father, Son, and Holy Ghost. I am God, but God is triune. I am the Revealer, to reveal this God to you. This is the God I reveal. The covenant is between man and a triune God, the same God of Abraham, Isaac and Jacob. Unity, but also a Trinity. The monument of Christianity, and of this particular fact in Christianity, is also perfect; the written record, the ceremonial rite, and the true Church or visible structure. To view baptism, therefore, as a question simply as to the use of more or less water, is to degrade it. To leave out this element of testimony, is not to see its whole value. So long as a man, or a woman, or a child, shall be baptized in the name of the Father, Son and Holy Ghost, so long will there be proof positive, that the God whom Christ revealed was a Trinity.

Now, if any one shall deny the Trinity, he must do one of two things: either, upon the ground of revelation, set up to be a better revealer of God than Christ was, (in which case, we leave him to such proofs as he may be able to give,) or, he must reject revelation, and take his stand upon reason; in which case, even he, will hardly deny that, at least, *that* field is as open to us as it is to him.

The Trinity of the One Deity, is the truth which the Church celebrates to-day. Because Jesus Christ revealed it and established it, no Christian can doubt it, and therefore, if the simple assertion of it be the object of our preaching to-day, here my sermon might very well end. But there are two senses in which we are to understand the word "*revealed.*" There is a body and a soul to everything. Man has an outward ear, and an inner mind or soul. The ear is the avenue to the mind or soul. The mind or soul is the man. The ear is the channel for reaching the man. What goes no further than the ear fails of its purpose and falls short of the man. The man has received a revelation, only when the sound has passed his ear, and the *fact* stands clear in his mind. The multiplication table is a *revelation* to your child. He cons it, and accepts it, till his ear cannot forget it, but it is then very far from being *revealed,* though he does not doubt it. When he eventually sees the laws which compel the results, when the mental forces lift him above his mere memory, then revelation fairly sets in, and he truly believes. In the nature of things, the hearing of the ear comes first, and the believing in the heart comes afterwards. For this reason, there are few of us perhaps who, as we advance in life, do not imagine our early training to have been imperfect, extremely defective. We understood nothing at the time, as we went along. Understanding came upon reflection, in soul-work and mind-labor. It could not have been otherwise; it always will be so. *That is revealed to us which we know,* and only that; and the process of knowing, is a subjective process, something to be done, each for himself. When that which is addressed to the ear and accepted there, is true, we go on to the knowledge, the real revelation, because it is true. As Christ said, if we will do His will, we shall know of the doctrine. That is God's law, that we need guidance till we can guide ourselves. We reach the real revelation at last, because we have received the substance beforehand. Hence, faith is not that which blindly accepts anything; faith is not credulity; faith never can be blind. The mere letter will always kill, and the more mere letter a man hath, the more killed he will be. Any system which denies us inquiry, is a system of death, not of life. That is faith, which not only accepts a thing as being, but knows it cannot be otherwise. Galileo had faith as to the revolution of the planets; when he rose from his knees, after saying they did not move, with the expression: "*Still they do move notwithstanding.*" Peter and John had faith, when the kingdom they had built in the air, out of Christ's words in their ears, had vanished, and they felt that what *was in Christ alone* was royal and glorious. *He who has the most knowledge, will have the most faith.* I do not mean that he who knows most of the world will have most faith in Christ. He who knows most of Christ, will have most faith in Him. He to whose inner soul Christ is most truly revealed, will have the highest faith in Him. Our faith in Him is skin-deep, because words of His have reached the ear, but not the mind and the heart. We are faithless, because we have given up knowing, in the thought that we already know.

Around the orbit of the human mind lie, and perhaps will forever lie, great facts, like the systems in the Zodiac round the orbit of the earth. They are there, and we cannot altogether penetrate them, and we call them mysteries. Still, great are the unfoldings of time. Age lends help to ages. Man defines for man, and though we see at first through a glass darkly, we are going on to know, as also we are known.

The doctrine of the Trinity, the fact that the divine unity is a Trinity, is a mystery, yet is there so much of it known, that the degree of belief with which we receive it, rises up into the regions of purest faith.

Still, I approach it with reverence and deep humility, mindful that the theme takes us into precious and perhaps toilsome thoughts, thoughts which will reach further than the expression, thoughts of which the expression, however perfect, will still be liable to be misunderstood. The manifestations of it in Scripture are manifold. The words which express Deity in the Old Testament, suggest a Trinity. The ancient languages were in their forms more expressive than ours. For God, the Mosaic record employs a form not merely dual, or plural, but triple. Moses, in prescribing the form of divine benediction, uses a threefold expression, the word God in each part having a specific and separate accent. The letter or symbol of God, which the Hebrews wore upon their phylacteries, was composed of three vertical lines, standing upon a common base.

Passing by the fact of Christ's baptism, of which we have spoken, the discourses of Christ, especially toward the close of His ministry, are filled with instructions relative to the Trinity, specifying the offices of Father, Son and Holy Ghost, expressing the Trinity, at the same time the unity, finally culminating in the command—wherever we taught of God, which must be everywhere, we must teach that He is Father, Son and Holy Ghost. Then, too, the significance of the fact, that the baptism of Christ was the occasion of the great manifestation of the Trinity. (Matthew 3.)

Then in nature, throughout all her works, God has suggested this idea of a divine Trinity in unity, and unity in Trinity. The difficulties which involve this fact in mystery, do not proceed from the fact itself, nor do they proceed from our *knowledge.* They grow directly and exclusively out of our ignorance, and that in two ways—first, from what we know absolutely nothing about, and secondly, from what we have taken for granted we know, *i. e.*, from our ignorance absolute, and from our error, *e. g.*, we do not know what God is. We cannot define Him. "He is far above, out of our sight." Then, we do not know what God the Father is, nor what God the Son is, nor what God the Holy Ghost is. We can only *know* a thing when we know all of that thing. We cannot know all of God, for only God Himself knows that. This is the one thing we shall be forever learning—*God.* Ordinarily we use the word God loosely, undefinedly. When we conceive of God the *Father,* we conceive of Him as if He were *the Deity.* We put a part for the whole. When we conceive of God the Son, we conceive of Him as if He were *the Deity.* We still put a part for the whole. When we conceive of God the Holy Ghost, we conceive of Him as if He were *the Deity.* We again put a part for the whole. We use the word *God,* in precisely the same sense as we use the word *Deity.* Or, otherwise to express it, we have no word expressive of the whole, which is not also used to express the parts. We say, "the Father is God, the Son is God, the Holy Ghost is God." Then the inevitable sequence in the mind is, there are three Gods, and how can three be one—hence comes confusion. We ask, can that which is not everything, or all, be God? Yes, it may be God, but not the whole of God. The Father is not the Son, nor the Holy Ghost. The Son is not the Father, nor the Holy Ghost. The Holy Ghost is not the Father nor the Son. The Father, Son and Holy Ghost together are *the Deity.* We cannot say the Father is *the Deity,* the Son is *the Deity,* the Holy Ghost is *the Deity.* We can say, the Father is *Deity,* all that the Father is, is *Deity,* all that the Son is, is *Deity,* all that the Holy Ghost is, is

Deity—and the Father, the Son, and the Holy Ghost, together, are *the Deity*. Take an illustration. Of a triangle—the first side is triangle, not the whole of the triangle, not *the triangle*, but the whole side is triangle, the second side is triangle, the third side is triangle. You see here we are obliged to use the same terms expressive of part, as we do in expressing the whole. And yet there are not three triangles, but one triangle, and there is one triangle only in the three together. Take the American flag; the red is flag, not the whole of the flag, not *the* flag, but all the red is flag, the white is flag, and the blue is flag, and yet there are not three flags, but one flag, and but one; because they are three. These three agree in one. They are the same in substance, the same in power, one is essential to the other. Where the one is the other is. What the one does the other does. Unless the three are together the flag is not, and unless they are three, they are not one. So God the Father is God *the Father*, God the Son is God *the Son*, God the Holy Ghost is God the *Holy Ghost*, and yet there are not three Gods, but *one God*, each of the same power and essence, only one not the other. Each in His separate office, these separate offices very clearly indicated by the Saviour—three because they are one, and one because they are three, all together the one eternal Trinity in unity, and unity in Trinity.

But, I apprehend, our great difficulty, in receiving the doctrine of the Trinity, is not so much in the doctrine itself, as in our various associations with that doctrine. We wisely associate Jesus Christ with the Deity. We wisely believe Him to be the Son of God. We worship Christ as *God* "manifest in the flesh," forgetting that it is *God manifest in the flesh*—*i. e.*, God only so far as *God*, could be manifest in the flesh. Because in Him dwelt the "fullness of the Godhead bodily," or *incarnately*, we forget that it was the fullness of "*grace and truth*." Because Christ said: "He that hath seen me hath seen the Father," we forget He also said: "No man hath seen God at any time." In these and other ways we fail to get a true conception of Deity, and then in the absence of such conception lapse into doubt and confusion. We do not define the difference between *the Deity*, and the fact of *manifested Deity*. We forget that it would not be *possible* for us to receive a full manifestation of God. It is literally true, as Moses said: "No man can see God and live." If Christ Jesus were God the Son, you perceive, from what has been said, He would still not be the whole of the Deity. But being God the Son, it does not follow that He revealed even the whole of that personality to us. You must recollect He is not God the Son from any idea of filiation. He would still have been God the Son, even if He had never been son of man. The word Son expresses an essence and yet a separate personality. That He did not reveal the whole of that personality to us, you have confirmed, not only in the nature of things, but also in the record of Scripture. On one occasion, in the presence of three disciples He was transfigured. There was a degree of manifestation more than ordinary, and that one degree more, overwhelmed the three witnesses. Shall we say there were no degrees of His glory beyond that? If they were not able to comprehend the lesser, would they have been able to comprehend the greater? You bring the sun, the solar luminary, down here, and we are not able to contemplate the sun. In His prayer for His disciples just before He was offered, He asked that they might be with Him, to behold that glory which He had with the Father before the world began. There was assertion, you perceive, of a glory which they had not seen, Christ was God manifest in the flesh, God the Son, not all the Deity. In the flesh He manifested not all there was of God the Son, only that which was necessary to His redeeming work and our salvation. Even of the manifestation He made, we yet see only the beginning. All we can see of God is in Him, but there is that of God, He laid aside, in order to make to us any revelation of God at all. What He wanted to reveal of God, what we wanted to know of God, was "grace and truth," God's character. "Grace and truth came by Jesus Christ." He veiled Himself, took the form of a servant, the more certainly to come within the limits of our comprehension. The lowest form He could assume was beyond our grasp. Had He been further removed, He could have made us no manifestation at all.

In order to make myself the better understood, let us take an illustration: Suppose, on one of the planets there was an intelligent class of beings, only very different from ourselves—suppose it were necessary to make ourselves known to them, and only one way was possible, and that possibility involving the mission of one person from us to them. Now man, though a unity, is also a duality. Man is not male, nor female, but the unit man, or humanity is man and woman. Man is not woman—woman is not man, but both together make *man*. Here, however, you have *man* used in two senses, one in a limited and the other in a distributed sense, and so it is better to say man and woman together make *manhood*. Hence, it might be said, man is manhood, woman is manhood, for we have attributes in common; the nature is identical; and yet we differ—so differ, that by no possibility can one take the place of the other. Now, again, it might be said, *man is a trinity*, which is much nearer the truth, for man is man and woman and *spirit*, or male, female, and *character*—for man is not God, nor devil, nor brute, in his nature, but with an essence of being peculiarly *human*, which essence makes a third element as separate, important and peculiar as either of the other two—so that, unless you express the character of man as distinguished from God, from brute and devil, you do not express man at all. Now, which one shall we send to those people upon the planet, to manifest manhood? We might send a woman. She would represent the whole manhood, and yet continue peculiarly and emphatically woman, too—*i. e.*, the fullness of manhood would be in her, and yet, *they* would not perceive it, because they could have no complete conception of it, till they had seen it in action as we see it, with all its developments and belongings—all its permutations and combinations. But suppose, instead of wearing her own form and language, she had to take their form and language. How the limitations multiply, and the difficulties of a perfect revelation increase! She would reveal the manhood to them, and yet not all the manhood. She could tell them wonderful things, and yet they not understand them—not because they were not manhood, but because they, in their limitations, could not receive her.

Now, this is the way I understand God—Father, Son, and Holy Ghost—the one not the other—not three Gods, but all together one God; the Father in His office, the Son in His, the Holy Ghost in His. The Son in

His office came to represent God to us, *i. e.*, God in His character, "grace and truth"—came to do a divine work for us. He did it; He did it under limitations our nature imposed, not His. Though He were exclusively and simply God the Son, yet He knew the Father, in a certain sense was the Father, and, in a certain sense, they who had seen Him had seen the Father, and yet no man had seen God at any time. The Father was in Him, and He in the Father. The Spirit was in Him, and He in the Spirit. The whole three one, the whole three Deity. He, God manifest in the flesh, the revealer, atonement, and mediator.

This is what God is, *a Trinity*. Christ came to teach us that. But for Him we could not have known it—but for Him we could not have known God was "grace and truth." This was part of the work He came to do. *But more especially*, this and all His work was, *that we might be taken into this unity*. Let us not lose sight of that, for if we do, we lose sight of the one practical object of the incarnation. He taught us, *and commanded us to teach one another*, "to observe all things whatsoever He had commanded us." You see it is easy to determine what religion is, not something made since Christ was here, but something made while Christ was here. The whole object of Christ, as of all revelation, is to bring us into divine unity, into union with the divine nature. Beyond all doubt moral nature is one, a unity—*i. e.*, the same nature that is in God is also in man. I do not say that man is God, but in His image we were created. God exists for man. Man is made to exist in God and with God. Every yearning of the human heart, the cry of the ages has taught us that. We had lost the unison and the knowledge of it. One great part of the object contemplated in the incarnation was to teach us of the *character* of God. The whole object of the incarnation was that we might be conformed to that character and so made capable of dwelling with God. It was not to reveal the whole Deity to us, but that much of the Deity, we were immediately interested in knowing. That prayer of the Mediator, just as He was finishing His work, thrills us with conviction of it. "That they all may be one, as thou, Father, art in me, and I in Thee, that they also may be one in us. I in *them*, and them in me, that they may be made perfect in one." Yes; this divine and perfect harmony and unity, between Creator and creation, between the Infinite and the finite, this is the one longing of time, that it might be, did God the Father send the Son, and give the Holy Ghost. Mysterious all the way through! How we, such beings as we are, can still be scintilations of the divine, only God *knoweth*. So has He been pleased to order. But that it is so, all nature and all grace, all earth and all heaven, combine to tell us. All the laws of fluids are in a single drop of water. A drop of water is not, however, the ocean. How God could put the properties of ocean into a simple globule is known only to Him. But there they are. We finite creatures are little globules, out of our place, out of God; soiled, corrupt, needing to come back and be taken once more into the fullness of being, into the infinite harmony, into eternal perfection. That perfection is a triune essence—Father, Son and Holy Ghost. So the Revealer, revealed. So reason deduces—so faith believes. The way for us to get into that perfection, into the full soul-revelation of God, is to observe all things whatsoever the Son of God hath commanded. May we all in the confession of a true faith, truly worship the eternal Trinity, and in the way which Christ hath commanded, be taken at last into the glory of the eternal Unity.

PROVIDENCE.

ROMANS 9: 21.—Hath not the potter power over the clay, of the same lump, to make one vessel unto honor, and another unto dishonor?

IN the chapter preceding this, St. Paul has been showing the Romans that they who are in Christ Jesus are free from condemnation. The truth of the proposition commends itself at once to any reflecting mind, when the Apostle explains that he means by being in Christ Jesus, walking according to God's holy law, living upon the spiritual plane. He who lives according to any law is universally uncondemned by that law. He is free from its penalties. He participates only in its blessings. A contrast then follows between the harm that comes of the flesh, *i. e.*, our perverted flesh, our unenlightened wills, our unsanctified affections; and, the good which follows from obeying the spirit, walking, as God designed we should, as nature invites, and wisdom suggests, in harmony with the laws of divine providence, laws embracing the highest good of all creatures, especially all intelligent and moral creatures, leading onward from one grade of excellence to another, from one stage of happiness to the perfection of angels.

This happiness and perfection for moral beings, this

life upon the spiritual plane, the Apostle asserts to be and to have been from all eternity, the one purpose of God in creating moral beings. In the nature of things, it must be so. The divine benevolence could wish nothing short of it, and the divine wisdom could not fail to make laws capable of producing it. This happiness and exaltation of moral beings was part of God's design in having any universe at all, and therefore, all things in the divine economy tend to help on the wise soul toward the desired end. In this purpose, joy and pain come together, and find a common mission—*pain*, to turn the soul back from wrong, and *joy*, to quicken its progress toward the right. So plain is this purpose in being, so emphatically is it the burden of all laws, the Apostle calls it "*predestination*." Thus any consummation contemplated in divine providence is "*predestination*." This world will eventually develop and come out into truth, and beauty, and holiness. It is *predestined* to do it. Predestination is in all things, *things working according to their laws*. The mention of joy and pain, however, leads us to define what moral being is, and that is a hard thing to do. It is that part of being to which more laws attach than to any other part of being. It is, in a certain sense, a perfected being, and therefore, in a certain sense, a complicated being. It is being involving greatest powers, and *therefore*, in misdirection, involving greatest danger. It is being, the inherent essence of which is self-action. It is being upon which devolves the necessity of knowing its own being, *i. e., having a rational consciousness of it*, and of acting according to its laws. It is being, which must learn its meaning, and guide its action by a knowledge of all other being. It is being, made for *truth*, and the glory of which is proportioned to the *truth* it embraces. A stone is not a moral being, because it is incapable of self-action. It can only act as it is acted upon. A horse is not a moral being, because it is not capable of a knowledge of all other being. It has no rational consciousness of its own existence, and its destiny is not affected by its own volition. Moral being involves social being, and out of society grows its weal or its woe. God is the highest moral being. He is moral being perfected. In short, moral being is a plane of existence, which, for you or me not to reach, is for you or me to be lost, and to be lost in proportion as we fail to reach it. It is a general conception of highest moral being, of God, that it is an arbitrary being—that it can make things be or not be as it prefers—that it could put something in the universe, or leave something out, or make something different, if it only chose. This is a mistake. Nothing *in* the universe is, or can be, arbitrary. Nothing can be without law. Whatever is, is necessary to the universe, without which there could not have been a universe. Only the universe itself is arbitrary. Whatever is there, must be so, because by no possibility could it otherwise be or not be. We cannot ask, therefore, why God, did not make us perfect, if He made us at all. He did make us perfect. He made us *perfectly* moral beings. We cannot ask, why He did not make us otherwise, for then He could not have made us moral beings at all.

Here we are in a universe of law, with a destiny in that law for us. We know that. That makes us accountable moral beings, or moral being itself makes us *accountable*. What destiny will we have? We can make nothing. We can change nothing, that is made.

We can make ourselves and our destiny. That is all. What destiny will we have? If according to the laws that are, then we are predestined to power and great glory. If not according to laws that are, then of necessity we are predestined to pain and humiliation, not because God wishes it so—*i. e.*, because he wishes the pain and humiliation, but because He *does not* wish it so. He wishes you to turn back again from the unwise and pursue the wise. The mission of what we call evil is good. Pain has the same general office as pleasure. He who is in the pain is very unfortunate and therefore so many agencies try to rescue him. We are in pain, because we are wrong and it is pain, if possible, to turn us into the right. Hence what we call evil, is *because* God is good. When it is said God *predestines us*, it is not that He picks out you and picks out me and says you shall walk this way and I walk that way. But when *I choose* to walk that way, then I am predestined, and when you choose to walk this way then you are predestined, because a part of this predestination is—*i. e.*, in the nature of things. You are predestined to choose. God's law is, that your will, within its sphere, which is very small, shall be supreme. God's benevolent wish is, that you shall be wise. These two, God's law and His affectionate desire, are the divine *will.* The *two* sides of the *one* thing. The gospel of Christ, all that incarnation of the Son of God, is as much a part of the universe as gravitation or electricity, as the mind or the soul. If you walk according to that, you are not condemned, because you are upon the spiritual plane. If you do not walk according to that you are condemned, because you are not upon the spiritual plane. It is not that God condemns or acquits, but the simple fact of your action itself. That it is which condemns or acquits. "I am not come to condemn," says the Saviour. He came if possible to show us the way out of all condemnation, came to save.

Now to make us conscious of this being, of the nature of it, we are set down in the midst of an economy. This economy we call *providence*, all of it, strange as it may seem, perfectly adapted to us, and we to that. It was made for this very end which we are contemplating. Whatever comes, it will define moral being for us, and it will fix our grade in that moral being. You can no more escape it than you can escape existence. You might prefer that you had not existed, but that makes no difference, only to prove that already you are upon the wrong side of predestination. *This economy, or providence, is God's household*—every particle of it—this world, all that pertains to it. He has some very idle and wicked servants in it, but they are *His*, not the less. They must give account. It will not do to make the Church His household, and all outside of it not His household. Then we do what God has not done, and will not allow to be done. We are all vessels in the household, every one of us. In that household is an infinite variety of wants, therefore an infinite variety of vessels or utensils, or servants, not one of them unnecessary, not one mean in itself, naturally, originally. Some may be more prominent and some more obscure, some more "*honorable*," and some less "*honorable*," but all alike designed, and each, in its proper work, equally to the glory of God. Over it God presides. He has a will as we have. He has purposes as we have. He knows laws as we do, only He knows more laws and all laws perfectly. He works by those laws, employs all agencies to perfect His plans. In His plans there are resisting agencies, so there are in ours. You work notwithstanding, and so He works notwithstanding, only He knows all laws and works wisely. We know only a few laws, therefore are very often defeated. When we talk of our will interfering with God's will, we place too high an estimate upon ourselves. We, individually, or, a whole generation of us, are, as compared with God, not so much as a mote in the sunbeam. One ant in your cellar could not materially disturb your domestic economy. Not one of us can interfere with God. *All* we can do is to affect our own destiny, or *possibly* to complicate that of some other atom like ourselves. This is what we understand by providence, God mingling in these affairs, preventing the wicked from destroying the race, and helping the righteous to build it up in peace and good-will, not creating any law, not violating any law, not doing anything arbitrarily, but just simply working, the same as a parent works for his children in benevolence and love, not only by agencies and laws within His reach, but by agencies and laws, existing for that purpose.

From this point, then, you can plainly see the difference between the man and the position of the man—between the being and the situation which defines the being. You plainly see that the position has nothing to do with the man, but the man every thing to do with the position. One man has nothing to do with another man's office, and no man in another office can be responsible for you in yours. Each man is but responsible for himself in his own office, wherever or whatever that might be. It is not for us to be longing for other positions, but to do our duty in the position in which we are. We may be prominent, or we may be obscure, but we may be as well off one where as another where, for it is all blessing to have part or lot in this household at all.

Now, it is this *position*, you observe, which is determined *without our consent*—not arbitrarily, not without law, but still not by our volition, only by the law of God's knowledge, wisdom and love, God's *supremacy*. But what we will be in the position, is left to us. It is this *providence* of God which determines this position. You may be born in one circle in life, or another. That is what is called an *accident* of life. It is not accidental in the sense that there is no known law which determines the fact; but accidental, in the sense that to be born at all you must be born somewhere. You may be born of parentage wise or foolish; with a constitution strong, or weak; with a mind of a high order, or of a low order; with passions more or less active. All these things will determine your degree in the scale of God's household arrangement. They will determine the offices you are to hold, or not to hold; send us out to prominence or obscurity, greater or less; to trials of one kind or another; surround us with responsibilities, more or less weighty. You may be a Pharaoh or a Moses, an Esau or a Jacob, it matters not which you are. There is no wrong in making you one or the other. Wherever you are, your surroundings and responsibilities are equal, and in that fact, the equality between surroundings and responsibility, we are all alike and stand upon one and the same level, and therein all men are equal. But these *positions* and *relations*, or our *place* in the household, is not *ourselves*. There is another element in us, over us, by which we are worthy or unworthy, by which we have merit or demerit, by which we are right or wrong, wise or unwise, saved or lost. There are principles attaching to us, moral essences that come in, known to us, to which *we* must have reference. There is justice and injustice, mercy and unmercy, love and unlove, self and unself, faithfulness and unfaithfulness, the well-being of others and the ill-being of others, the honor of God and the dishonor of God. You see how this spiritual being strikes the region of spiritual laws, how moral elements in us respond to moral laws outside of us. Here you strike your personality, your individuality, *yourself.* Position is a common fact; Providence has determined that. What you are in that position, you must determine. If you can be wise at all, or serve God at all, you can do it in one place as well as another. If you choose to live upon your animal or carnal plane, you are predestined to sink down. If you choose to live upon the spirit plane, you are predestined to great glory.

All this, however, would only fix the fact of your choice without involving the idea or fact of responsibility, or guilt. And this develops another element, and a higher element, another fact, and a higher fact—the element of conscience on the one side, and God communicating with that conscience on the other, not only nature inside of us, and nature outside of us, but God in active paternal love, working on the one by means of the other. We come to the fact of a moral sense God has put in us, something responsive to the right, a something which we must pervert and blunt and resist in order to go wrong, something with which we must live in a constant state of protest if we continue in the wrong. *It is this constant state of protest, this violation of your conscience, which makes guilt;* which is the sin against the Holy Ghost. God is made for the soul, and the soul is made for God, and there is communication between the two—just as vegetation is made for the sun, and the sun is made for vegetation, and they are responsive one to the other. You come then, here, to the supreme fact, the fact to which I wished to bring you, the fact stamped upon this day, *Whitsun* Day, *the gift of the Holy Ghost, the divine power and love, dwelling in us and with us,* God, a Father, and Counsellor, and Guide. Heaven and earth, not two but one. Man and God, not at enmity, but reconciled—man taken into God, through Jesus Christ our Lord.

We are prepared, now, in a measure, to understand some of these expressions of St. Paul. He says, some false reasoner, some bungling thinker, looking out upon this being, will conclude, because places in God's household are fixed—therefore, they who are in these places are made in them what they are morally. Whereas, it is only when you strike what they make themselves, that you strike the moral at all. Looking upon the history of the Jews—God's calling Jacob rather than Esau, will imply that Esau was condemned, because Jacob was chosen. Whereas, there was no condemnation about it. Only one was wanted. The very fact of choosing implied a rejection, but no depreciation. Esau was not fitted for a given position, and therefore to that position was not called. He had no faith. He saw nothing of divine things. He cared nothing about them. He chose to live upon the animal plane, and God wanted something upon the spirit plane. Jacob was fitted, and to it he was called, and in it he was as responsible, as Esau in his. Eventually he perverted his privileges, and fell to a woe greater than any Esau ever knew, and God did not make Esau unfaithful, any more than He afterwards made Jacob unfaithful. He blessed both and if the children of both exist to this day, they exist in the common mercy of God, and it is difficult to decide which are the better off. This same wrong thinker will continue his gaze, and imagine that God arbitrarily made Pharaoh what he was, whereas, it was the exact purpose and wish of God that he should be different, who employed all possible means to make him different. Because being, in spite of everything, a given material, God worked Him into fabric, as God will work all material into His fabric, for nature knows no waste. This wrong thinker will conceive God arbitrarily made him such material in order to have him to work up into His fabric. Out of all this, he will infer, that every man is just what he cannot help being, and therefore, is not accountable for his actions. He cannot help asking, " why doth God find fault with us, since no man hath resisted His will?"

Yes, my hearer, if you are not responsible before God, how pertinent that question is—why doth God find fault with you in your error, your wrong, your trangression? Do you wonder St. Paul indignantly and emphatically repels such a thought? " Who art thou, O man"—or *what* a man thou art! how little of a *man* there is in you, to reply so against God—against all His providence, against His very design in giving us any moral law at all. What else does a moral law imply, but a responsibility? What a man thou art, to make out God like us—playing providence, inconsistent, unequal, unjust, calling upon us for a service we have no power to render, and demanding of us a life it was never intended we should live! Let the simple fact, that a holy life is demanded, prove that thou art *inexcusable,* O man, whosoever thou art, that thus repliest against God. Has not the potter power over the clay, of the same lump to make a vessel unto honor, another unto dishonor? Does he not know, exactly, what this economy requires? Did potter, out of any lump, ever yet make vessels which had no purpose at all? Did potter ever yet make vessels just simply to be destroyed? Is the clay not honored, in being fashioned to any service for the master's use? What a man thou art! You might as well complain that the great All-Father who made man in the beginning, male and female, has now, in His providence, made you a man and not a woman. What a blessing it is, God does know what to make us. What a wonder it is, the race keeps on just equally divided, male and female still. But for this divine hand, guided by an omniscient wisdom, how soon would the whole race cease to exist. How soon would the world lapse to its primeval being, and the original purpose in any world at all, be defeated. How soon would it be requisite to form another creation, and try another experiment. Do you see no providence? No wisdom in providence? What a blessing it is that He who knows exactly whether to make us male or female, knows exactly also, whether to put us in one position or another, so that our whole economy shall be kept up. And how blessed we are to be where God has put us, and to be what He has made us, rather than to be anywhere else. With what earnestness and love should we study His will, and yearn for His glory, since the true service of the Creator, is the exaltation of the creature. What a blessing it is, not only that when God does make us, He makes us male and female, but that He makes most of us under those conditions in life which compel us to use our God-given energies, under conditions which compel us to development. How strange it is, nearly all of us are vessels unto *dishonor*, *i. e.*, vessels for use, for practical, every-day purposes. How much wiser God is, in making the world, than we would be, if we had had the making of it. How foolish we are, not to study His will, and let Him make it as He would delight to have it.

Now what I wish particularly to assert, what I believe the whole tenor of Christ's life and doctrine asserts, and what Paul wishes to assert, is this. We are all one family, under one impartial Father, every privilege of His grace and providence as much for one as another. This world, with the human family in it, composes God's earthly household. For all of it Christ Jesus died. For the whole of it, and each member of it, *the spirit of God liveth.* What else does that Scripture tell us which records the outpouring of the divine grace at Pentecost? "How hear we in our tongue wherein we were born? Parthians and Medes and Elamites and the dwellers in Mesopotamia and in Judea, and Cappadocia, in Pontus and Asia, Phrygia and Pamphilia, in Egypt and the parts of Lybia about Cyrene, and strangers of Rome, Jews and Proselytes, Cretes and Arabians, we do hear them speak *in our tongues* the wonderful works of God." Yes! *Every man heard, wherever he was born,* whether he were Jew or Pagan, whether he believed or not, *all heard.* The *Holy Ghost spake.* Yes; brethren, that Pentecostal fact, is pregnant with truth which we have not all learned. God henceforth dwells with *all men.* Nor is there an ear which understandeth any speech or language, to which that spirit does not speak. In whatever language your soul speaks to you, or you to it, God's spirit is there telling you of God's wonderful works. God's spirit is your enlightener *and if you only would,* would be your perfect Counseller and Guide, to this blessed predestination, this glory, eternal in heaven.

As there is no part of the material universe, the light, the air, the laws of nature and providence, the benefits of which you do not share, so from no part of the moral provision, the soul-provision which God has made, are you excluded. As in your bodies God does much without your knowledge or will, and then leaves you to do the rest for yourselves—so for your soul God has done much and leaves you to do the rest, leaves you to make use of the elements He has bestowed. He has made a law of Redemption in Christ Jesus. You are redeemed whether you will or not. And you shall have the tender offices of the Holy Ghost, whether you accept or repel, yes, even whether you know there is a Holy Ghost or not. The office of the Holy Ghost is to place your spirit in communion with God. The incarnation is " God, manifest in the flesh." The office of the Holy Ghost is to take of the things of Jesus, because they are the things of God and reveal them unto us.

So true is the remark that has been made, that God can do nothing without law, we find that the Holy Ghost was made known to mankind only when Christ had furnished a power by which the Holy Ghost could work. It is said that the Holy Ghost "*was given*" at Pentecost; but had there been no Holy Ghost antecedently? Then, by whom spake the Prophets? By what power had so many spiritual facts been accomplished? The

Holy Ghost had, *in the incarnation*, a new lever, so to speak—a new means. His power was accordingly greater and His manifestation corresponding.

Hence the power of Christianity over heathendom—not that God's Spirit is not with the heathen, but that the thing to be revealed has only dimly been manifested. They are as the whole world was before Christ came. Carry them Christ, and not some horrible sectarian effigy, and we might look for great results. Even among ourselves, if the presentation of the Church were in spirit and in truth, practically and theoretically, objectively and subjectively, only Christ, we should experience greater things.

Hence the office and duty of the Church to preach Christ, leaving results to the Holy Ghost.

This whole subject is peculiarly prolific, branching as it does into the thoughts suggested by the Gospel for Whit-Sunday—the Comforter, the oneness of God and His children.

These three things,—we and Christ and the Holy Ghost,—are for each other. The office of the Holy Ghost is to spiritual things what *light* is to physical things. You have an eye, which was intended to give you knowledge of outward objects. Out before you is a beautiful landscape. But it is night. The eye is useless. The landscape is as though it was not. But the sun arises—light, silent, serene, unites the two, and while it is that power without which all else were useless, it is that power which says nothing of itself. So the office of the Holy Ghost is to take of the things of Christ and reveal them unto us. Many a man can see no beauty in a landscape--many a man can see no beauty in Christ. But by the love of God we all have this light if we will only use it. If you will accept that law, if you will take Christ for a Saviour, if His atonement can be your plea of acceptance, if His precept and example can be your idea of *acceptableness*, your hope of glory, then you can be saved. Your position in life is just the best one you could have, if it be one which God has given you. It will give you opportunity to be saved, and test whether you are faithful or unfaithful. You may be a king, a governor, a head of a family. You may be lonely, obscure, unknown. All that matters nothing. Not always is that which is most distinguished, the most truly honorable. The ornaments in our parlors have their places and their purposes. But those obscure agencies which maintain the comfort and order of our dwellings are more truly honorable than they. The blackened utensils which give us food at the appointed hour, are more honorable than the gilded clock which only tells us that the hour has come. In God's economy nothing is mean. It is a glorious thing to serve God, and he who stands in any lot to do that, to bless the race of which he is a part, to live out a poem of usefulness and holiness, is as honorable a spectacle as any on which the eyes of men, or of angels can rest. And He who stands in any lot, unmindful of God, forgetful of his soul, neglectful of divine and holy things, have what he may, or think what he may, is already condemned. It had been better for him if he had never been born, not because God will take anything from him, but because he has not reached out after what God longed to give him. He has sinned and continues to sin, the one sin, against the Holy Ghost, the one sin which hath never forgiveness, because it precludes all conditions which can make forgiveness of any value.

Brethren, where do we stand to-day? Are we saved? Are we lost? What mean the life, the death, the cross, the resurrection and ascension of the Son of God? What mean the whisperings of the Holy Ghost? What mean our days, our years, our lives? What mean our positions? Are they those God has given us? are we using them for His glory? What record are we making above—faithful, or unfaithful? Solomon says, "a faithful *servant* shall share with the heir in the inheritance." Christ Jesus said, "I call you no more *servants*, but *friends*, and *sons*. The Holy Ghost says, "If we are sons, we are also heirs, joint heirs with Christ, to an inheritance incorruptable and undefiled, and that fadeth not away." To that inheritance, that sonship, God calls us. Let us hear, believe, obey, and live, day by day, studying to be faithful in doing our very best, in that state of life to which it has pleased God to call us.

THE PRODIGAL SON.—No. I.

Luke 15: 11, 12, 13.—And He said, a certain man had two sons, and the younger of them said to his father, Father, give me the portion of goods that falleth to me, and He divided unto them His living. And not many days after, the younger son gathered all together, and took his journey into a far country, and there wasted his substance with riotous living.

This parable of the Prodigal Son, is the third of a very remarkable series. The three form a constellation upon which the eyes of eighteen hundred years have rested, with all the emotions of joy and hope. The three are so many parts of *one* discourse. The thought in them all is the same. Each one only increases its degree. Perhaps, within so small a compass, there never before was so much taught. This chapter embraces, in a certain sense, the whole Gospel in itself. *The burden of it is, the love of God for all His children—a love above all loves, the one thing which, be life what it may, it alone never dies.* Around the thought is woven every conceivable circumstance of aggravation or unworthiness, on our part—that the *Fatherhood* of God may stand out supreme and absolute. *That* it was intended to teach. *That* it does teach. All else is only accessory. On a certain occasion, Christ said He had not come to condemn the world, but to save the world. That seems to have been the one yearning, burning thought of all His life, and it is worth while to observe *here* how *spontaneously* it gushes from His warm and sympathetic heart. In these parables there is nothing of learned elaboration. They are as simple as the utterances of a child. There was no time for premeditation—but their grasp is infinite. It embraces God, and time, and the human race.

The parables were a response to the Scribes and Pharisees. We must recollect that, or we shall miss much of their meaning. The Scribes and Pharisees had found fault with Him for receiving sinners, and communing with them. These parables were the instant reply. They as much as say, what else should I do? Who can need my help as much as they? What would a salvation be, which deserted us in exact proportion as it was needed? That, surely, would be a human way of doing things—of loving those who love us, a selfish way, not imparting blessing, but valuing people because we could of them receive blessing—being kind as long as they did not need the kindness. But that is not God's way. *God does not look upon sin so much as a fault, as a misfortune.* Of all things in the universe, it is the unnatural thing, the undesirable thing, on both sides. It is that thing which disturbs all relations, and defeats all purpose. Man was made for God. A thousand divine objects are contemplated in man's existence. An abstract existence, an existence just for himself, even if it were possible, would make him fall short of all design, and therefore, not fulfil his existence, not unfold his being. God is thus interested. His affections, His sympathies are enlisted. If a man lose a sheep, it is the lost one he must go after. If a woman lose a piece of money, it is the lost piece she must be occupied about, till she find it. If a father lose a son, it is that son his heart follows, till he return. The question now is, not at all about any desert in the lost, whether it did right or did wrong, voluntarily or involuntarily, there is loss. The question is wholly as to the owner, the Creator, the Father. What is He? What is His nature? *Can* He help? *Will* He help? Would it be worth while to have a Shepherd, if He could afford no aid? Would the coin exist if it had no value? Would it be a coin without an image and superscription? Would a father be a father, if he did not love? Would there be any evidence of a superior nature, if, able to help, He still refused? View God as the mere possessor of beings, which He has gathered for His own selfish purposes, or as a Father exercising affection, endowed with all the attributes of love—view man as having nothing, whatever, in common with God, or as having merely a sort of divine stamp upon him, or as endowed with the same nature, and possessed of faculties and yearnings, exactly responsive to those of a Father—still, in either case, you must see how it is, of necessity, the lost, sick, erring one, for whom God cares.

I ask you to take particular notice of these thoughts. They are peculiar to Christ. We Christians do not, or at any rate, did not always understand them. In the face of the Gospel, where the questions of total depravity and original sin came from, is inconceivable. The Gospel is the "*good news*" of restoration, the call to us to come home. It presupposes the thing Christ presupposes in these parables—a right to us that God has. That right is now twofold—first, by creation, second, by redemption. It asks for the third, the right by our volition. It presupposes in us, an adaptation, first, to God's purposes, as the sheep and money are contemplated in our economy, and second, a participation of nature, and consequent responsiveness, as a child to a parent. When God made us, as the rest of all His works, so we were very good. If we lost in Adam the divine image, then in Christ it was restored. We are all children, God's own beloved children, participating His nature, germinally it is true, but still actually having parts and faculties contemplated in the divine life, and intended for the divine life; made in God's image, employed in any other life, their object utterly defeated, and their possessor utterly a wreck, existence a burden, the soul, made to be a conscious joy, turned into one undying remorse. But, if it be in any other life, it must be there by its own act. If it go from God, it must go in spite of God's remonstrance, of God's intention, of the divine desire. The divine laws permit it to go, because moral force forbids coercion; but the divine benevelence wishes it not to go, and so surrounds it with restraints and warnings. The sin is, in not heeding the warning, in despising the restraints, in not responding to the divine nature, in being indifferent to the better and glorified being God intended for us. But, even when we are there, we are still God's. He is, while a *grieving* Father, still not a *hating* Father. He ceases not to yearn and to watch, and when we return, the first to see us, to greet us and bless us.

Now, the race has ever been divided into those who were in their Father's house and those who wandered away, the religious and the irreligious, the son at home and the prodigal. You have here, therefore, "the two sons." The first remains at home. You see, sin is not the natural and first condition of man—God did not make you and crush you, start you out to begin with crooked and broken, asking of you what in the nature of things is impossible or unreasonable, when our *translation* says, "the *natural* man receiveth not the things of the Spirit of God: for they are foolishness unto him, and neither can he know them, because they are spiritually discerned," it does not translate St. Paul. He says the man buried—abandoned to his gross animal nature does not receive, and that is very true. But that grosser animal nature is itself a development. It has grown there. It is by neglect or perversion of powers God made for very different purposes. This human nature, contemplated merely as a *natural* fact is a wonderful combination, or a combination of exalted and wonderful faculties. It implies just the very destiny the Gospel contemplates for it. When you contemplate it as redeemed by grace, and aided by the Holy Ghost—the first bias or tendency is toward God—and where total neglect, or wrong education do not more than counteract that tendency the development is in that direction. I believe, and I think your experience and observation will sustain the thought—that the first impulses of youth are pure and noble. Have you never taken the hand of a young man in the first conscious flush of his manhood? What impulses beat within him? What schemes and achievements he proposes! How unselfish? How little he thinks or cares for what it is to cost. How sanguine, how he imagines all the world as pure and unselfish and noble as he is himself. When we recollect our own aspirations, when we sit down and contemplate youthful inspiration, how impossible not to feel that the image and superscription is from God's own stamp. How we who are older often stand and laugh at his inexperience, how we chill his ardor, how we give him his first lessons in selfishness, in suspicion and mistrust! We whose business it is to build before him splendid idols, to guide his aspirations to grand and happy realization, to analyze life for him hat he may distinguish the real from the delusive. We shall come to this, if it please God, when we come to speak of that older brother, that cold, selfish, calculating mortal who thought his very staying at home was a virtue. But I confess I have no sympathy with that spirit who is abroad in society who poisons life in its very fountains. How is it possible for our children to believe in virtue when they hear in our very houses that the whole earth is a hot-bed of all evil, of deceit and hypocrisy. Do children never reason? Do they not often catch their first lessons in evil from our own life? Do they never ask whether we are sincere in our professions of affection and piety? When we hear people say every day that the world is devil-riden, do they all speak out of their own experiences, are their words the overflowings of their hearts? Take one single example. At this moment the world is afflicted with divorces, with divided families, with evils direct and indirect, not the least of which is the delay of marriage and in many instances its abandonment altogether. But why should not the evil exist and soon increase. I think if you listen you will find married life often laughed at and misrepresented by us who call ourselves Christian people. In our houses and our papers it is made the subject of jest, a happy home or a happy man is spoken of as the rarest thing in existence. We picture husband and wife as always quarreling, or at any rate, as seldom happy, when not one of us out of all we know could count a dozen homes that are miserable, a dozen men and women who, even if they are *not* superlatively *happy* together *would be* superlatively *miserable* apart.

We know that divorces are the exception, a small per centage, but we speak of them as the rule, and so familiarize the mind with the fact, and so, while complaining of the world's corruption, are doing much to corrupt it. No, I say that life in its beginning is pure and noble, and would be vastly purer and nobler, if we would believe in purity and nobleness. If our ideals were as high as our childrens, their *realization* would reach beyond our conceptions. If the troughs from which they drink are ring-streaked and spotted, what wonder they become ring-streaked and spotted themselves. The one want of our world now is, a real virtue, and real belief in virtue, when virtue is supposed to be a deeper apprehension of that for which we are apprehended. If the elder brother were better, the younger perhaps would not think of leaving home.

But let us go back to the thought that the first impulses of life are pure and noble. You see it is not merely that we are as a sheep to a shepherd, without any nature in common. It is not merely as a piece of coin to a king, with a mere image and superscription, but it is a participation of real being, a responsiveness. Now undoubtedly it is the *duty* of the child to be worthy of its parentage. It should aim at such appreciation of the father's exalted character as to improve every privilege, every faculty, and so to honor the father. You see simply to fail there, simply not to contemplate, not to resolve upon high action is itself to be delinquent. *The boy or the girl that can be insensible to a father's care and a father's honor, has taken the first step in ingratitude and dishonor.* You observe, life implies even in its very beginning, something to do, action. We generally imagine we have something to do to be lost, but the fact is, we have something to do to be saved. Salvation is recognition of the divine nature and development into it. It must be not merely action, but high-born conscious action. Even neglect is guilt. We will not stop to define guilt. It is difficult to tell what it is. But guilt is a thing felt. It is an effect, natural and instant. It is part of the perfection with which God has clothed all His works. If you do a mean thing, you feel mean, unless you are so inexpressibly mean as not to feel, not to feel guilt is to be most certainly guilty. We shall come to this when we come to the citizen of the strange country, those so lost, so utterly "*past feeling*," as to be taken in by sin and naturalized. That is the extreme degree. But the neglect of which I have spoken is the first degree. In that you have the beginning of an alienation from home. When there is no *love* of a father, there will soon be a desire to be free from the restraints of a father. When there is *no* love of home, there will be a love of some other place that is not home, a thing we who are supposed to have homes very often forget, and so fail to make the homes of our children what they ought to be. It is not enough to tell a child they should not find their pleasure abroad. We should see that they do find their pleasure at home—pleasure pure and holy—pleasure we create and provide—pleasure that is worthy of us and worthy of them—pleasure that contemplates at once their young life and their future life. I do not say it is an easy thing to do, but I do think we could succeed better if we would try. I do not think we spend time enough with our children, and teach them to find real happiness with us. We should show them the real pleasure there is in the things they ought to take pleasure in, our real pleasure in it.

There is, however, to all inexperience, evermore the desire to go out and try for itself. Any of us, even after years of experience, are apt to imagine that some other place is better and easier for us than that in which we are. The young especially must ever be trying experiments. It is the essential property of inexperience, of ignorance. Perhaps not one of us ever started out in life without the feeling that we had the world in a sling. No matter how many have failed before us, we alone cannot fail. Men start that way in business sometimes, and demonstrate over again what has been demonstrated a million times before. Every life is as fresh and as much a new life as if there had never been a life before it. There is a longing to be free, and an utter ignorance that freedom is conformity to law. The child knows better than the parent. We all know better than God. We ask our portion, and God divides to us His living—"*His life*" it is literally. God gives us our nobler faculties, our far-reaching perceptions, our responsiveness to nature—this being so gifted, so capable of grand accomplishment. This is "*our portion*"—a royal gift, the image of our Father—this scintilation of the divine. We do not know that it all has its own laws, that it demands its lawful exercise, just as the eye must not only *use* light, but use it *wisely*. We do not know we can be wrong, without *intending* to be wrong, and that the wrong is defeat of all intention—just as to stare at the sun, is to put out the eye. The child needs the parent—man needs God. To turn aside from the divine restraints, to set up wilful, personal pleasures as an end in itself, to ignore all guidance, that it is, to gather all together, and go into a far country. What object more pitiable than the child left to itself. What self-destruction. Mind untutored, passion unrestrained, affection, talent, undeveloped. What a curse to itself! What a waste, what a "*riotous living*," what an *unsafe* life, or *unsaved* life! for, if I recollect, that is what the word *riotous* means in the text, *unsafe*, *unsaved*. If you are wise, you can predict the destiny of almost any household you know. The boys, the girls, their tastes, their habits. You see their tendency, you have seen enough to know results. Where righteous restraints are not sought, you see the good shrink every day less and less. You see the evil abound. We are not talking now of the *guilt*, of things, but merely of the certainty of results. The world has its attractions, the flesh its pleasures. We think they are as good as heavenly attractions and soul-pleasures, but mark, they are very different. They are the attractions of *the world*, the pleasures of *the flesh*. They have their grades. You can begin at the opera, and go down through the first class theatre, and second class, and third class, to the dance house and dens of low degree. Which, now, will you call the place for a child of God? "There is no harm in them," we say. Is there any blessing in them? Are they in the right direction? I shall not deny that music hath its *holy* charms. Music, *in itself*, never did anybody any harm. It is the divine thing which, somehow, man has never been able to curse. Even in the dance house, it is the only pure thing there. If the opera were music, it might do very well; but opera means dress, and lust, and vile thought, giving to many an innocent spirit, not merely its first intimations of evil, but so clothing it as to beget a relish for it, a relish which, everybody knows, ends not once nor twice, but many times in the dance house, and the Potter's field. I shall not deny that histrionic art may be, and has sometimes been, instructive and edifying, that there are now and then, beings with transcendent genius, who, above all artifice, or mere tricks, can thrill our soul. But *we* have never seen any of them. They are not one to a generation. Still, they may be, and I believe are, as frequent as the best specimens of anything—but, is that the *field* for a *divine* life? Is that the best phaze of this mortality? Is it the home of mind and wisdom? Of purity and exalted virtue? The pleasure of it, I shall not dispute, but pleasures run all the way down, and all the way up. You have to choose which field of pleasure is yours. Is that a near country to you? Are you a citizen there? You may begin with the paltry novel, and go down through all sorts of trash, but is there no prostitution of mind in it? Are there no grand poems, no high philosophies, no wide-reaching science—all as angels, beckoning and asking to be entertained, that we, too, may be as angels? The question is often asked, is there any harm in these amusements? The answer must vary, according to the inquirer. To many, I should say, unhesitatingly, *no*—many persons are as pure there as they would be anywhere, perhaps, for two hours, at least, be in better company than they would have at home, be in better humor. The kennel is the proper place for a dog, and the sty the proper place for swine. But can it be your place? Everything is good enough in its proper place. The question is not whether it is good enough for you, but whether you are base enough for that. Sodom was good enough for the Sodomites. Lot was not much better, or he would not have been there at all, and even if he was a tolerably good thing himself, he was in the wrong place, and no wonder it took a miracle to save him. In such a land, in any land of mere animalism, of idle fashion, of sensual indulgence, the Christian must be indeed in a far country. For you to go there, you must carry the splendors and riches of a better country. You can go there only to desecrate the divine portion your Father gave you. You were made for thought, for study, for high communion with divine things. In such a land, *you must soon* begin to be in want. There must soon be famine, death of all that is morally pure and spiritually good, and wishful recollections of the home land, the fatherland you have left.

What a blessed thought it is, to those of us, who have children, that if we can give our children the true culture, if we can implant within them pure thoughts and holy recollections, they can never forget them. What a thought—that wander as they may, revel as they will, the still small voice never dies. Train a child in the way he should go, and when he is old he will not depart from it. That promise is a tower of comfort and strength. It is based upon a law. I often wonder whether any man can wholly forget God. I think not. When I look at some of those citizens, naturalized in vice, citizens of the far country, I think they too, themselves, must sometimes think of their father and their home. Christ does not intimate it here—but it is possible.

Still, this prodigal need not go down to poverty and vice to waste his substance. Many a rich man has for his riches parted with every noble faculty. In the far country forgotten his lineage and his father's house, forgotten the dignity and honors and walks that belong to a Christian. Have you never seen men in the pursuit of bubbles, not only forgetful of God, but forgetful that they are men? You can see it every day. We sometimes meet men that fairly stagger all our conceptions of manhood; men with so little perception of divine things, we wonder if they are men. I read a piece in a paper a few days ago which caused me to pause and ask, whether it were possible that the writer of it ever had a conception of manhood. You have seen men with all affection and manly sentiment frozen, miserly, miserable mortals, afraid of death, willing to give all their possessions for a hope beyond the grave, who feel they have missed the true mark of life, that somebody is anxious for their shoes, that nobody really loves them, that they have done nothing for which anybody should love them, whose place will soon be filled, whose life will leave hardly an echo behind, over whom time will close like the sea over the way of a ship, mind gone, soul gone, life gone, men far from home, hungry and faint, that cannot fill themselves with the husks that swine eat. Have we not all seen spirits sick and wearied, consumed with a sense of disappointment and humiliation. Such is sin, only once desecrate the blessed Eden in which and for which God created you and you go forth, the flaming sword forbidding forever all return. Still do you mark the gradation and degradation here? Do you see how the original divine pasture has been wasted? Do you observe the contrast and interval between that grand ideal, thy first self, and this wretched wreck, thy second self, this, *not* thyself, not thy Father's child, could He love thee? Would we there be with the living? Think of Him. He needs us not. He hath a home and other sons. How we have disgraced Him, ground our nobility into the dirt, and like a profligate prince, dishonored royalty itself. Is there any hope?

Do you observe then, that though our Father looks upon us in our sins, as unfortunate, rather than faulty, though He is not angry, yet our misfortune is real, our woe is not the less? Do you see though God has not created it, and will not add anything to it, there is enough of it already? Can you go on and make it more? Do you see what alienation from God means? Suppose you become like one of those citizens of the far country, without any father, without any God, remorseless, soulless, dead, *fit* to deal in crime. Is there no punishment in that? Have you lost nothing? Do you see you have lost your soul; and do you see, when I tell you God will not punish you, that is not telling you that you will not be punished. Think, should your mother be taken from you, of *never* seeing her again. Think of the little sister that went the other day, pure, spotless, *never* see her again. Never. But suppose when they are clothed in transcendent excellence, you are clothed in transcendent soul-poverty and wretchedness and there is a great gulf between you. Think of *never* seeing God, of an infinite gulf between you. Do you see what that gulf is, the loss in you of the portion, the divine portion your father gave you? But, you say God will not eternally punish; no, God will not punish at all. But do you see the sinking that is there, first of all, the neglect to love, then the alienation, then the far country, then the want, then the hiring out to the citizen, then suppose you were a citizen, should go so far as to be truly a citizen, to feel satisfied there, not to know you are lost, then you see there is no hope. Do you see no eternity beating there? Well, you are not there. If you have not left your Father's house, let me entreat you not to leave it. He is a good Father. With him are joys forevermore. If you have left, if you have any recollections of your home, any longings to return, pause, resolve to return. Stay not, nor rest, till once more in your Father's arms, the sobs of repentance are mingled with the affectionate greetings of your Father's forgiveness.

THE PRODIGAL SON.—No. II.

Luke 15: 15–19.—And he went and joined himself to a citizen of that country, and he sent him into his fields to feed swine. And he would fain have filled his belly with the husks which the swine did eat, and no man gave unto him. *And when he came to himself,* he said, how many hired servants of my father have bread enough and to spare and I perish with hunger! I will arise and go to my father and will say unto him, father, I have sinned against heaven and before thee, and am no more worthy to be called thy son, make me as one of thy hired servants.

This is the continuation of the parable of the Prodigal Son, upon another part of which we were meditating last Sunday night. We traced the wandering sinner through the alienation from his father and his home, his realization of the portion his father gave him, in his sense of independence taking his journey into a far country, there devoting the wealth of an angel to the pursuits of sin. We traced him through the wasting of his heavenly portion, through the dearth of everything there that could respond to his better being, down to the sense of want that overtook him. I asked you to mark the gradation, or *de*gradation that was here, the gradual but sure *sinking*, lapsing, gliding downward. That is what spiritual death means, the *wasting* away of life, *falling*, the decay of noble faculty, of high-born aspirations, the passing from a higher to a baser being.

But there was a deeper lapse than that, "He went and joined himself to a citizen of that country." What is meant by that? You recollect in dwelling last Sunday night upon the thought of the "riotous living," I spoke of spheres of worldliness, within which for any gifted or pure being to be, was simply a prostitution of all gifts and of all higher being. Yet *there* is a land within which myriads of this human race dwell. You look out upon life, dissect society, the community, and you find classes, degrees of ungodliness, ranging all the way from what is supposed to be refined worldliness, down through hypocrisy, through all sorts of license, through immorality, through vice, to crime, to all that is ignorant, vulgar, sensuous, utterly and to all appearance hopelessly abandoned. There you have one inclined plane, crowded, not with kinds, only with degrees. You find there, not so much human nature, as the perversion of human nature, the neglect or abuse of divine faculties, the "portion" of goods originally given utterly squandered, the patrimony all gone, the family records lost, the family spirit dead, till they *seem*, indeed to be not the children of God. Here you have the *descendants of prodigal* beings who wandered here and never returned, beings born here, educated here, *i. e.*, beings who never knew their origin, not that they were born in poverty, in ignorance, in vice, what they are in they do not know to be ignorance, poverty, and vice.

You must have observed what a naturalness there is sometimes to such people. There seems to break in upon them no echo from upper worlds. The moral sense, if not dead, is dormant. Though the Holy Ghost is there, there is little by which the Holy Ghost can work. To you, how *unnatural* it seems, that any being could live so forgetful of a better being, so unregardful of God, of all divine things, and it is unnatural. Take it, in what is its least repulsive phase, in what is very often an attractive phase. Take it in circles where wealth abounds, where the pomps and vanities of life flourish, where social etiquette, abandonment to pleasure, the pursuit of what others think are the *supreme good.* Mark the *shallowness* there, the frivolous vanity, the shining veneering, the absence of solidity—of all indication that the strong and true things which constitute humanity, were ever there. There is not unfrequently a sparkling brilliancy, sometimes a glimpse of true beauty. But try to present there a thought. What a waste of labor! How the toil reacts. That being ranges not within the limits of thought, and I do not mean simply religious thought, but solid thought of any sort. The whole of that being is sensuous. It has not penetrated into immortality. It is animalism, painted, draped, and decorated. It creates and sustains the *froth* of life. It is for them, that all which panders to that kind of being, exists. It comes so natural to them, and it appeals so forcible to unculture, to inexperience, to youth, and all beings in which the higher nature has been reached, that many of us suppose that to be human nature.

We take that so much for granted, that instead of endeavoring to make it impossible by culture, we turn to abusing it. We guard people against it, without cultivating those faculties, which would render all guarding unnecessary; like an unskillful pilot, we watch the wrecks, when we ought to know and follow the channel.

Then, from here, go down, through the multiplied manifestations of the same thing. There are men who live *only to be able to live* in that kind of life, men who devote all the soul power of which they are conscious to be able to maintain appearances. Hence we get men in trade with great faculties of combination, of penetration, of execution, who oil the wheels of commerce and keep trade in motion, men who never think, nor care, for any interests beyond their own, men like the big pikes in a pond, that eat up not only all the little fish, but even the smaller pikes, men that create monopolies, which in their turn create and stimulate all selfishness and wrong, men who have too many *great* things to do, to think of religion, of humanity, of philanthropy, of right, of God, men who often have mind-culture, but not moral culture, men who have only one-half their being developed, and that feebly. Here we get to high-born faculties, in all office, perverted to petty and selfish ends, in every department of life, talent devoted not to the highest and universal good, to the true and the right, but to the expedient, the near and local and temporary, the form and not the substance, men who betray trusts and sacred interests—men, to be like whom, other men commit crimes. Then you go down to where the tinsel begins to peal off, to where the repulsive begins to appear, but observe, *repulsive* not always to those who are there. If you have been long in a vitiated atmosphere, you are not conscious of its exhaustion as the man who steps in from the pure air outside. They are used to it. They are indifferent. Here the misunderstanding begins to be intensified, because the ignorance is more palpable. They neither covet, nor could they enjoy your refinement. They think people of culture and religion are their enemies. That arises from the undefined consciousness that they are at enmity with all social good. You get down now to where society for its protection begins to issue *licenses*, to where the police begin to be needful. You get down now to those vocations that are illustrated by saloons, by gambling dens, by all infamy. You get down to where courts and jails are demanded.

Within the limits of our cities, even you get to a territory here that is thickly settled.

The point I wish you to observe is, the naturalness that is there, the fact that men and women are *citizens* of that country. You perceive it is not what God made them for. It is by leaving out all that distinguishes them from the beast. It is the enthronement of all that is merely animal. When we look upon the world, and see so many hard fates and cruel destinies, we think God is full of wrath, and wonder how a God of love could create souls for such woe. But that is not what God has done, so much as what God has been trying to prevent. When you look only sometimes, and see families broken up, all unlove and unrest there, it is because they have lived in their lower nature, and forgotten God. It was against this God provided such endless means, such an economy of reason, and moral sense—even this Gospel itself. That is our slavery. We have spent our divine life. We have joined ourselves to a citizen of a country that is ruled by the devil, the cruelest of all masters. He makes fair promises, but He sends us to feed swine. That is all the stock he has. He deals in animalism. Its food is not soul food. No spirit can feed upon its husks. Souls have tried it, but all have failed. We sometimes call it human nature, but the truth is, it is human unnature. Mark the force of the swine in the text. You know the hog is the illustration, the epitome of all that is mean and loathsome in animal being. Man, having parted with his divine portion, sinks to the very dregs of animal being. To part with your birthright, is to sell yourself to one of these citizens, is possibly, *to become* one of these citizens, to become *naturalized* there, to be ruled by lust and passion, to wear a yoke more galling than death. You see people trying to become naturalized there every day—young people imitating the frivolous and profane, people sometimes supremely *ridiculous*, because you can see it is not natural. *Christian* society is only immolation of those who are of the earth, earthy. Many of the fashions and customs of life are imported from foreign and heathen circles. One of the deplorable facts of to-day is, that there exists little of what may be strictly called *Christian society*, anything that pervades life as such. The world has more power, in certain directions, over thc Church, than the Church over the world. Much of the dress and extravagance, in which we indulge, is very unnatural. It is the testimony of the absence of heart power, and soul power, and brain power. It creates and substantiates the impression, *the suspicion*, that religion is not where it claims to be. Hence the thinness of our churches. Hence the impotency of church machinery. Hence the want of success in reaching the cancer spots of society. Hence it is, that wise laws are not made, and those that are made fail to be executed. Hence so much that is done is unwise.

While we are here, let us look at an important thought. From what has been said, *we may infer that there are all degrees of appreciation for divine things*, even down to that degree of which it may be said there can hardly be any appreciation at all—down to that degree which justified the Master in saying to His disciples, "*Cast not your pearls before swine.*" In forgetfulness of this, there is absence of much wise action on our part *relative to the masses*, and much of Christian effort *which is wasted*, because *it is unwise*, well meant, but having in it more zeal than knowledge. We aim too often at a higher good, *forgetful that if we would do any good at all, we must first accomplish that of a lower degree. The Saviour Himself always acted upon this plan.* Whenever men and women presented themselves for His aid, *He invariably imparted it up to the degree in which they first asked for it*—to my mind, one of the most instructive facts in the Bible. When the ten lepers came to Him, He said nothing to them about sin; He never said anything to *any of them* about their sin; He never makes them promise to come back and follow Him; He always takes for granted the better nature in them; He assumes that that nature must work, if it work at all, by laws of its own. Yes, "go and show yourselves to the priests," "go and wash in the pool of Siloam," go and get clean by all means up to the best you covet. When you are there, the better degree will bring you to a degree still better. The blind boy will come back and worship. One out of the ten lepers will come back for a higher blessing. *Now, we* go down into lanes and alleys, into rat-pits and dog-kennels, and read the Bible and hold prayer meetings, and all that may be right enough, but it is not all that ought to be done. Now, is it *the best that could be done.* How hopeless it is, experience tells us. We scatter the rats and the dogs to other quarters; we make their former locality available for better business. The Five Points Mission House is a grand institution, perhaps as grand as any in New York. *It aims at education.* But I contend that a Christian people should not be felt merely in isolated and sporadic endeavors. If we could unite all our charities and stand together as Christian people we should not only be more effective, but more charitable. Why are *our laws so powerless? or why have we so few really salutary laws?* Why is ignorance increasing upon us and pauperism increasing upon us? These are questions which are alarming already, and which as a people we must before long seriously contemplate. I think as Christian people and as Churches we ought to be more interested and more active in all the questions of social science. Many social evils are, I think, because Christian people are not making themselves felt as they ought to be felt. We feel our duty is discharged when we have paid our taxes and that is what makes it so hard to pay them. We have no interest in that toward which they are supposed to be paid. We never look after the money to see whether we have any equivalent in actual benefit returned. When we take up a *principle* we dabble with it, like a blind chemist trying experiments. It is not for our brother and sister we care, not for the multitudes, not for a better condition of society. *We have no soul invested.* In my judgment we never can reach the religious sensibilities *of the multitudes,* till we have first reached the minds and morals. We may reach here and there an individual case, but we must do as the Saviour, have compassion upon the multitudes. It is very true our soul is worth all the money we spend in converting it, but if wisely directed, if Christians, instead of quarreling over abstract theories, and acting in sectarian and solitary, and not unfrequently, on very slender bases, could unite all energy and realize that, after all, our interests are common and our work too a common one, I think we could send a tide of life, through our laws, through our police agencies, through our philanthropic institutions, and withal derive a high life ourselves, quicken the divine faculties within us, and have not only more religion to impart, but richer appreciation to which to impart it. We should all reach proportionally a higher story of our being. The thought of the condition of society at its lower extremities is breaking the hearts of many good men, but the thought which paralyzes their energies is, the impossibility of weaning Christians from their unprofitable quarrels, and uniting them in wise, strong and concerted activity. The misfortune is, we look out upon the world not with the anxiety of him who feels he is his brother's keeper, not with warm solicitude for our Father's honor and interest, but as "*hired servants*," with the selfish narrowness of our little divisions. We have our schemes, our respectability, our ways, whatever they may be, to secure, and beyond that nothing. All, at last seek their own and not the things of Jesus Christ.

You know what a household becomes left to *servants*, and you see what God's household must be, left to "*hired servants*," with enough and to spare, with means of grace and privileges and blessings beyond, not their needs, but their craving, with vastly more than they themselves appreciate. There is great force in this thought that the Master puts into the mouth of this awakened prodigal, "How many *hired servants!*" How many souls think that way when they awake and think of us. Roused by bitter experience, by dark providence, by, *to him*, mysterious extremity, he reaches depths of being, longings beyond utterance. He misunderstands his father. He does not see the glory of a sonship. His first thought is of us,. the hired servants. And verily, we have enough and to spare. When I look out upon the manifold gifts of Christians, when I see the time they have at their disposal, the education they have received, to a great extent unemployed, lending light, transcendently beautiful to be sure, but only to very limited circles, not employed as a talent *lent* of God, not invested in the well being of those who have no helper, when I contrast this with the myriads who would be glad of the crumbs of our superfluity, I think they have a right to expect more of us, and we owe it to God, to ourselves and our neighbor, to be more diligent and devoted in the work our hand ought to find to do. We ought not to be idling, "*hired*" servants.

But let me remark again this thought, that there are all degrees of appreciation for divine things, has its bearing upon this part of the work of the Church or the Christian, called "*preaching the Gospel.*" Some men think that to preach the Gospel, we must always, in every sermon, lay out the whole Christian scheme, so that if, for the first time in his life, a straggler happen in, he may hear the whole Gospel. That would do very well, if it were not that, to my mind, *that whole Gospel* generally leaves the Gospel out. To me, most of the preaching, since I was eighteen years of age, has been telling us what sinners we are, not what a *Father God is.* It has been *theology*, and not *Gospel.* It has run upon a certain class of texts, leaving about ninety-nine one-hundredths of the Bible unopened, and unknown, and a large portion of it is, to great multitudes of us, still unopened and unknown. If the preaching of our times is changing at all, it is in this, that it is bringing some of those other texts to our minds and hearts. When we preach the Gospel, we have to assume *some knowledge* in our hearers. I assume, in my preaching, that we all know we are sinners. If we know not that, the case is hopeless, after all the preaching that has been done. I take for granted we are all prodigals—or even if there are some of us, *those elder brothers*, that have always been at home—then, even to us, our Father would speak. I take for granted that sin is the worst yoke man ever had upon his neck; how it galls, none know so well as those on whose neck it has rested. Why should I scrape the sore, and pour vinegar upon the raw and festering spot. I think that is where we who preach the Gospel err, in not knowing how raw it is, in not knowing that men feel it, that they do not want it to be so—in not knowing that it came there in their ignorance, in some dark day, under some crushing temptation—that they were born in a far country; that cruel, mysterious providencies left them without instruction, without culture, without those restraints, which would have made them angels. Stranded there, without a messenger from home, or a guide to lead them back. *We have not sympathy enough*, and so do not know that the one thing we want, is an oil for the wound, a balm that can heal—just this message of Christ—"Neither do I condemn thee." "I will; be thou clean." Though thou art far off, thy Father is watching and longing—oh! the days and the nights of agony I have spent over what I know already, my sins, the tears I have shed over the same message, tears of joy, tears of streaming peace, this prodigal son. Oh! when I had come to myself, and then wanted God, it was here I had found Him, *my Father*. It was this that convinced me that Christ was my Saviour, because He convinced me God was love, that was "good news," and when I came to see His own bleeding side, His cross, and the grave, when I came to see how my wicked, prodigal heart, brought Him there, my sins burned like fire within me, and if it could have done any good I *could have crushed myself;* but cured, and clothed in my right mind, and at rest, in the thought that, while only fit to be crushed, God was the only being in the universe who would not crush me, then I felt it was worth while to live, and give soul and body to the service of God, in the service of my fellow man, in telling them that every day they staid away from God, they wronged their own soul, in telling my fellow men God loved them, for that could make them repent; in showing them what was in Christ, for that would make them ashamed of themselves—just as I do this day with my little children; when they transgress I do not tell them how mean they are, but I tell them of something pure and noble, and sweet and holy, and it makes them self-convicted, but hopefully and sweetly penitent, and, my dear hearer, in my judgment, if the love of Jesus, if a sense of the love of God, do not break your heart, do not make you sensible of your ingratitude and sin, then nothing upon earth can do it. No, I do not think the elder brother knows his Father the best, or loves his prodigal brother the best—or even if he knows it better than I, I think Jesus knows it better than any, and He holds up everywhere, and all the time, only God's pardoning love. His own life and death are illustrations of that love, and to see that, I think, is to be led to repentance, to abhor ourselves, and cling to God, to be born again, to put on Christ, to renew our mind; as the Master so sublimely expresses it here, "*to come to ourselves.*" When a man gets there, he is a converted man. He is the best kind of a converted man. He may think he wants to be a hired servant, but God will not let him be. He shall be a *son*. He shall not be looking downward to see what the least requisite for his Father's Kingdom is, but always upward, how near to, and how worthy of that Father he can become.

"When he came to himself," what a world of meaning there is in that! What a body of theology is there! Do you see this palsied, leprous, sin-stricken mortality, is not thyself? I have known a youth leave his father's house, his boyhood home, and in the mazes of a large city disappear. He went out with all the benediction a parental heart could bestow. He had been reared tenderly, perhaps what we might call indulgently, the pride and hope of a large family circle. After long, long years, in which evil association, dire temptation, vice in all degrees had done their worst, on a dark, cold, wintry night, that father's door-bell has wrung. Shortly after, an altercation is heard with the servants in the hall--that father goes out and sees a tattered, trembling, driveling form, asking for the father's forgiveness before he died. Was this his son? Was this the being in whom so many hearts had made so large a venture? Was this he whose form was so erect, whose heart was so noble, whose soul was so pure, whose life was laden with promise? No—it was the wreck that was left of him. His crime had been that he had changed into another being. He had cheated himself, and cheated his father, and sinned against God. In his case, he never came to himself; it was too late to save him. Shall I say he never came to himself? Perhaps, in that dark night it was himself that struggled back into himself. In coming in repentance to his earthly father, he found forgiveness and peace with God. But if he did not, it was not because God could not forgive him. No, that Father-heart was rich in mercy if he could only know it. I say what a body of theology is in this thought—does God's spirit ever leave us? What is it brings us to ourselves? What is it brings that Spirit there? Oh, the death and sacrifice of Christ! Oh, the gift above all gifts, God to dwell in earnest love even with those who do not love Him. Through that do you see God abroad everywhere, pleading, working through every faculty of manhood, quickening the memory, through the law of association bringing back the past, applying all providence, as links of iron, to hold us to truth, to goodness, and to God? That is what we forget, that spirit of God there, that He works, that it is His office to apply the things of Jesus, and that all those things are love. Yes; my friend, when you are where you know you ought not to be, when providences, dark and mysterious, quicken your thoughts, and send them back over the past, or out over the future, what is it all but God's spirit calling you to repentance. "When he came to himself," He was hungry, but against whom had he sinned? Against his father. Who ought to be angry? According to all our notions, that father. Who ought to be his best friend? According to Christ, that Father. Who did he most of all need? that Father? Oh! my hearers, God is the one Being that serves us all, the one Being we cannot get along without, the one Being we may be sure will never fail us. He is the one Being against whom we have sinned, but He is the one Being who is not angry, who does not hate. That is the curse of sin, that is when the devil is a liar. He steps in between us and God and says we cannot return. This is what faith is, this is the one work for us to do, *to believe Jesus, to believe* IN *Jesus,* to accept His invitation, to resolve to return. Do you see there the one thought, "you must come to yourself." You must accept the overtures of the Spirit. You must repent and say: "I will arise and go to my Father." Make up your story,—"Father I have sinned against heaven and before thee, and am no more worthy to be called thy son, make me as one of thy hired servants." But why so long a story? You shall not need it, God knows it already better than you can tell Him—yes; even with all you would tell Him, you do not know how much you have sinned. You do not know how unworthy you are. As the years go by, and you see your Father's love and your Father's purity and understand Him, you will the better understand what you have been, and while every day will only refine the soul within you, every day will the more deeply humble you. In your humility will be exaltation. Now you ask, "make me one of thy hired servants." Your Father will not let you ask that? By and by you would not ask it yourself. There will come a hungering and thirsting beyond what you now know, and that hungering and thirsting will be, in deed and in truth, a son of the Highest. May the Spirit of all truth, quicken all our souls, and send us out with one constant longing, to come nearer to Our Father who is in heaven, to be more like that One, elder brother, who gave Himself that we might live—the Saviour, Jesus Christ.

THE PRODIGAL SON.—No. III.

LUKE 15 : 20, 24.—And he arose and came to his Father. But when he was yet a great way off, his Father saw him, and had compassion, and *ran* and fell on his neck and kissed him. And the son said unto him, Father, I have sinned against heaven and in thy sight, and am no more worthy to be called thy son. But the father said to his servants, Bring forth the best robe and put it on him ; and put a ring on his hand and shoes on his feet. And bring hither the fatted calf, and kill it, and let us eat and be merry. For this my son was dead and is alive again. He was lost and is found. And they began to be merry.

YOU readily recognize this as part of the record of the Prodigal Son. He is first represented in his alienation from his Father and his home. Then, in consequence, sinking to great want and extreme degradation. Then we see him at last meditating upon his evil career and dark condition, thinking of home, and resolving to return. In this text we see him carrying his resolution into effect. "He arose and came to his Father." We reach the very climax and pith of the parable. He comes, not to an angry father, a father to be appeased, but to a father anxiously watching, more glad to welcome the sinner, than the sinner is to return. This is the lesson of the parable, the love of a heavenly Father for his sinful and erring sons.

Possibly an error we have made in reading this parable, has been to consider it a mere story, illustrative of God's general love, *but because a story*, filled in with parts having no immediate parallels in divine facts. If such has been our conception, it has been a misconception. Of all the beings that ever walked our earth, none spake like the Son of Man. He was wonderful, in thought, in word, in deed, uttering no idle word, and in any record leaving no necessary word unsaid. If this parable had been uttered by any but Christ, we should have had many faults to find with it. We should have thought it not sufficiently explicit. We should have loaded it with elaborate technicalities, till its truth, its beauty and its force had all disappeared in one mist of complication and uncertainty. "*He arose and came to his Father.*" But before that, "*he came to himself.*" Did he do that in his own strength, by his own unaided volition? It would appear so, from all that is contained in the record itself. Persons who do not believe in all our Scriptures, but persons of wide observation, seeing, in all climes and ages, men truly turning to God, longing after God, say, the *natural man* turns to God and longs for Him. But, while it is true men in all climes and ages do turn to God and long for Him, it is still *man under grace* that does it. This human race has never been under more than one dispensation. That has been a dispensation of love, of mercy, God through Christ reconciling the world to Himself, out of that love wherewith God "so loved it as to give His only begotton Son." It is convenient for us to talk of three dispensations, but all these have been but phases or developments, successive unfoldings of the one universal dispensation. Men have been known to talk of the uncovenanted mercies of God. There are no such things as *uncovenanted* mercies—mercy is one and forever, and all the mercies of God are *covenanted* in Christ. The Abrahamic covenant was only a type or shadow. The Christian covenant is all there ever was, or ever can be, and that embraces a race and a world. The *covenant* mercy *in Christ*, as much envelops the earth as the atmosphere. It applies to every man as much as electricity or gravity, or sunlight, or space. Christ's atonement took away the sins of a world. It made all men brethren, but not only so—the love of God contemplated the *infusion of life within us* as much as the *removal of punishment from us*. Even more. There is *salvation* as well as *redemption*. The atonement, therefore, procured the Holy Ghost, the Lord and giver of life, *to dwell with man*, to teach him the true and the right, to urge him toward its attainment, and is the source of all the right, and true, and good, in the world, find it where you will. I do not think the spirit of God ever leaves any man upon earth. That spirit appeals to us through every providence that overtakes us, through every channel of our being, from the worlds that swim in space to the flowers that bloom by the wayside, from the winds that sigh through the trees to the funeral train that winds through the streets. Because it was a fixed fact, this redemption and this gift of the Holy Ghost—fact that our action or inaction cannot change, because it was universal, always acting, there was no need that Christ should be ever telling it. He only demanded and taught, as God has in all ages demanded and taught, as we do to-day demand and teach, an action in us commensurate with and directly responsive to the facts.

In the Bible we are not told on every page that the Holy Ghost is there to give it life, to give us vision to receive it. In our sermons we are not always telling that the Holy Ghost is present to apply the truth. We know that, we feel that. If the Holy Ghost were not present we could not perceive that anything is truth, there could not be any truth to apply. When on some delicious day you stand and gaze on an exquisite landscape, what is it you see? The tree, the valley, the hill, the shadow, the marvellous combination of beauty. But does that make the landscape? What if the sun were below the horizon; where would the landscape then be? Could your unaided eye create it? Not at all. The one agent and producer of the whole, is the one thing silent, unobtrusive. Your eye sees, because it uses the light. The soul sees when it uses the Spirit of God. Through Christ they are made for each other, and the Holy Ghost is with the soul without saying anything of Himself, just as the sunlight is with the eye without saying anything of itself.

"He arose and came to his father." God asks that of us all because we are all under grace, because every man has the Holy Ghost there to help him, because every man is under the one covenant God made with the race in Christ. Man now is not man after the first Adam, dead and helpless, but man redeemed in the second Adam, man like Adam before his fall, with germinal life, with perception of and capacityfor life. Man better off than the first Adam, because he has been bitten by transgression, like the prodigal, and knows the deadliness of the serpent's bite, and can look to that Redeemer who was lifted up, even as Moses lifted the serpent in the wilderness, if *he only will.* This is why God pleads with us in the Bible as He does, to repent and turn to Him, why he finds fault with us when we do not repent, why there can be no forgiveness for that because it is the sin against the Holy Ghost.

"He arose and came to his father." That is what

God wants every sinner to do. We can come pleading the atonement, pleading all the promises therein made. We can come to a Father reconciled. This is the very Gospel itself to tell us of the reconciliation and urge us to come. But we can only come in repentance as this Prodigal did, and as he furnishes us a clear illustration of what repentance is, *a change of mind.* You see him in his unrest and alienation, striving for an impossibility, a happiness in his animal nature, a life without God, a being with all that is immortal stricken out of him, a being resisting the Holy Ghost. You see then the one common experiment of ungodliness, the deadly attempt at impossibility to live without God. If man *could live* without God and be happy without God, if in the nature of things you *could be safe* in opposition to all higher being, if your *good could* be accomplished outside of God's plan, none would rejoice in it more than God. But it is the impossibility of the thing, the madness of trying it, that grieves God. You must perceive that, you must see what a folly you have committed, what an ingrate you have been, what a guilt you have incurred. This is the beginning of repentance. You see the Prodigal conscious of his mistake, guilty, not so much before God, as in his own consciousness, before the tribunal of his own soul, self-accused, self-condemned. This is the work of the Holy Ghost, *conviction,* marvellous and mysterious work. It makes the soul its own judge. This makes him exclaim, "I am no more worthy to be called thy son." He sees it, his own meanness. He knows he has forfeited all his right and title. He must accept all now as a gift. When he first went out in his pride he *claimed* his portion. His poor silly heart has made him think he was strong and rich in his own right. He sees now *all is of grace.* He must accept. St. Paul says, "the *gift* of God is eternal life, and this life is in His Son," and verily so it is. It is not ours by birth, or by purchase, or by works, but out of the riches of divine grace. Truly, too, it is ours now by the best of all rights, for what a father gives *ennobles* and makes us truly rich, rich in gratitude and affection and in all endearment. This *is* repentance, not only the sight of the wrong and evil, and sensual and wicked, for if we see only that it is the dark side, that which makes religion a fear, but repentance is vision of the true, and right, and divine, that which makes the service of God perfect freedom, but which makes us see at the same time how far away we are from a true service. You perceive only a nature quickened can attain it. Hence a mystery is solved, the purer we grow, the unworthier we seem. The more truly rich we are, the more we ascribe to God. Thus, true exaltation truly humbles, and true humility truly exalts. The archangel while highest and grandest is still humblest and simplest. Hence, too, we get to a true idea of God, while He is the absolutely supreme. He is the absolutely accessable, while the absolute Ruler, at the same time the universal server—while infinitely exalted, still responsive even to a child. Infinite love at last embracing all being.

"But when he was yet a great way off, his father saw him and had compassion." That expression in itself were enough to tell us of God's yearning to get us all back to Himself. This were enough in itself to dissipate all thought of God's anger, of a Father in wrath. That man should have that notion of God that He is angry, is perfectly natural. If your child should wander out in disobedience and transgression; should it commit some flagrant misdeed; its first thought would be of your displeasure. It would keep away from you. But to whom else *should* that child instantly go? Who could be a better friend to it than you? And, if you were a true parent, who could desire it to do just that very thing more than you? What a relief it would be to those of us who have children, if we could only feel that in all their errings they would come instantly to us! Who could pity them so much? Who could guide and counsel them so well? Oh, what a thought it is, that God is a Father! His justice satisfied! His anger all removed! What a Gospel is in those words!—he saw him when he was a long way off, and *ran* and fell on his neck. Oh! how far did Jesus come, away from that glory above, past cherubim and seraphim, past angel and spirits of the just, down to us, tattered and trembling sinners, to tell us *that*—God, "*our Father!*" How He exhausted language and resources in teaching us. When he would teach us to pray, while he bids us shut ourselves by ourselves, He does not say, "*my* Father," or, "O Lord God of Israel," or, "O thou that dwellest in Zion;" nay—but still "*our* Father," not unwilling to hear, but more ready to hear than we are to pray, watching, anxious, *running,* in a transport of joy, falling on our neck and kissing us. No wonder the Saviour labored so hard to impress it. Good news as it is, men are slow of heart to believe it. When Adam sinned, he ran away from God and hid himself—the very natural thing, but the very worst thing he could have done. Notwithstanding that earnest, pleading Saviour there, we even now come tremblingly, "perfect love" not yet having "cast out" all "fear." Why can we not believe? There is no reproach, no accusation, no upbraiding, no reaping up. What can so touch the heart, and break the heart, as love and kindness we know we do not deserve? Would it not be strange indeed, if Jesus, being lifted up, should *not* draw all men to Him? The Holy Ghost works through love. Not only so. What can so break the heart as kindness, which, having been rejected and despised, now wells up out of its own native fountains and overflows in forgiveness and blessing?

No wonder the prodigal does not finish his story. He does not say now, "make me as one of thy hired servants." His father's love chokes him. That would be unworthy that father's child—to ask it. He must be nobler and higher than that. At first he would come back and *work* for something. But oh, how little he could work for! It would not touch the riches of such a father. Oh! my hearer, if God gave us only what we could work for, we should be poor indeed. But you see, God is so truly God, His Spirit teaches us to be sons. We must share the *riches* of that Father. We must be like Him, holy as He is holy, perfect *as* He is perfect. All that the Father hath is ours. All that we can receive, all that we can be, and the more we can receive, and the more we can be—so much nearer and dearer to Him. No more now about any *wages*, and yet every day finding relief in service. Every day doing more, and yet every day feeling how much more God hath done for *us*. Every day closer to God, and higher up in Christ, but every day more and more dependent.

Now, too, once there in this higher and truer service, how all things minister to us. "The Father said to *His servants*." Everywhere in the economy of God, every instrumentality ministers to the redeemed. This is the purpose of all things. Earth was made for man. As we grow in truth, in wisdom, and become more truly sons of God, how many more things there are in nature and in God's word, than we supposed was there; and how much God has for us which we are not yet able to receive—oh! the ministering agencies we might command, if we were only worthy! This life of God is not merely turning from sin, it is being clothed upon with the fullness of God, it is being lifted up in true glory. "Bring forth the *best* robe and put it on him," says the father. God's purposes are to make us sons indeed. As we have been clothed in brutishness, He would have us now meet and fit for the society of saints in light. Oh! to think of the beings there, exalted, transcendent, pure, what a service is theirs—so far above us, how can we enjoy them, how shall they enjoy us? He would have us with a robe of *acceptableness*, that which shall make us not strangers in the courts above. That robe for every soul is Christ. Observe, at first an imputed righteousness, in progress of eternal cycles to be *an acquired righteousness.* As being unfolds, it is to be Christ in us. All that was in Christ reproduced, all the virtues, all the graces, the majesty and power of the divine life, all toward which Christ so earnestly exhorts us, and unless we are putting on that higher life, we are still lost; churches and creeds count for nothing. "If ye love them that love you;" etc., "be ye perfect as your Father," etc.; you see the need of this, when you come to consider that grumbling elder brother. How far away he was from his father. What a gulf between them, though he had never been a prodigal. Unless we understand this, we shall misunderstand much of the Scripture. We are to be clothed upon, not working for salvation, but working out salvation, putting on salvation. That is salvation, to be what Christ was. That is *sanctification*, to be putting on that. This is what so many of those Scriptures mean, especially St. Paul. Take such a passage as this from the Ephesians: "For this cause I bow my knees unto the Father of our Lord Jesus Christ, of whom the whole family in heaven and earth is named, that He would grant you according to the riches of His glory to be strengthened with might by His Spirit in the inner man, that Christ may dwell in your hearts by faith, that ye, being rooted and grounded in love, *may be able to comprehend with all saints* what is the breadth and length and depth and hight, and to know the love of Christ, which passeth knowledge, that ye might be filled with all the fullness of God." Or, take such a passage as this, which expresses, as it were, the whole object of redemption, of the Church, and of religion: "And He gave some apostles, and some prophets, and some evangelists, and some pastors, and teachers, for the perfecting of the saints, for the building up of the body of Christ, till we all come in the unity of the faith, *and of the knowledge of the Son of God, unto a perfect manhood, unto the measure of the stature of the fullness of Christ.*" What a robe is that? What a sonship is there? It is to be from the crown of the head to the soul of the foot, a whole nature absolutely reclothed. He is to walk in a being *adorned*, glorified—not only bring the best robe and put shoes on his feet, *but put a ring on his hand.* No longer a nature poverty stricken, but a nature enriched and adorned, with a riches that can satisfy, a soul feasting on "fat things," a feast made of the Lord, with a spirit merry and glad, with a Father rejoicing and all the family of God rejoicing. Oh, my hearer, it is *worth while to come home.* It is coming to a heritage of glory that shall never be taken away and never be diminished. The crown and the palm branch and the harp, they mean something in that kingdom of our Father. See the glory of not having it as wages. It is given without measure. See the glory of its being a gift. Your title to it is clear; nobody can take it from you. There is nothing about it, that shall ever molest or make you afraid. A life with God! Has any body ever told us what heaven is? We are told that here, in mortal language, nobody can tell. "It hath not entered," etc. We know that here upon earth, there are losses and disappointments, wrongs and deceptions, woes and sicknesses and sorrows. There, nothing comes that can deceive or make a lie. There the wicked cease to trouble and the weary are at rest. Tears are wiped away from off all faces. No more sickness, nor woes, nor darkness. Well, that is infinitely much, but it is not all, God shall cause us to eat and be merry, to feed on things divine and rejoice for ever and ever. There is to be music and dancing; Heaven, joy and peace in the Holy Ghost. This it is to which God invites us. This it is to which Jesus died to bring us. Oh, suppose, your little child were out, having lost its way, or afraid to come home, fallen among cruel and wicked souls, cold and naked and hungry, buffeted by the winds and evil passions, with no arm to shelter it, no living breast to pillow it. What would you not give to get it back? Such a joy is God's when the sinner returns. But what would that child not give to get back? Such a relief and joy is that of the sinner that returns! What thing in the house could be denied it that could minister to its comfort? Such a welcome has our Father, for every penitent; such a home, for every rescued, reconciled child. Suppose that child were hardened and would not come, suppose it were insensible to give love, then what a grief would be yours, what double need of grieving. Such a grief is God's, over the thoughtless, thankless, sinning prodigal heart. Can any of us here today have such a heart? Then listen, sinner, Jesus calls you. Hasten, for thy Father is waiting. Thy ransom is paid. Thy welcome is before you. "The spirit in thy heart is whispering sinner come." It is the joy of that spirit to say through Christ to all God's children, come. And oh, beloved, may we all remember what we were, and what we are, and what we may become, remember, Him who brought us this glad news, and purchased us with His own blood, that we may be the children of the Highest. Wrapt in that robe which He gives to them that believe, may we, not be *hired servants,* but true sons, risen with Christ.

THE PRODIGAL SON.—No. IV.

Luke 15: 25, 32.—Now, His elder son was in the field, and as he came and drew near to the house, he heard music and dancing. And he called one of the servants, and asked what these things meant. And he said unto him, Thy brother is come, and thy father hath killed the fatted calf, because he hath received him safe and sound. And he was angry, and would not go in, therefore came his father out, and entreated him. And he answering, said to his father, Lo, these many years do I serve thee, neither transgressed I at any time thy commandments, and yet thou never gavest me a kid, that I might make merry with my friends. But as soon as this thy son was come, who hath devoured thy living with harlots, thou hast killed for him the fatted calf. And he said unto him, son, thou art ever with me, and all that I have is thine. It was meet that we should make merry and be glad, for this thy brother was dead and is alive again. He was lost and is found.

On three former occasions we have dwelt upon the record of this Prodigal Son. First, upon his estrangement from home, and its consequent debasement. Second, his coming to himself and resolving to return. Third, his reception at home. Last Sunday night, our souls were moved in contemplating the watching, hastening, yearning love, wherewith his father forgot the past, and welcomed him to a happier and worthier future. We reached the prime thought the parable was intended to express, the great fatherhood of God, with all its wealth of affection, the fountain of exhaustless blessing. There the parable might have ended, for the joy was full. But the wisdom of the faithful Saviour saw a lesson beyond it. It is needful we should know, that the true sonship consists, not in any outward relations, but in pure filiation, in a participation of nature. This is the counterpart of God's love, the object on account of which He loved us. The father's action toward the prodigal shows the love of God for us all. The conduct of the elder son shows the want in us of such a love toward each other.

You will recollect, in the earlier part of the parable, mention was made of an "*elder brother.*" As the recital progressed he disappeared, till now he emerges to-night, the occasion to us of sad reflection, but not, on that account, necessarily the occasion of reflections any the less instructive. I remarked, on a former occasion, that possibly, by the fact of this *elder* brother's remaining at home, might have been meant to convey the thought that, now through the redemption, our first estate is one of sonship—that, as a matter of fact, we are created, not only with capabilities, but with affinities for things divine; that truly *man* is the grandest *creation* of which we have any knowledge. While that is true, still, as compared with God, what a worm man is! What an interval between him and Deity! How everything *in divine action* is wanting to him. The best we can say of him is, that he *has a perception* of the divine, not that he *is* divine. Very often in his *best* estate, he but reveals the poverty of his being. He is grand when compared with all that is below him. He sinks into pitiable proportions when compared with God. His glory above that of all earthly creatures is, that *he can become like God.* His glory is, that for this end, all things earthly minister to *him.* He alone has religion. Likeness to God in him is religion.

You will recollect this parable was occasioned by the murmuring of the Scribes and Pharisees. They could not understand Christ's sympathy for publicans and sinners. They did not see how, if anybody needed the physician, it surely was the sick; that if anybody needed God, it was surely these very souls who knew Him not—the lost sheep of the house of Israel. But not only this, the Scribes and Pharisees, professors of religion, set up to be God's children. The Saviour does not dispute their position. But they undertook to say that others were not, and for that reason ought not to be considered children, sons, as well as themselves. *This* Christ disputes. Their thoughts prove that even if they were sons, their sonship was of no high order; they *had* little of God, and *knew* little of God. The true sonship *is likeness to God.* This the Saviour wished to show. It is this, this part of the parable illustrates. It is easy to see, therefore, who is meant by this *elder* son.

If we carry the parable off into the mere generalities of Jews and Gentiles, of Pharisees and sinners, I think we shall lose its efficacy. The parable is built not upon any mere accident, but upon law. It applies to all ages, and therefore, to us as much as to the Jews. The elder brother means the Church, the *representative* Church, —not the Church considered as visible or invisible, but the Church, acting, assuming, administering. The younger brother means the worldly or unconverted.

The record of this elder brother, is a condensed Church history, so far as the Church has a history that can be recorded. You know that any history is not the record of real life, but only of some accidents of life. Natural history can give little incite into the actual condition of an age, or a people. We read of kings and armies, of wars and laws, of progress in outline. Certain facts represent a great multitude of facts. So in Church history, and this record of the elder brother represents much of Church history. He had been in the field. This implies he had been at work. The Saviour does not intimate that there was any mistake about that. He had been seeking to augment the estate. But to what purpose? with what motive? Was it that he might magnify his father, or that the estate and his father might magnify *him?* These are questions worth asking. The world has often had occasion to analyze the claims and actions of the Church. It has often come to the conclusion that they, whom the Church was carrying, were more in number, than they, who were carrying the Church. When you look at those Jews; yes, when you look at ages long subsequent to *those* Jews, when you look through the Middle Ages, when you come nearer home than that, when you contemplate the imposing names and pretensions of Church dignitaries, when you contemplate the official zeal and anxiety for creed and Church and custom, we may well ask, is it zeal and anxiety for God, or for themselves? Suppose, in such a case as Wolsey's, and in many others just like it, a real work had been there to be done; suppose a real cross had been there to be carried; suppose there had been any shame to be despised, had they been there at all? The world *will* ask such questions; it *does* ask them. We may think it is rather unkind in the world to do it. Still, it is only the world, and we can hardly expect of it anything better. It is very natural, but would it not be wise for the Church to ask it herself sometimes? I know that when we do ask it, we are soon said to be no friend of the Church. We are supposed to be gloomy, ill-boding prophets. The query, however, seriously entertained, *would* cause us, *might* cause us, to see how it is, *our grand things* cannot, after all, glorify God. So far from attracting the world, for the world's own sake we ought not to have them, because they *will* put the wrong construction upon them. We might see that "God, who made the world, being Lord of heaven and earth, dwelleth not in temples made with hands, neither is worshiped with men's hands, as though He needed anything." We might see that, after all, it is not strange that the grander we become, the less efficient we are—that the more of our glory we have, the less there is of God—that the more stone we possess, the more we want bread. I cannot dwell here, for there is enough here in itself to occupy the half-hour, but there is thought suggested here, which followed out, would show us why the Church should be like Christ in all things, would show us the fallacy of all that undertakes to teach us that God wants our earthly things. Soul is never sensuous, nor carnal. For that reason, the more we represent it, the less we have. It cannot be, but that the further we go in that direction, the further we go from God. In this direction we will perceive why *sacrifice* and *mercy* are always in inverse proportions, and why God loves *mercy* more than *sacrifice.* It is well to be in the field, but it is better to be there in holy motion, in godlike purpose—there as Elijah was there, as Jeremiah and Paul and the true sons of God have ever been there. We cannot help feeling, if we could give ourselves, as Christ gave Himself, for the glory of God, it would be easier for us all to live and all have more true glory at last.

He draws near and hears music and dancing. When he learns the cause—"*Thy brother is come,*" he is angry, and will not go in. Instantly a sort of low jealousy arises. He puts on an air of conscious injury. He acts as if some injustice had been done him, as if the enjoyment of another was something taken from himself. Mark, the parallel has relation to the Scribes and Pharisees. Mark its force, as applied to that immediate occasion. They imagined they had ever been in the house—they transgressed no commandment. They come now and find the Gentiles taken into the covenant, the Samaritans and sinners all taken back, and placed within the reach of heaven. Emmanuel sits there with publicans, while the Church authorities and dignitaries appear to be slighted. Instead of inquiring the cause, they unreasonably complain. If we let this man go in, the Romans will come and take away *our* place and nation. They have certain *assumptions* of their own importance and authority, certain assumptions as to what God's kingdom is, so rooted and grounded in them, they are incapable of inquiry. You observe, the kingdom they had built was not God's kingdom, at all; that which they supposed needed to be guarded, was *the* thing for human good, needing to be destroyed. Virtually they have taken the management of the estate in their own hands. The father is ignored. They assume his prerogatives. They make laws. They prescribe what God shall do, or shall not do. *They take the keys.* In reality, they are worse than the prodigal. He asks for his portion, and goes off and sets up for himself. They stay at home and turn their father out. You see, then, how it is, that spiritual pride is the deadliest of all pride. You see running through that fact, the words of Christ—"Verily, I say unto you, the publicans and harlots," etc. You see that the pinnacle of the temple is a dangerous place. But what have the ages ever been doing, but repeating this folly. What does the Pope claim to-day, but "*the power of the keys.*" Would you like to be the Pope? Yes, but look at every sect. They are all only so many Popes. Each one is perfectly sure it knows what man wants, and what God ought to do, better than God knows. How strange it is, that all the reformations of the ages have had to leave behind the elder brothers. The Jews would not accept the Gospel. They got angry and staid out. The Romanists would not come into the Reformation. They got angry and staid out. So all reformations have left some of us behind, and, from many signs of the times, we are entering upon a dispensation of grander proportions than any the world has known, from which many of us are to be left behind, because we will get angry, and refuse to come in. Can nothing new happen in this human family? Is every son and daughter gathered back? And if not, are there not many *surprises* yet for us all? And ought it to be a surprise, when God is what He is, when Christ is such a Christ, that these sons are constantly coming back? Who should be better prepared, or who has a better right to enter in and rejoice, than all the elder sons. Observe, we all rejoice when another soul joins our sect, but this is not the point here. We get angry when the limits of the great Church are extended, when an old fence is destroyed. Mark the progress of the last three hundred years. Multitudes died in battle to prevent the progress of the Reformation. Then, at every step, it was assumed by the elder brother that there was no step beyond. The recognition of Jew and Romanist as citizens, the toleration of Quakers and Methodists as religionists—each had its struggle, each was occasion of fearful prognostics, each was thought to be the sweeping away of all religion, till, as I remarked a few Sundays ago, the Europeans cannot understand how we have any religion at all, because we have no State Church, or State Religion. But shall this Gospel-view shoot out no new branch, develop no new life, attach no other chapter of this lost humanity? It is remarkable, of all the reformations against which the elder brother has grumbled, that they have carried men to a larger liberty, opened a new territory, and brought forth a richer heritage. It is ever a *fatted calf* with which God is welcoming the return of his children. It is singular how, in holding on to the tradition of the elders, we often sneer at the very word "*progress.*" How we forget that man is more than we, and God is more than we, and time is more than we; how, in turning them out of our thoughts, we have not a true faith, as an anchor within the vail, and so literally chain ourselves to littleness. If there are laws in the universe, then this law of growth is certainly one. If there is one, this elder brother has uniformly forgotten it is this, and hence we find actually existing, moral fossils, as well as physical fossils. We can find a petrifaction of perhaps every form of religion that ever existed; forms of religion that the world has long, long centuries left behind, still exist, and it is one of the most remarkable facts which all time presents. It is singular, too, that every transition period has been a period of anger, and hence too often the history of religion is the history of controversy. That ought not to be. It is not in Jesus. The elder brother is he by whom the work has been sustained, and he should be the first to enter in and rejoice. But, observe the language of this selfish, angry elder brother. "Lo these many years do I *serve* THEE." Was it indeed his *father* he had served? Well, we have thought of that. But he does not say, "these many years have I *loved* thee." *That* not being in his heart, it is not upon his tongue. "Neither transgressed I thy commandments at any time." Yes, and neither had he ever got beyond the commandment, and for that very reason never *up* to it. To him the law is still a necessity. He is truly a servant, not a son. Service to him is not "perfect freedom." "And yet thou never gavest me a kid." Indeed, and on whose bounty had he been subsisting—whose riches had he been sharing? And if he had never made merry with his friends, what was it that prevented, but his own narrow nature, so unlike his father, it had prevented his entering into sympathy with him. "But as soon as this *thy son* is come." He does not say "as soon as this *my brother* is come," "as soon as this my brother is *returned and got home again*." Here he shows us again the *heart* within him. No response, no echo there indicative of love, of anything akin to God, and then, he reaps up the prodigal's life, runs over the horrid catalogue, dwells with emphatic satisfaction upon its darkest feature. Ah! how like man is that! When we get into trouble, how ready is everybody to tell us the cause, and how few ready to help us out? What a contrast here with the affectionate action of the father himself! Mark the silence of Christ here, He virtually admits the truth of the elder brother's cruel charge—*i. e.*, cruel in that he brought it up at all. You recollect the action of the Saviour himself, when He was called upon to judge a trembling sinner, how He said, "neither do I condemn thee." Admit then that this prodigal was mean, wholly undeserving, admit that he was *no better* than the elder brother, still does this fact make the elder brother *noble?* does it make him like his father? Is he set free from meanness? Is he a true son? Why is he in his father's house, heir to such a heritage? Is it by his merit? Is it not equally by the father's long-suffering and affection? Is it not simply of free grace; even if there is a difference, cannot infinite love cover one as much as the other? Nay—if the Prodigal were more penitent, was he not more deeply covered? If much had been forgiven, might he not for that very reason love the more, and if he did, even upon mortal reasoning, was it not a reason why he should be more loved? Ah! brethren, this is what we so often forget, in our controversies, that none of us are in God's favor except by His mercy, and if He chooses to have mercy, who of us shall say nay? Do we not often, tacitly, but still actually, reckon upon our good works, as though we could possibly have any? Theoretically we believe in justification by faith. Practically we set up a claim by works, that is to say, we give to faith the efficacy of a good work; we place a merit in it, and then we make God our debtor for what we do for Him. But what are our good works? What can they be at best? "The *tender mercies* of the wicked *are cruel;* the *refinement* of the vulgar is *vulgarity;* the *righteousness* of the self-righteous is *sin.*" You see nothing can go higher than itself, and what if we know not the purity and holiness of God? Why, we shall not only think God is indebted to us for keeping commandments, but attach a merit to our abstaining from certain evil practices. How often do we hear men speak in tones which indicate, that they think they have done more for religion than religion has ever done for them.

Then, again, look at the tone here of this elder brother. It indicates that he thought the Prodigal's life of indulgence had been a blessing, a life of enjoyment, something that for some reason or other denied himself. Just as we, in our way of talking, often imply that to be religious is *to make a sacrifice,* give up something good. I think multitudes of people have that idea, that by becoming religious they will lose something. They are not taught by us that they are to rise to a higher plane of being and therefore to a higher enjoyment. We somehow, by our hankering after the world, imply, that the worldly and sensuous have higher pleasures than ourselves, and so in reality we often make religion a perpetual penance, a price we are to pay here upon earth for great happiness by and by, make religion a sour fault-finding—a joyless, monotonous *service.*

I do believe if we could all live upon the plane on which God desires us to live, on which Christ lived, the Church itself would convert, the life would persuade, and preaching need be nothing but instructing.

As it is, in the absence of that higher life, all preaching is proportionally paralyzed. In thinking that the wicked can have a life that by any propriety can be called a life of enjoyment, I do not wonder we misunderstand God's mercy, that it seems to us as if He offered a premium to sin by rejoicing when the sinner returns. We do not see that worldliness and all sin is soul-sickness, and that the more sick our child has been, the greater the rejoicing when the recovery is accomplished. It was this which made the elder son lament the fatted calf. What would he have said, if he had gone in and seen the robe, and the shoes, and the ring. But, "to whom little is forgiven, the same loveth little."

Listen to the reply of the father: "Son, thou art ever with me, all that I have is thine." If you have not enjoyed and do not enjoy, whose fault is it? Surely you would not narrow the universe down to yourself. Surely you would not deprive me of joy, because you are too narrow to receive any more. "It was meet." I do not say it was my will. I say nothing about my authority. It was fit. Love could do no otherwise. This is love. My heart yearned so, as a father I must. "This *thy brother*." The fact that he is a brother ought to make you rejoice, too. "He was dead, and is alive again. He was lost and is found." But, you do not love him—you do not love me; you love yourself. Perhaps you love nobody. If so, then, how are you worthier than he? If so, then, though you have never left me, you have staid home to little purpose. You know very little about me. This is life eternal, truly to know the true God and Jesus Christ whom He hath sent.

Thus, brethren, you see, the Saviour while expressing the fatherhood of God, also tells us what a *son*ship must be, likeness to God. You see, He tells these Jews what a sonship is, that without which we are a sounding brass or a tinkling symbol. Thus we come to this essential query, What, if we do belong to the Church, but have not the likeness of God?

Thus, we learn these lessons: First—we may be in our Father's house, and yet be very unheavenly. Being a Church member is not necessarily being Christ-like, and Christ-likeness alone is salvation. Without that we cannot see the Lord.

Second—we can have no heritage separate from and independent of our Father's and our brethren's; or, in other words, we can have a heritage only as we "enter in," upon our Father's and our brethren's. Their heritage is ours. If our religion is mere sectarian pride, or Church zeal, then there is no practical difference between us and the ungodly. Without the true sonship, the world will see, what the world does so often see, the same passions and ambitions in the one as in the other, only playing upon different grounds. With the true sonship, we possess all things.

Third—nothing can be gained to God, or to our fellow-men, by narrowness. But much may be lost. This parable was spoken against the Pharisees. The Saviour called the Pharisees "hypocrites." We think a hypocrite is a person who *intends* to deceive. This is a mistake. It is a person who is self-deceived, and he is very sincere in his self-deception. This marks for us one great difference between a true and a false religion, One is open always to growth, the other is determined to stand still. One carries the ages forward, the other the ages leave behind. When we return from our field it is right to hear the music and dancing—our ear *should* be open. It is right *to be sure to find out what it means.* But if we be assured it means the return of any sinner; if, the gathering in and healing of any nation, any member of this human family; if, the extension of the kingdom of love, which is the Christ-Kingdom, then we ought to go in. Our Father entreats us. All that He has is ours. If there is any broader truth, it is for us—if any greater freedom, it is for us—if any feast of fat things, it is for us, unless we are angry and refuse to go in.

Fourth—love is the fulfilling of the law. Love is her own reward. You need nothing else than to be with your father all the time, every day, every night, throughout all vicissitude. This is a whole heritage in itself. It embraces all that the Father hath. Rejoice with Him every day. Let your service be above all fear. Let your religion be a rejoicing. Have faith in your Father, in His love. Let the world see that you are satisfied with what religion gives, that to you it is love and joy and peace, that by it you can make, and do make, your Father's service more attractive to all your brethren.

Finally, the whole parable teaches us, *that God is love,* that all we are brethren, that God loves one of us as much as another. We are all about equally deserving, *i. e., all undeserving.* But true sonship consists *in being like Him*—merciful as He is merciful, perfect *as* He is perfect, not perfect according to any law or creed of ours, but as God is perfect in love and holiness. It is not prodigality that opens the way to His heart. It is not sordid, selfish, stay-at-home religion that makes Him love us. It is likeness to Himself, as it is in Christ, which makes us *sons.* Once here we shall love one another. This God desires in us all. For this He is working. For this Jesus came, and all the means of grace exist. Peace on earth, good will among men. This the ages shall produce. This, because He is love, and because He lives. *He will not resign His estate. He will not allow us to ruin it.* We must come up to Him. He is not coming down to us. He lives, and intends to keep *the power of the keys.* We do not want it, nor want it anywhere but in His hands. We *do* want to know *that it is in His hands.* Knowing that, we can walk by faith. We can go to our field, wherever that field may take us, and work in faith, and while working, rejoicing that the prodigals are coming home, that our Father is rejoicing—that the great family circle is being completed. By, and by, as our day declines, and the shades of night gather us homeward, as we approach, may we hear the music and the dancing. May our souls be thrilled with a holy delight. May we, too, enter in with all those who have gone before us, and hear Jesus, the author and finisher of our faith, our forerunner in glory, bid us enter into the joy of our Lord.

EPIPHANY.

MATTHEW 2 : 11.—And when they had opened their *treasures*, they presented unto Him gifts ; gold, and frankincense, and myrrh.

IN the progress of time, we are brought again to the season of the Epiphany. This word "*Epiphany*" means *manifestation.* More directly, it is connected with the incident of which we read in the Scripture, the presentation of Christ to three wise men, or, more exactly, the three wise men led to Christ. This presentation is supposed to be typical of the fact that Christ was manifested for Gentiles as well as Jews. Otherwise expressed, it is typical of the fact that Christ came *to* and *for* the whole race. This Epiphany to the wise men, thus embodies a central fact. As often as its celebration occurs, it revives to us a central idea.

In my judgment, all things, *i. e.*, all actual facts, elements, so to speak of Christ's earthly being, are typical. We use the expression, sometimes, that Christ was the end of all types. A better expression would be, that He was the consummation and perfection of types. Antecedent types embraced Him. He embraced great facts. He was the door to great territories of being—reaching out through all time and all eternity, for man. In other words, God being perfect, therefore infinite, one part of His being was in harmony with every other part. What He did, could not help being linked with all things that were, and were to be.

The simple incarnation itself was transcendently instructive and prophetic. You have in it a divinity, born of this humanity, through the operation of the Holy Ghost—a divinity passing through the vicissitudes of development, subject to all natural and mortal contingencies, as we have recorded in the Gospel for this day. "Christ was subject to His parents." "He *increased* in wisdom and stature, and in favor with God and man." The divine grew with the human, till it, at last vanquished all ignorance, all suffering, all ENMITY, and triumphed everlastingly. As if God would tell us, thus are born all things divine, and thus shall God grow in this humanity. So with this Epiphany scene, the nucleus, as I have said, of a *central* thought. There are wise men as opposed to ignorant men, from regions afar—wise men that are *kings*, for wisdom alone is royal, *rich* men, as wisdom alone is rich, wise men, seeking something better, as wisdom alone seeks. Led by a brightness in the heavens above, out-hung by God for all that can see. The divine brightness responding to the human longing, till it is brought to incarnate Deity, that Deity veiled in humility, yet worthy to receive the best offerings that wisdom and riches can give, the richest products that this land of mortality, our native land, can yield. He, greater than all kings, and richer than all riches—they unable to add anything to Him, but honoring Him most, and exhibiting their true riches in coming to Him at all. This, I say, is prophetic. All this you have expressed in this simple utterance of Scripture, "And when they had opened," &c.

But He was there *to be manifested.* As He was the "*desired of all nations,*" so God intended Him for all nations. In this human heart was a longing; He was God's response to that longing. This world wanted life, as all true wisdom has forever testified. Christ was *life*, the divine life, that was wanted. St. John says, "the *life* was *manifested*, and we have seen it, and bear witness, and show unto you that *eternal life which was with the Father*, and was *manifested* unto us." The divine life is alone eternal, and the eternal life is alone divine. That alone is life. In another place, St. John says, "He was *manifested that He might destroy the works of the devil.*" There you have what a manifestation of Christ is, namely, a manifestation of *divine life in the flesh*, and the object of it, namely, the redemption of man from the power of Satan, the two sides of the same thing, all of it culminating in the great fact, man truly royal, but all royalty and all it involves, *freely tributary* to the *King of Kings*, the Everlasting God. Man wholly God's, by creation, by redemption, and now by his own conscious volition, *freely* God's forever. God's kingdom thus, not a kingdom of force, but a kingdom desired and implored, every subject convinced there is nothing else *fit* to reign over it, and only more and more desirous that God should more and more reign over it, by more and more rejoicing in it. Hence, in the very incarnation itself you get the pledge of all the promises made by the incarnation, a kingdom of true glory for man, with God, that shall know no end—Deity in this humanity—Deity incarnate. That is all you have in that manger scene. Then, by it, this humanity lifted up to God.

But in these very thoughts of a kingdom growing, of life, and then of "the works of the devil," of Satan, of death, you get very distinctly the idea of two sides. Yes, you get many distinct ideas. Old theologians used to spend a great deal of time in discussing *the origin* of evil, the supremacy of God, the free agency of man, and other abstract and kindred subjects. They did not take facts, or laws, seen to exist, and themselves work by them, but were, as we should be, in neglecting the law of gravitation, and endeavoring to go behind it, to remote causes, and ask *what* it is, or *why* it is? The First Cause in everything, is hidden from us; but the truth is, the bare existence of light implies darkness. If you think of a universe, you must contrast with it the thought of no universe, nothingness. It is only by knowledge, you *create* the idea of ignorance. The brute beast knows nothing, *not even ignorance*. The negative is always first. Space must be before body, darkness before light. Such is the universal order; it is in the very nature of intelligence. To ask, *why?* is a childish asking. The very thought of *God,* is a pledge that all things are supremely *best.* To find out the position, that which is, to accept it, to place oneself in harmony with it, *that is wisdom.* Religion is, finding God, and opening our treasures, presenting to Him the best of them all. Only *wisdom* can do that.

Jesus Christ was the first *revealer* of this, and its first illustrator. Whatever of it other men did, these Magi themselves—*e. g.*, they did mechanically, as it were out of certain instincts which they did not and could not define. The peculiar work of Christianity has been, because it was the peculiar work of Christ, *to bring the positive nature of man to closer communion with God, to increase the positive nature, for that is to commune with God—i. e.*, it is communion with good, or goodness, and so far with God. The coming of a Saviour at all implies *sin.* Sin is ignorance, darkness, hence transgression of law, because we know not that *law* is, know not *where* it is, nor *what* it is. The Saviour does not go to work analyzing sin. There is nothing to analyze. Sin is negative, the absence of virtue. He does not condemn us for being in it. It is because we are in it that He has come. But this is the condemnation, light has come, and we *love* the darkness rather than *light.* The degree of your love of darkness is the degree of your condemnation. That love of darkness is all the Saviour even denounced, the taking for granted, that our dixit, our doctrine, our system, was the *truth,* life and light. Pharisaic formula, Pharisaic pride, *that* the Saviour denounced. It took for granted its little system could comprehend God, and by refusing to stir out of that, thereby stood condemned. That was condemnation, to be in it. It is condemnation to any man that is in it, whether he is inside of a Church, or not. Pride, self-sufficiency, self-conceit, that is always opposed to God. It matters not what shape it takes. But to everything else, Jesus always presupposes a better nature. The poor Magdelene bowed at his feet, scorned by Simon, how like God, to her yearning, He freely and instantly responds. The poor woman overtaken in sin. "Neither do I condemn thee. Go, and sin no more." You know you have sinned. That is condemnation enough. Feel your meanness. Rise into thy better self. See the true life. See that, without which you feel degraded and are degraded, without which you are not up to where God wants you and where you wish yourself to be. Always taking for granted, you perceive, the power to see, the faculty by which to pursue and lay hold of the better life.

And hence this sublime naturalness in Christ. Why, what is man? Is he a bundle of nothingness? Has he no faculties? Are body and appetite and passion, is mere animal, manhood? Is mind nothing, and all the moral faculties nothing, and all this affectional nature nothing? Did God mean nothing by them when He created them? What does God mean, when He says that in the image of God He created man? You absolutely can have no conception of God, except as you reach it through this thing that we call manhood. It is only as you have a proper conception of *man* that you can have a proper conception of God. If you leave out these elements of mind and morals and affection, you have not man at all. It is of these you think when you think of manhood. It is these without which you could not have the idea of *wisdom*. These, for you or me, create wisdom, or goodness, make one of us worthier than another. They explain the idea of religion and create your eternity different to mine. What is the wonderfulness of the life of Christ? We have been in the habit of putting it in His miracles, in His precepts, more especially in that thing of which He said very little and which *I am certain none of us understand, His atonement*. But the great wonderfulness of that life is not in one or all of these. No! we have erred and failed to glorify Him in placing it exclusively there. It was this which caused the poet Lessing, (infidel, I suppose we would call him,) to write, respecting us:

> " Christianity, not manhood, is their pride.
> E'en that which from their founder down has spiced
> Their superstition with humanity;
> 'Tis not for their humanity, they love it;
> No, but because Christ taught, Christ practiced it.
> Happy for them He was so good a man,—
> Happy for them they can trust His virtue.
> His virtue? not His virtue, but His *name*,
> They say shall spread abroad and shall drown
> And put to shame, the names of all good men:
> The name, the name, is all their pride."

But, brethren, there is a great deal of truth in that, "*Happy for them He was so good a man.*" It was His goodness, His *naturalness*, that was so wonderful. *He was the expression to us of a full manhood*, and therefore the expression to us of the Father. He was the *perfection* of the image in which God created us. He was the brightness of the Father's glory, and the express image of His person, the ideal and model we once lost, and which God wishes us again to reach. There was nothing stilted about Him, nothing was artificial, nothing borrowed and put on, nothing conventional. His mind—what a quickness and grasp it had! His moral faculties, what a harmony and purity was there! His affections—when has the world seen anything like it! Against these the surges of time have rolled, and peacefully subsided. It is against these alone the gates of darkness have not been able to prevail. *Our doctrines have never defended Christ.* They *have defended our notions, and in defending them made us deny Christ.* What is it that has made infidels, so much as church quarrels, and church dignities, and church machinery, and church pride? What has made infidels, so much as the unlikeness of Christians, so-called, to Christ? Nothing. Nothing is so opposed to all leanness and narrowness as Christ, and nothing is so opposed to Christ as leanness and narrowness.

Somehow, in himself, man feels a sort of consciousness of two selfs. One that is animal and gross, and sordid, that is not himself. One that is noble, and pure, and loving, that is himself. One he wants to increase, one he wants to crucify. In Christ man sees his better self. Men love Him, because all that we can love is in Him. There you feel you are near to God. Being there, you *are* near to God. That was the object of Jesus' coming, that you might get there, and being there, so, be near to God.

Now, what does he tell us is the first great commandment, *the* thing absolutely and universally imperative, the sum and substance of religion? "*Love God with all your heart, and all your soul, and all your mind.*" He does not merely mean to say that love of God is imperative, but He defines what a love of God is—consecration of *heart*, and *soul*, and *mind—intellect, morals* and *affections*. There you have the three essentials, elements, of *man*, the three essential elements of moral being. Man is a trinity. All great unities are trinities. Man is intellect, morals and affections. To cultivate these, to develop them, to make them harmonious, is to be religious, to serve God, to be uplifted to God. These are the natural productions of this our native clime. These are our treasures. These are the offerings we are to make to God—the gold, and frankincense, and myrrh, to offer which is itself to prove that we are royal—this it is to lay our dominion at the feet of Christ, and have Him "*Lord of all.*"

Now, I think these thoughts to us are very valuable, and these things are the things Christians have *not* always done, and are not now everywhere doing. *There is no other way in which God can be manifested to us except in a redeemed manhood.* There is no way in which you can make an Epiphany of Christ *except as your manhood is redeemed*, exalted, and made like Christ, *i. e.*, except as your manhood is clothed in Christ, and you see what I mean by that—*in what Christ was.* This is that prayer of Christ, "That they all may be one, *as* thou, Father, art in *me* and I in thee, that they also may be one in *us*." This thought is not a prevailing one among us, and for lack of it, we are often hindering Christ more than helping Him. What has the Church done from a period very near the beginning? Simply made a creed and said, "believe that, and you are saved." Now, in the beginning, creeds were very essential things; that is to say, they were truth formulas, and as such, creeds are at all times essential things. But no creed can hold all the truth. Man cannot make a cup that will hold the universe. Life is always broader than our homes. After getting the creed, it, and not the truth, was the object that must spread. "The name, the name," as Lossing said, was all their boast. In progress of time, the truth *in it* was lost, and hence, to spread the Church was *to spread Christ*. That we are at to-day. To great numbers of us, an Epiphany of Christ means a spread of our Church, whatever that may be. But, thank God, the world, now-a-days, never asks and never cares what Church a man belongs to. If he is broad, and strong, and noble, and manly, if he expresses their ideal of a Christian, they seek no further, and if he is not that, they pity the Church that has to carry him. It may be, I cannot say, but it sometimes seems to me, that they whom the Church is carrying, are more in number than they who are carrying the Church. In other words, let a man get the idea that his Church is the only Church, or let a man in any Church, get the idea that the Church, all together, specifically so-called, alone is Christian, and will narrow him, and so far make him a burden to all alike,—a vitiated globule, and so far a disease to the whole body.

Some of you ask me, do I think, humanity and morality, and intelligence, and charity, are religion? Let me ask you, do you think that is religion which leaves all these out? Did Jesus Christ leave them out of the Sermon on the Mount? or out of any hour of His life? Do you suppose a righteous Jew, or a truly wise man from Arabia, God is going to leave out of His heaven? Look at that *star* leading the wise men. Will we never learn anything from the Bible! That star was the Holy Ghost, God's own power, which never rests till it stands where Jesus is. To Him, all wisdom must come, *because the Holy Ghost leads*. Hath God no star except the feeble lamp that you and I hang out? Is there no God the Holy Ghost, mightier than you and me, and broader than all our churches put together? Hath that Holy Ghost anything to reveal, except that incarnate God, the things that are of Jesus Christ? Why, my brethren, we forget how, with all our churches and all our creeds, God is getting on often in spite of us more than by means of us. Look at Christian life—life, rather, within the Churches. Is it indicative of deep-rooted and far-reaching thought? Many are the thoughtful wise men *out*side what we call the Church, who hang their heads in sorrow over some of us inside of it. Is all knowledge embraced by us? Is intellect and reason, alone comprehensive here? Again you ask, will knowledge save us? Again let me ask, can we be saved by ignorance? When I see Christian people wasting precious time on frills and ruffles, whole hours and days, *all sacred*, going up in trifles—when I see the levity that pervades Christian society—I feel they are not Christian, believe what they may. We belie the name that saved us; we cast a shadow across the glory of Christ. We make infidels, for us to turn round and abuse them after they are made. The pure gold of God's manhood we bury in the dirt, and offer the Saviour a lip-service and the service of forms. Is that an Epiphany? By us, at that rate, there is not and never can be an Epiphany of Christ. There is an Epiphany of our carnal, grosser nature—that's all. Then look at morals. Has the Christian Church a monopoly of them? Is life in Italy purer than life in Japan? Would you send a Chinaman to *Christian* Paris, as we send so many of our sons and daughters, for his model in morals. I do not mean to say that life among Christian people is immoral. I do not believe it is. But neither is it saying much to say that *it is not.* What I would ask is, is it uniformly above the level of bare morality. That is the question for us. You ask whether morality can save us? I say no, you are not saved, if you are no higher than that? Arithmetic is mathematics. But he is not a mathematician who is no higher than arithmetic. We should not be characterized simply by naked virtues. Morality is not a very exalted level. It is the first level this side of immortality. The Christian should be up in the graces. The moral qualities should mount up and blend with the affectional. The frankincense should rise into the fragrance of the myrrh, and all go up together, an offering of our whole nature to God, like the evening sacrifice. Can we say, to-day all this pervades and characterizes the Church? It pervaded and characterized Christ. How then are we an Epiphany of the Son of God? *You see, that Epiphany must be perpetual. It must be actual.* It is the road to the millenium. That which makes this Epiphany is *the Church,* no matter what we think about it. The Church is God's star to lead to Christ. The Church is that agency which is leading the world up to God, and not any agency which the world is leaving behind. Whatever is dark is not in it, or of it, whether it be mental, moral or spiritual. Whatever is of truth and light, is in it, for they are Christ's, and all Christ's is God's.

Now, I do not mean to say, there is more light outside the Church than there is in it. That is impossible. There is an old saying, "there is no salvation outside the Church." That saying is true. But the Church is where salvation is, and nowhere else; where light and truth are, nowhere else—where Christ is, and nowhere else. The true Church has several times gone around that which was ostensibly the Church, that Church which was standing embalmed in pride and self-conceit. It did it in the times of Christ. He passed by the Jews. It did it three hundred years ago—we passed by the papacy. God grant there never may be need of its doing it again. But that it might not be, we must understand that God will never stand still with us, *but that we must find out God, and advance with Him.* Do you see anything in that you have to do? I was struck with a remarkable sermon from a prominent Jew, not long since. He tells us some very unpalatable truths. We have had a way of asserting all progress as Christian, and the Christian Church as the source of modern civilization. He undertakes to prove that nearly all progress has been made in spite of the Christian Church. He says, so far from forcing progress upon the world, progress has been forced upon her. He says, every attempt at a free inquiry into anything, has been silenced by the Church, that Christians now have a kind of fear of philosophical inquiry. He talks of Galileo, of the Inquisition, of Smithfield. He asks, who denied civil liberty to the Jews, in England and elsewhere? Christians. Who opposed liberty of conscience? Christians. And so through a variety of questions—and I confess, that the most painful thing to me about it, was, that most of it was true. But he denies that we have any Christian civilization. Therein he is wrong. Who taught men to resist the inquisition? Christ. Who taught the world it was better to die than to be submerged in self and wrong? Christ. Who gave the Jews civil liberty? Christians. Who died for liberty of conscience? Christians. Who leads the van of civilization to-day? Christians—but not any *sect*, I grant you that, thank God for that, but that star of God; and what I want you to see to-day is, that an Epiphany of Christ is not a manifestation of any narrowness, no matter where it is, or what it is. Let me ask you, then, in conclusion, have you any wider and clearer idea of what you are to do for God, of what an Epiphany of your Master is to be? I am afraid that to-day many Christians will be entertained with a rehearsal of what the Church has done, of the great glory that remains. I too thank God for all that has been done. But I feel down in my heart that *we* have not done it. *God has done it.* We are unprofitable servants, and the manifestation that is, is nothing compared with the manifestation that ought by this time to have been. And then, I am afraid, that much will be taken for glory which is not glory, and much be praised as done, which had better never been done at all; and this is natural enough, for, only once think that you are wholly refined and learned, and good, and that is proof positive in itself, that you are neither the one nor the other. We have a way of talking too much about our ecstatic experiences, a way of blazing abroad our good deeds. But that is the world's way, not God's way. When I look around the world, I feel as if our ideas of Epiphany were inverted. As if God wanted beautiful churches, and fine music, and splendid ceremonial. All that cannot help Christ. The material gold and material frankincense, and material myrrh, could do nothing for Christ. They left Him just as poor. They could not give Him where to lay His head. The gold of apostolic mind, the purity of apostolic life, the sweetness, and benevolence, and affection of redeemed hearts—these brought peace to man and glory to God. It is that we need to-day. Most men live in their grosser and meaner nature, because they have nothing better. Men would not be vulgar, if they could be taught true refinement, and men would not be irreligious, if you and I could show them the beauty of holiness. We are at our wits' ends to find means for building churches, and sending missionaries, and yet we are amazed at the small results of the churches we have and the missionaries we send. Beloved, we have lamps enough, we need only more of the oil of the divine life. Not a Christian listening to me to-day, but is a missionary. Some of you have golden chances. You can preach better sermons than I can, down where there are eyes watching, down where there are hearts that are aching; you can *manifest* the true *life.* You get it from Christ, and to manifest *it,* is to manifest Him. When your thoughts are occupied with high and sacred themes, when, in order to attain to the graces which Jesus teaches, you forego your worldly interests, and crucify your flesh; when over your life exhales the aroma of benevolence and affection, then you are a co-worker with God, and are hastening the day of the Eternal Kingdom. Thought, to-day, is the solid currency of the world, the emblem of nobility, and so if you have time to waste, if your mind is uncultured, if you are low and selfish in your pursuits, if you know how to watch others more than yourself, then you are not a Christian at all. The Church has to carry you. Great thoughts are beating at the human heart, and you have nothing to do with them. You are bringing reproach upon your Master. You are a sign-post in the wrong place. You will not destroy the works of Satan, nor reveal the glory of God. You never will see it. It had been better for you if you had never been born. Oh! may we all be wise men, may we all be like the Magi—come to Christ. But be sure of the treasures you bring. If you learn of Him, then you can go out and *be* part of the great Epiphany, and yourself have part and lot in the glory that remains. Let us learn something from the star and the wise men, the incarnate Christ, the gold, and the frankincense, and the myrrh.

THE DIVINE LOVE.

JOHN 3: 16, 19.—For God so loved the world that He gave His only begotten Son, that whosoever *believeth in Him* should not perish, but have everlasting life. For God sent not His Son into the world to condemn the world, but that the world through Him might be saved. He that believeth in Him is not condemned, but he that believeth not is condemned already, because he hath not believed in the name of the only begotten Son of God. And this is the condemnation that light is come into the world and men loved darkness rather than light, because their deeds were evil.

THIS is part of our Lord's discourse with Nicodemus. It embraces the whole Gospel in itself. To a mind, *not preoccupied with doctrines and theories,* as the mind of Nicodemus was, it is peculiarly simple and plain. Nicodemus was a Jew and a theologian, like us, bound hand and foot with traditions. The feature of Christ's life which affected him, was, the fact of miracles. Through that, Nicodemus got an inkling that Christ was a teacher come from God. He just had vision enough to see that Christ's wonder-working differed from that of all others, chiefly in that it was merciful and beneficent, and so commended itself to His moral sense, *as worthy of God.* The feature of Christ's life which most affects us, is not His miracles, but the fact that being a Jew, He was neither a Jew nor a theologian, His thought was neither colored nor distorted by time or place. His life was moulded by neither His age, nor His nationality. He was *human* and belonged to mankind. His truths were coins which have heaven and God stamped upon them. Their substance was not earthly, but spiritual. *He was Himself the greatest of all conceivable miracles,* and view Him in any light we may, we too can say: "We know Thou art a teacher come from God."

Like the rose, or the morning light, these propositions of Christ carry with them their own endorsement. Who is God? God is love. This was news even to the Jew. It is news yet to a great many Christians, for simply assenting to it, is not by any means the same thing as understanding it. It is remarkable that all theologies and religions have called God from the depths of their darkness, created Him out of their fears and their passions. With what light we have had, we have projected simply our own shadow, and *called it God.* Both Jew and Gentile, as was natural enough, consulted their fears. Not understanding themselves, or nature around them, they turned all providence into evil, look upon mankind as under a curse, and called God a *Judge,* regarded Him as an *angry* being, anxious to *destroy* rather than to preserve. He was a God to be *appeased* and that too by ordinances that were either foolish or deeply revolting.

Imagine Christ's words falling there and saying: "*God so loved the world.*" When man has long delved for the truth, how simple it seems, when at last it comes to him. If we had truly reasoned, we would have seen that wrath, anger, hatred, or any unlove, were really a weakness, and therefore impossible in God. They are merely the absence of mercy, patience and love. If they had looked into the divine dealings with our race, they would have seen mercy, restraining and guiding love, in them all, an attempt to prevent evil consequences, and so to redeem and bless mankind. They would have seen that every element in man and every element in nature, under the direction of wisdom, under the influence of *reason*, of love, were burdened with divinest ministration. All that nature wanted, all that God asked, was that man should not be a brute, that he should mount up to a recognition of his soul-nature, his true man-being. The very point contemplated in his being was his recognition of his moral being, his realization of soul. It was only as he got away from his fears, his passions, his grosser self, that he could find God. What he needed was not facts, but *the power of seeing them,* not truth, but the power of perceiving truth. He and all other things were *so* made, that he should find his soul level, his moral or spiritual existence. *The essence of moral being is that the* SOUL *find it and accept it.* Divine love and wisdom, God Himself, could not frame any other uuiverse or make another moral being. You perceive, individual volition creates moral being. Take that out and there is no moral being. To have finite spirit existence at all, it was *needful* to have it just as it was. There was no unlove whatever in making the world as it was and in creating man as he is. It *must* so be, or *never* be. That lies in the very fact that God is God. There is a conception of God—*i. e.*, to say, a *misconception* of God, that He can do any arbitrary thing, that is, that He might, if He chose, please to do anything, irrespective of all law. If that were so, then He might some day choose to break His promise and forget and forsake us.

We see, of *necessity*, the law of truth, forever forbids that God should ever break His promise. So God is omnipotent *under His own law*, by and within a law, and the world was made, and man made upon it, under the law of divine love, and divine wisdom, the best world and the best humanity that could by any possibility be made, so that in a certain sense, whatever is, is right. If consequences, dark and fearful, intervene sometimes, still there is no anger anywhere, because *that* is the negative of God, but *love* everywhere, because like light that is the essence of Deity. God is a spirit of positive and pure essence. *He is transcendently happy and glorified*, BECAUSE *pure spiritual essence can produce nothing else*. That is what Paul calls "*predestination*," that is the ultimate end and object of its existence. The kingdom of God, used in its spiritual sense, is thus of necessity a kingdom of pure souls, or purified souls, souls quickened by the divine life. Souls without the divine life are not partakers of the divine blessedness, but just the reverse, and a law of proportion pervades both sides. He who is nearest to God, or who has most of the divine life, is most blest, and he who has least, is most *unblessed*. The soul *that has the divine life* is in a state of salvation *and the soul that has it* NOT, is in a state of condemnation.

In creating soul, then, *it was needful* to create us bodies as well, and *needful* to create us in just such a world as ours. The soul-life can be reached only through the body-life. All being is a sort of inclined plane, but because our gross senses cannot mark the gradations, they break upon us only at long intervals, and so, being appears to be a series of steps rather than one continuous plane. These steps again, are sometimes so broad and deep, they appear to be, and in reality *are*, to us great planes themselves. The two great planes of our being are the bodily and the spiritual. The bodily plane is our first plane, the gross outward, animal plane. It is not an end in itself, but a means to an end, not without its own purposes, but still auxilliary to higher and ultimate purposes. It has little or no meaning, except as you contemplate its highest meaning. Just as, if you contemplate existence lower than man, you find its purest significance only in man himself. Why the delicate shades of color, the delicious odors of flowers? Why the fitness in lower animals for our own domestic, or economic purposes? or a thousand other things, except as you refer them to a spirit to which they can and do minister? So you get the full meaning of our bodily plane, when you reach our spiritual plane. Paul says, these two "are *contrary* the one to the other." He does not mean, that God made one as a hindrance to the other, but only, that to be inside the one is to be outside the other. Ignorance, our first estate, is contrary to knowledge. Vulgarity is contrary to refinement. Poverty is contrary to wealth; the body-plane to the soul. The body-plane is negative; the soul-plane is acquisition. Negative, in all things, is always *first*. Our bodily plane is the first in order, hence it is called "*the natural man.*" *Merely in that*, the man is *not a man*. It is true there is a soul linked with it, but it is an embryotic soul. Its perceptions are undeveloped. As the body has been born after laws of its own, the soul must be born after laws of its own. Each begets after its kind. "That which is born of the flesh is flesh, and that which is born of the spirit is spirit." Since God is a spirit, and His Kingdom a kingdom of spiritual things, we must be born of the spiritual life, in order to be in, or of, that kingdom. The lower cannot judge, or be participant, in the higher, any more than our domestic animals can judge, or be participant, in our intellectual and human life. Hence, Christ said to Nicodemus: "Except a man be born again," or more literally, "except a man be born *from above,* he cannot SEE the kingdom of God." As the animal senses in a babe are unfolded, till the mortal gradually reaches a realization of the world in which he is, so the soul-senses must unfold, till the *immortal* reach a realization of the eternal world. "*You must be born again.*"

Now, nothing is wanting to this spirituul development any more than anything is wanting to bodily development. Laws pervade all planes of being, only each after its kind. There is a fitness, a provision, an adjustment of all elements. Born into this world, nature, or God, provides a food for us, but not only so, provides that our little body shall crave that food, and reach out, unconsciously it may be, but still naturally to receive it. Not only so, but the same laws which bring the body, bring also the food to nourish it. So with the spirit, its kind of life is provided for it, by the law of God's love, called by us the *atonement.* There is a "*law of life*" revealed to us in Christ Jesus. How that law comes, except as everything else comes, out of the love of God, we know not. But, "as Moses lifted up the serpent in the wilderness, even so must the son of man be lifted up." By that law, the Spirit of God is with every man that is born into the world, says St. John, "*to light it*," guide it, awake it, and set it in *conscious* co-operation with spirit-life, and you may discuss human depravity as you please, I contend the soul of man looks up for God, just as the flower looks up for the sunlight. The fact of a religion of some sort, or degree, upon the whole face of humanity, is proof positive that nothing can crush the crying out of man's heart. This is the office of the Holy Ghost, to take of the things of Christ and reveal them unto us. All these things are of the *spirit-life.* Christ is to us, not only procuring cause of spirit life, but illustrative of it; in other words, the atonement is not only a removal of death, but a *manifestation* of divine life, at once like a parent to a child, means of support and a pattern of life. He is not only the only cause, but he is also the only pattern. Man did not know God, does not now know Him. "No man hath seen God at any time. He only who is from the bosom of the Father hath declared Him." Christ said truly of Himself, We speak that we do know, and testify that we have seen—nobody else did know or had seen. To take anything else for God, is to mistake the whole spirit-life, and hence, while God so *loved* the world as to give His only begotten Son, it is only, and of necessity must be only, he that *believeth* on Him that can be saved.

The truth is both beings, *i. e.*, bodily and spiritual, begin at the lowest conceivable point, *i. e.*, they have beginning. Its original, normal condition, in both cases, is germinal. It is nothing, except so far as it is an embodiment of capabilities or possibilities. These capabilities or possibilities, in both cases, are matters of our own decision, or at any rate, are dependent upon our own action. Here you strike moral being, in this self-action. The normal intention of nature is a healthy body. The normal intention of God is a healthy soul. This out of the divine benevolence. What God *wishes.* But it is subject to law, and laws must work, and hence we get two senses of the expression, "God's will"—what the affection of God yearns for, and what His laws determine, two very different senses, and yet senses very often confounded. In one sense, God willeth not the death of the sinner. In the other sense, He will by no means spare the wicked. With respect to our bodies, if we live wisely, we develop into health and vigor, into all that makes life rich enjoyment. If we live unwisely, we simply *lose our health. But observe what that means.* It means weakness, pain, suffering. You see the absence of health is not only not enjoying, but it is *suffering*—something, as it were, of a positive nature, and, worst of all, as the health goes, it is proportionally the loss of ability even to regain it. The powers of nature, so to speak, die, and their death is pain. It all comes about of *transgression,* violation of law. You call in a physician, for there are *redeeming* agencies in all nature, for this law of life in Christ Jesus is only according to universal analogy. You call in a physician, but he does not create a single pain. He does not reproach the patient. If he is a true physician, he is truly sympathetic. His office is one of mercy. He would die, and physicians, very often do die, to alleviate, not what they create, but what they are unable to prevent. The parallel in spiritual things is complete. The soul, too, must live by law. In *transgression it dies.* From its ignorance, you perceive, if from nothing else, transgression is natuaal. Transgression is sin, and sin is an inevitable fact. Some people go off at this point, and create what they call "the doctrine of original sin," and there is no objection to that, if anybody pleases to do it, only, original sin, you observe, is a *fact;* but, discuss it as you will, its roots lie in the nebula of first causes—into which man cannot pry, and whoever undertakes it, will only "darken counsel by words without knowledge." All first causes are hid from us. There *is* transgression, or sin, or soul-sickness. But observe what that means. In its least degree, it is ignorance of God, and that is absence of transcendent enjoyment. But it is worse than that. The absence of love is the presence of unlove, and that means, not simply immorality and vice, which, indeed, are very bad symptoms, but it means soul characteristics, like enmity, spite, cruelty, revenge—that which turns a man into a demon, that which gives us our idea of devil, devilishness; that, whenever you see it, whether in Pharisee circles, as you observe it in the Jews in Christ's time, or in later times, or in any form of the Inquisition, or in fashionable circles, as some of us see it every day; or in trade circles, as it is in gold rooms where men curse and cheat each other; that which is *selfishness*, that which eats joy out of life, that which repels mercy and truth, that which creates what men have agreed to call a *hell.* That is *hell.* You ask me, what becomes of these men, what hell is, or where hell is. I cannot tell, but there is a hell, a great scorching furnace, which you create and feed, and carry with you, down in your heart. It burns like fire. It gnaws like a worm. It is as if the universe had judged it, and condemned it, and cursed it. *It is condemnation.*

Observe, God does not come down in a thunderbolt and crush the soul. No Angel is there to forge a chain for it. It has done it all itself, not so much by something it *has done* as *by* FAILING *to do something it ought to have done.* The United States Government has not *condemned* the savage Indian upon the plain to his barbarous life. The municipal authorities have not *condemned* the drunkard, the vile wretches that rob and murder each other in the dens of our city. The police authorities in New York did not condemn that poor woman who went home one morning last week from a masked ball and blew her brains out. No, all the forces of civilization have for their very object the prevention of these very things. There are men and women who would die if all these creatures could be redeemed. It is of the nature of love, you see, to pity. Only a pure soul and an exalted soul could pity them and give itself for them. Of all pitying beings God is greatest, He sends His Son. *The Physician comes. Not to condemn.* Comes *because we are condemned.* Comes to write *love* upon every element of being. Comes to inaugurate means by which all condemnation may be forever escaped. That is condemnation, to be *there,* in our unspiritual being, whether we know it or do not know it. To perceive the life He brings, to accept *Him,* to leave where and what we are, to put on what Christ is—*i. e.,* to repent and believe, is to enter into life, to have salvation, but to love the darkness, rather than the light, is to continue in the condemnation, ruined, lost, and because soul-powers die, as well as body-powers, it may be, so far as we can see, to be ruined and lost forever. And then it so happens, that to get upon a plane, from any cause, is very likely to remain there. Somehow, our antecedents do greatly control our actions. You cannot bring the wicked man from his associates or his associations. They hold like iron fetters. You cannot make the vulgar sensible of the delights of refinement. You cannot make the ignorant sensible of the blessings of knowledge, nor the ungodly conscious of the joys of the redeemed. "The natural man judgeth not the things of the spirit of God." "They are foolishness unto him," and so it is, the kind of life, our deeds, or call it by what name we will, the life upon which we have embarked, whether consciously or unconsciously, is likely to be our kind of life forever.

Now let me ask, can you get no definite idea of these words of Christ? "God so loved the world, that He gave His only begotten Son," (only God could,) "that whosoever believeth in Him should not perish, but have everlasting life. For God sent not His Son into the world to condemn the world, but that the world through Him might be saved. He that believeth in Him is not condemned, but he that believeth not in Him is condemned already, *because he hath not believed in the name of the only begotten Son of God.* And this is *the condemnation* that light is come into the world and men loved darkness rather than light, *because their deeds were evil.*"

Yes, sin is the most unnatural and repulsive theory that walks upon the face of the earth, that into which you could not possibly get a man to go, if it were only possible to show him where it is he is going, that, in which of all things upon earth man is the most unfortunate and most to be pitied. But, what blessing, what mercy, what love, what a God! to come to us! to tell us He does not hate us, that He loves us and cares for us! Oh! man, did you ever think, how, if you had been left to me, or to your fellow men, how you had been ground down, how a great angry Judge had been set over you, how you would have been turned into a living fear, going to heaven not from any love of what God is, but from a great dread of what He is not. Do you see how religion is, direct communion with God, with goodness, not a church routine, another *work* added to that burden which makes life so galling. How blessed to know God loves you, that He is willing to give you eternal life, that all you have to do is to accept it. You cannot buy it, you cannot work it out. You can only receive it, and God will give it just as fast as you will receive. "The gift of God is eternal life, and this life is in His Son." You are to see that, see the divine life that is in Him, what the Saviour calls "*believe*," then you are not condemned. You must be able to say, in a deeper sense than that in which Nicodemus said it, "I know Thou art a teacher come from God." All your intuitions and longings, will feel, that He is the Alpha and Omega, not from any theological dixit, but from the eternal nature of things. That belief, that Christ is the Son of God, and that through Him you are a son of God, that belief, not merely an assent of your mind, but a conviction that penetrates every tissue of your being, a conviction beyond expression, makes you a member of Christ, whether you are a member of the Church or not. The Church is an artificial association of believers. If you have the divine life, you are a member of the invisible Church of necessity, and though a connection with some branch of the Church visible is to some degree imperative, it still is optional. *It is not what are called "doctrines" that constitute salvation.* Doctrines make Churches, and very often ruin souls. Your believing anything does not make that thing true, does not affect the truth at all. So far as truth is concerned, it matters not what you believe. So far as you are concerned, it is of the first importance that what you believe is truth. If you do not believe in the Holy Ghost, the Holy Ghost can still find you. If you do not believe in a hell, that will not keep you out of it. If you believe the Church can save, that will not save you. Our business is to learn, not to write anything down and say, "I believe that." No Church can make a creed for even all its own members, because truth crystalizes in different ways in different minds. No truth is valuable in itself, but only in its combinations, and because it enters not into the same combination in any two minds, we have so much trouble in all our Churches, and the more truth we get, the more trouble we will have, till we get truth enough to know that doctrine is not Christianity, and that belonging to any Church is not necessarily belonging to Christ. Any truth is infinite, and for that very reason its form must change. Any form is but a shadow cast before, and forms are therefore valuable. Our business is to find out the facts they do foreshadow. Christ is not doctrine, except as the greater comprehends the less. *Christ is a life.* "Do the will of God," He said, "and you shall know the doctrine." "The Spirit of God shall guide you unto all truth," not all at once, but very slowly. Put Christianity into doctrine and you have the Churches, with the world saying, "a pretty set of Christians you are indeed." Put Christianity into life, into love, into unself, into self-sacrifice, into that which is pure, and true, and noble, into a likeness of Christ, and the world says you are a Christian, without asking what Church you belong to.

Mark how Christ and all good are synonymous. Mark

how the "truth as it is in Jesus" differs from all other truth—not that other truth is not true, but of a different kind. Truth as it is in Jesus is true virtue, true purity, true love, true *life*. Did you ever reflect upon the remarkable fact, that nobody has ever said that Christ was anything else but good? Even the malignant Jews had not intelligence enough to bring a charge of real evil against Him. They could only bring a charge of *heresy*, as a great many *churches* would bring, if He were to appear among us to-day. Christ was God manifested. We know not what God is, but the more we know of God, so much the more we see in Christ, or the more we see in Christ, so much the more we know of God. *Calling* Him God is not *believing* Him to be God. Mere assent to anything is not belief. Our likeness to Him is the only measure of our *belief* that He is God. Belief, or faith, is soul vision, soul vision is life. "Without eyes we shall want light." Belief in Christ is vision of the soul verities in Christ, so as to produce a life in us, a longing after it, "hungering and thirsting," as Christ called it. It is obedience to God, and trust in God. It is loving God and our neighbor. It is communing with God, and walking with God. It is the reproduction of the Christ-life, the life of faith, of prayer, of sacrifice, of love. It is the crucifixion of carnality, and the enthronement of spirituality. Our victory over the animal or natural plane, is the measure of our entrance upon the spirit-plane. All time, all providence, this economy of temptation and trial, is designed to test and demonstrate which plane it is we are on. Not to have the upper spiritual, or divine life, is to be lost. You observe, it is not simply that we are hauled off somewhere, or are cut off from an economy of usefulness, but that something is lost to us. What is lost to us, no mortal can tell you. God is lost to us. Heaven is lost to us. An eternal weight of glory is lost to us. That is what grieves God. Suppose you had an idiot child—how your heart would break in thinking of it—so much joy and knowledge cut off from it, communion with *you* all lost. Suppose you contemplate your knowledge or education, whatever it be; suppose you contemplate your refinement and culture, whatever it be. Suppose you realize that to lose these would make you vulgar and ignorant, could anything upon earth induce you to lose them? You perceive the loss of them, would make you lost.

Now, as compared with God, with the heavens above, with holiness, with life—that is where all of us are by nature, where so many of us, like the vulgar and ignorant, are contented to remain. How is it with us here to-day. You observe, God does not accept you, because you are acceptable, but because you *desire* to be acceptable, not on account of your attainments, but on account of your progress. He knows how unworthy you are, but He can wait. That is His mercy, He will wait, and does wait. Christ is advocate. A thousand years will be nothing, if they can bring you to all you want to be. God will not *upbraid* you for your unworthiness, but the more you can see that unworthiness, so much the more will you reach out after Him. That reaching out is sanctification—immortal progress. What I want you to see, is, that we all have something to do to be saved. Not, as so many imagine, that we have something to do to be lost. Men feel sometimes, I have never robbed anybody, I pay my debts, I never swear, nor drink, nor slander my neighbor. All very well, but, salvation is not what you do not do. What do you know of spiritual things, of the love of God? How far do you see into the things of Christ? How much like Him are you, forgiving, sacrificing? Salvation is not a fixed quantity, doled out by a church, limited by a creed. It is sanctification, more and more unto the perfect day. It is struggle against self, and earth, and our carnal nature. It is enthronement within us of Christ and God.

I wish to impress upon you all, a sense of the solemnity of life, that life means something, that it was given for a purpose, that purpose growth—that you cannot buckle a doctrine around you like a life-preserver, and say, "here I am all safe." I wish to impress it particularly upon the young. Redeem your time. You have a future to frame, an eternity to fix. Your heart, your soul, your mind. Christ calls you to Him, to take His yoke, because it is easy; His burden, because it is light. Calls you to consecrate your time, with all your energies and faculties. You see men sometimes beating about, not knowing which way to turn, and taking, at last, just the very thing they ought not to have. Is it any wonder, when they have perverted all their powers, and wasted all their days? You cannot gather figs of thistles. Sit at Jesus' feet. Hear what He says as a message to you from God. Know that God loves you, and that if you will only love Him, you shall not enter into condemnation, but shall pass from death into life.

THE SPIRIT ABOVE THE LETTER.

II CORINTHIANS 3 : 4, 5, 6.—And such trust have we through Christ to God-ward, not that we are sufficient of ourselves to think anything as of ourselves; but our sufficiency is of God, Who also hath made us able ministers of the New Testament, not of the letter, but of the spirit; for the letter killeth, but the spirit giveth life.

ST. PAUL is here, I suppose, partially defending himself from certain reflections which in one way or another had been raised against him and his ministry. The people whom he addressed were like all the people of his times, like the vast majority of the people of all times, blind people. They had been used to certain formulas, and to certain rites and ceremonies, in which they rested, and which they regarded as the counterparts, or development, or end and object of the formulas. They had been in the habit of contemplating the sources whence the formulas sprung and the channels through which they had been handed down, as essential adjuncts to the formulas themselves, putting trust in man, not realizing that God was the only original source, and that any earthly sufficiency came alone from Him. Moses himself was only *one* divine agency, and that only to the Mosaic degree. He, advancing from the nebulous condition of conjecture and tradition, wrote down certain principles or laws, as nearly as it was then possible to write them. His people, looking upon the Mosaic writings as absolute, failing to see the reality of which they were but dim reflections, gave to them an outwardness and literalness, which eventually dwarfed and shriveled the faculties, moral and spiritual, they were originally intended to quicken. Christ came, elucidating, literally fulfilling, the old formulas. The Jews, even the Apostles, did not understand Him. St. Paul goes out preaching Christ, the spirit above the letter. He met an experience similar to that his Master had met before him. Those experiences have been repeated to some extent in every age and generation since, and are being now repeated more *universally* perhaps than ever.

The very Gospel itself was an exhortation to man to awake and arise. It addressed itself to those faculties in man, which made him *man,* as distinguished from mere mechanical, animal being, faculties which had been dormant, latent, or only rising into life, in rare and distant instances. It addresses itself to precisely those faculties to-day. The wonder of the Gospel, like the wonder of all nature, is, that the more we see into it the more we see there is *in* it. We find it illimitable, or if limited to us at all, limited not in itself, *but in our own want of capacity.* The little flower is beautiful even to a savage, but transcendently more beautiful to that mind which brings to it a knowledge of those laws of light by which it was produced. So with every truth formula in the Bible; and as no man knows yet all about a flower, so no man knows yet all about the Bible. The age to which we belong, above all others, begins to realize this. *Men are now asking for truth, of every sort and every degree, because it is truth, irrespective of any formula, or any authority, merely human.* The tendency of the ages hitherto has been to tie the race down to what they *suppose to be reverence,* by what *most certainly was credulity.* They talked of belief. They meant blind acceptation. We sometimes meet the impression that we are putting trust only in man. I think we are everywhere refusing to put trust in any mere mortal authority whatever. The tendency of our times is, to develop man to the degree of self-consciousness and thought. The general effect of all tendency hitherto has been that of turning men into children. The general tendency now is that of turning children into men. Hitherto all independence in inquiry has been looked upon with distrust. The Churches have thought it a thing not to be allowed. Our age is impatient of any man who has not learned to think, and passes him by as one who, if he will not help the race, can hardly claim to be helped by the race. Of the two tendencies ours is infinitely preferable, but there are dangers in it. Against these the Christian above all men should be guarded. The *Christian* not only ought to be, but will be, in the vanguard of light. He not only ought to be, but *will be* guide to others. *That is to be a Christian.*

All around us the formulas and traditions of the past seem to be breaking up, like the ice before the advancing spring. Men and women, good people too, are everywhere uneasy and fearful. They hear their creed assailed, their notions impeached, and, like the Jews of old, they are alarmed. They forget that God sitteth between the cherubim. They sometimes fear that the Bible itself is to be overthrown, set aside, that people will get along without any religion. They do not see that the Bible is as fixed as mother earth, and that religion within us is as essential to our being as the sentiment of love or the nervous system. Such trust have we through Christ upon God. Christ demonstrated this law to us, that truth, in conjunction with mind, hath the power a seed hath in conjunction with earth. It springeth up into life. In doubting that, we are like certain temperance people, who tell us, *all men are* going to take to drinking, singularly forgetting that even fifty years ago there was not the beginning of a temperance society, or anybody to sound an alarm, that temperance societies themselves are therefore proof positive that *all men* are not going to take to drinking. Motion is never the sign of death, but of life. If the tendency of our age were confined to a sect or locality, even then it would be hopeful; but when we find it universal—in China, in Japan, in the Jews, in whole nationalities and continents; when we find it in every sect in Christendom, in every shade of belief—we cannot, or ought not, to fail to look upon it as God once more moving upon the face of the waters, God taking a larger and grander step toward the eternal consummation, the establishment of order over chaos, the enthronement of man over nature, the creation of a being upon earth with whom the Creator can commune in spirit and in truth.

St. Paul realized, as his Master had taught him: We are but sowers. All seeds produce after their kind. The thing is to see whether we are ministers of the new covenant. To be ministers of that is to be ministers, not of the letter, but of the spirit. This is what we are called upon to do, to go down below the surface, to get at the deeper things of God, that our children in their turn may be wiser than we. We all of us live in externals to a vastly greater extent than any of us are aware. There is an infinitude in everything beyond that we perceive. This *manhood, e. g.*, is not merely animal. It is not animal at all. We look sometimes upon degraded humanity, a mass of bloated passions and driveling weaknesses, and say what a thing this *humanity* is! That is not humanity. That is animalism with the humanity taken out of it, animalism under indulgence such as God never intended even for animalism itself, animalism in a sphere which animalism *alone* desecrates. Neglect a *garden*, and you have neither grass nor trees, but only *weeds*. It is true, God has put the animal and humanity in conjunction, but humanity is intellect and soul, humanity is moral force, is perception of divine and eternal things. So nothing upon earth is just what it seems to be. Commerce, again, is not simply trade. If it is, it is decay and death. Because the nations have too often made it an ultimate end in itself, it has not failed to make an end of the nations. Commerce is civilization. Art is not merely architecture and painting. Art is soul-life. It is *perception* of nature, and *expression* of nature. True art springs from true life of its kind, and reproduces after its kind. With respect to realities, the great essences that lie beyond the outward appearances, the wise, the seers in all ages, have been endeavoring to give expression. The great moral lights, have endeavored to give expression in like manner, through what we call language, to moral truth. Their sayings became formulas, not perfect, but only approximate, not realities, but only reflection. Simply to rest in *them* is not to perceive them at all. To mistake them is to defeat their very purpose, to turn into a millstone round our neck, what was intended as a vehicle to help us to glory. A wise man in attempting to give expression, or as we call it, definition, to this thing we call man, said "man was the only animal that controlled *fire*." To this a blind man remarked, "that it was not true, for on a given occasion where a fire had been left on a shore by some travellers, the monkeys had kept the fire going by placing sticks upon it, as they had seen the travellers do," a remark which proved he had not the remotest conception of what the wise man meant. The control of fire does not mean merely the placing sticks upon a fire already built, but it means all that can be accomplished by man aided by fire. It means everything from the finest needle to crystal goblets and porcelain vases, everything from cotton spindles to locomotives, and steam engines. It means things of which we yet have no conception, because any truth is an infinity. The truth is one thing. An expression of truth is another thing. The *letter* is one thing. The spirit is another. To rest in the letter is to die. To catch the spirit is to be quickened.

That is what Paul means. Be not like that man. Every expression in the Bible is the husk of an endless truth. Open it, enter in, and live. You begin then to see what language itself is. We say it is the sign of ideas. It is much more frequently the sign of the want of ideas. At any rate at best, it is but a sign. There is nothing in the arbitrary sound, or the arbitrary form which *necessarily* conveys our idea.

A Greek text is the same thing to the illiterate as no text at all. The French, the German, the English, can only be understood so far as we learn and accept what the French, and German, and English, respectively, mean. Any language is but a conventional currency, a thing by means of which we agree to effect certain exchanges. It is a currency without a specified value. Its value to you is never that of the person imparting it, but only that you yourself are able to give it. To us the word *meat* would mean *flesh*. In certain parts of England, and some of the provinces, it would mean *grass* as well. It is used in that sense in the Bible. "*He giveth to all* their *meat.*" Nature and life, and the Bible, never respond to any man, except in voices the man himself evokes. It is so with everything. The wild Indian absorbs only the worst part of our civilization, *i. e.*, he absorbs only our uncivilization. When foolish people go to Europe, they pick up nothing but mere folly. When the ignorant immigrant lands upon our shores, he asks not for our schools, our thought, our culture, but only for such things, too much of which he has had already at home. You select from life, not what you most need, but according to what you carry to life. Hence, we never can convey our ideas, except up to the capacity of the person to whom we are imparting them. You cannot tell your child all you know. Hence the Jews misunderstood Christ. Hence these Corinthians misunderstood St. Paul. Hence we are always misunderstood, and forever misunderstanding each other. Hence the fearful quarrels and wrongs which kept this life seething and boiling. A lamp is of no use to a blind man. All the light possible for you, is in the capacity of your own eye. Hence the extreme importance of teaching people to think. Hence the extreme importance of reaching the brain and the heart, rather than the ear and the eye. The one killeth, the other giveth life. Every man's horizon is limited by his own hight. To tie him up in sect, in formula, is to keep him a child. Hence, no man's criticisms of another man, of any truth, of his times and the movement of his times, can be higher than the man. If you would know what any man's opinions are worth, you must, first of all, know *the man*. The teaching and preaching of anything, is not so dependent upon the teacher and the preacher, as upon the hearer. The Jews went to Christ to trip Him in His word. We read people's opinions to see where they differ from ours, not so much with an object of mending our own, as of finding a handle with which to complain of theirs. Christ invariably recognized this. When He began to speak, and when He closed His speech, He said it was addressed only to those who had an ear to hear. They were all that could hear, and that is the extent of any man's hearing. Old things then, as now, were passing away. All things were becoming new. Then, as now, there was no reason why the old formulas and creeds should not be left behind. Not that they had no truth in them, but that men should go on to perceive the truth beyond them. So, to-day, if you have been living in the letter, and desire to live there forever—the signs of the times can bring you no hope, and fill you with no joy. Those words of Christ, "Be of good cheer, I have overcome the world," can have for you no meaning. You do not see how Christ has overcome the world. But if you have the spirit, you know God is coming closer to man, and that the present is big with the glory of the future. If you know how to think, and catch the spirit above the letter, you will be safe and blessed. "Whosoever hath, to him shall be given."

This answers the question, then, so often asked, "Can truth ever change?" You see the answer. Truth never changes. God's foundations, what we call *fundamentals,* remain forever. Our measure of it must always change, unless we would be forever dead. Nature every day is changing her forms, and because she is forever exchanging, nature is forever life. Perhaps it is the destiny of truth to be forever assuming new forms. Truth is not only infinitely elastic, but infinitely compounded. As I remarked last Sunday, no truth is valuable simply in itself. It is valuable according to its combinations. You must be forever assimilating new truth, as you are every day assimilating new food. Stop the process and you die. The race is as one man, and so there is forever progress, and forever change. It is so not only in religion, but in all the great facts of our economy. *Wealth* was once cattle and clothes, peacocks and apes, pearls and fine linen. Now it is bonds and consols, stocks and factories. The lesser is included in the greater; the old is in the new, but the new was not in the old. *Art* was once pyramids and sphinxes and temples. Now it is locomotives and spindles. Once it was Madonnas and saints. Now it is Niagara and the Rocky Mountains, the Yosemite Valley and photographic production. The fundamentals of wealth and of art cannot and have not changed; they never do change; they always bear the same relations to life; but the form is changing every day. A merchant of the middle ages could not understand even the terms of modern commerce, any more than a warrior of the middle ages could fight with the weapons of modern warfare. But the essence of commerce and war has not changed. The form has passed away; the spirit abideth. So with what we call comfort, so with even life itself; the forms and accessories are always changing, the thing itself abides. All changes have for their object the increase of the reality, and in the aggregate succeed. It is folly to imagine that the ages past were better or happier than our own.

Now some of you ask whether we can never know

anything. I would say, "Yes; we may always *know* most certainly that we do *not* know anything." The error of the past has been that we have pronounced definitely upon subjects that we certaiuly knew very little about. Salvation itself has been fixed, as if some of us had surveyed it with a chain and compass. The most hopeless feature of the prospect before us to-day is, the unflinching blindness which accepts things because we are told them. Go into the rank and file of any Christian denomination and you will find the grand reason for their belief to be that their sect believes it.

There are Christian Churches, so-called, in which the clear assertion of a great truth would create a panic, in Mexico, in Ireland, possibly nearer home. In India, in Constantinople, in Rome, the blinder a man is the better believer he is. In other words, you will find they do not *believe* at all. If you are a wise man, if your spirit burns with Christian impulse, you will understand those expressions which tell us Christ had compassion upon the multitudes. How His divine accents struck Jewish superstition with alarm, but how His sympathetic heart grieved over their blindness. You will ask how the germs which are certainly in man, can be caused to shoot into divine development, but you will see it never can be by refusing to use the noblest faculties with which God has endowed us. The position of asking for the truth for the truth's sake, is the most hopeful the race can reach. All liberation is in it. Every blessing of the past or present, exhaustless riches of the future, are there. Peace upon earth is in it, good will among men. Without it, we are cannon loaded for each other's destruction. With it, we are trees laden with each other's life. Only take for granted it is our neighbor who is in ignorance and error, and there is instant repulsion. Take for granted *we* are in ignorance and error, and there is instant attraction. Yes, only take for granted you are the only favored of God, and you will assume the prerogatives of the Almighty. Take for granted you are helpless and needy, you will look to God in faith and reverence, and all divine prerogative will distil upon you in blessedness and peace. Once get a man to loving truth for its own sake at any cost, and you place that man in direct communion with God. For this, God intended us. To this, Christ and the Gospel introduced us. To this, I think all the truths wrapt up in denominational forms, are bringing us. I do not regret denominational forms. The only thing that is wrong in *sect,* is *sectarianism.* Church authority, the greatest misfortune perhaps that ever settled upon man, cannot choke thought. When men tell you faith is dying, they mean their blind authority is dying. They mean *faith* is truly beginning to live. Put a thought into a heart now, and no mitre can smother it, no crosier can reach it. If it be worthless, it lives as long as any little life it may have will last, and then dies. If it be truth, a grand Œcumenical Council, grander than that at Rome, proclaims it, and it goes forth in all the vitality with which God has clothed it. One thing the great abundance of Christian machinery has done for us, is to teach us the little reliance to be placed in any machinery. We are trusting more to truth, to man, to God. We begin to realize that *Christ* lives, that movements come when God orders them and that it becomes us, not to resist, but to learn. The world to-day is not asking whether we are of Paul, or where Paul got his authority, but saying as Paul said: Be the authority what it may, ye are witnesses, epistles, "written not with ink, but with the spirit of the living God, not in tables of stone, but in fleshy tables of the heart." This also hath Christianity accomplished. This is part of its glorious work. Only this work must be more, and the glory more. The work of Christianity is this very work of guidance. Christ is the creator of new force. The work of the Christian is to be the radiator of that force. The form of Christian work, like all other form, must change. In the early age it was the simple proclamation of bare historic fact,—the incarnation, the death and resurrection of Christ, the releasement from Judaism and Paganism. To-day it is the proclamation of all that the incarnation included, the unfolding of those forms in which Christ left His revelation, the bringing out into actual life, universal life, the precious life of the Son of God, the bringing it not merely to a few, but to the many, curing the leper, unstopping the ears of the deaf, and opening the eyes of the blind, not only raising the dead, but loosing the grave clothes themselves, and setting us free in that blessed liberty wherewith Christ alone sets free. It takes more to be a Christian to-day than it ever did before, and one thing that grieves me is, men outside the Church, men of thought, men of culture, point to so much of so-called Christian life, point to sectarian narrowness and bigotry and ignorance, and ask if that is Christianity. One thing that grieves me, is, Christ is still wounded in the house of His friends.

Some of you tell me, "This is making Christianity a difficult thing." No, my friend. You are only speaking out of your misconception, of which I was speaking just now. It is only making it, not the thing you have been supposing it to be. You ask, "Who can attain to all this?" Nobody can attain to it, if they spend their divine faculties on the decorations of a hat, or the elaborations of Parisian fashions, or the contemplation of railroad stocks. Everything begets after its kind. If you sow the wind, you reap the whirlwind. Nobody can attain to it who is governed by laws that come from France and New York, and know nothing of laws that come from God; nobody who can waste time and energy upon the mere signs of life, and dwell in ignorance of life itself. This is our misfortune: even when we do begin to see, how long it is we see only trees, as men, walking; how long before these dull orbs can gaze upon the glories of God in all the charms of unveiled sight. I do not say there is nothing in forms, for the form of much so-called Christian life proclaims there is no life in it. The real creed of too many of us is, that faith means earthly enjoyment, and that it is easy to enter the Kingdom of Heaven. What is that Kingdom? Have you ever reflected upon what Christ said, that the Kingdom of Heaven was within you? Have you ever thought that there is no more Heaven for you than you are capable of receiving? St. Paul says, not as our translation hath it, the *natural* man cannot receive the things of the Spirit of God, but the gross man, the man buried in the things of time and sense, the sensual man, cannot receive the things of the Spirit of God. Were I to preach to you a sermon to-day against the pomps and vanities of the world, you would say, as is so often said, "Yes, these ministers must be at their trade." But do you see that the pomps and vanities of the world are only the graves of mind and heart and soul, that they are not wrong, so much as that they proclaim you are right? You talk of going to Heaven. What Heaven? You think it is easy to enter. Did Christ say so? Around you are glorious visions, if you could see them, and eternal facts, if you could know them, and angelic experiences, if you were worthy.

> "Children of grace have found
> Glory begun below."

And if you find not that glory here, you never will find it in any hereafter. Every fact is only a result. Heaven itself is only development.

> "The Hill of Zion yields
> A thousand sacred sweets,
> Before we reach the golden fields
> Or walk the sacred streets."

And the streets and fields above are never trodden by unwilling or unhallowed feet.

The thought, then, I would leave with you to-day is the thought that religion means culture; life means growth; Heaven means spiritual glory, the vision of God. Upon you that are young, I would like to impress that thought. You have years; you have strength; you have opportunities. To-day as every day, I would ask you to come to Jesus. He hath the words of eternal life. I would ask you if, through what I have said, you cannot understand much that He said? "Strive to enter in," if you cannot see the force of that earnest life, that pleading, patient, hopeful spirit. I would ask you to reflect upon the meaning, the spirit, of such words as prayer, meditation, thought, communion with self and with God. You will see that you must give up either a *thoughtless life* or a *hope of Heaven*, one or the other. You cannot serve God and mammon. You will serve one or the other. I would say, Come to this Bible. There is more upon every page than any eye hath seen, much your eye *can* see. Through what I have said, hear its echo. "Set your affections on things above, not on things on the earth." "The Kingdom of Heaven is not meat and drink, but peace and joy in the Holy Ghost."

And, one and all of us, What are we living for? To what extent are we *believers*, to what extent disciples, *scholars* of Him who was the Son of God, whose life, whose doctrine, whose very Gospel is an exhortation to be in deed and in truth the children of the Highest? May God give us grace to come to Him, and, coming, give us vision to see, faith to know most certainly, that He alone is the Way, the Truth, and the Life everlasting!

RENOUNCING THE WORLD.

MATTHEW 4: 1.—Then was Jesus led up of the Spirit into the wilderness to be tempted of the devil.

You readily recognize this passage as introductory to the record of Christ's great temptation in the wilderness. The whole three and thirty years of Christ's life constitute what He gave for us men, and for our redemption. But He was now about to enter upon that part of His life more particularly called His *public ministry*. He had just been baptized of John, at the Jordan, where a miraculous testimony had been given as to His person, His character, and His office. A definition of Him, so to speak, had been made. From this scene He is carried, still by *divine* influence, into the wilderness to be *tempted* of the devil. This temptation embraced three prime elements. First, "Command that these stones be made bread." Second, "The pinnacle of the temple." Third, "All these kingdoms will I give thee if thou wilt fall down and worship me."

The whole of this *temptation*, being, in itself and in its circumstances, extraordinary, what we might call miraculous, it is impossible for us in all respects to explain it. How Satan could approach Christ, how his propositions could be presented to the mind and spirit of Christ, we cannot tell. But if Christ were the Son of God, the Messiah, promised of all ages, the Great Redeemer of a fallen race, we can conceive a sort of necessity for His being subjected to such a test. Marvellous as the temptation is, more marvellous, indeed, would its absence be. The fact that He was subjected goes far to prove He was all He claimed to be. It gives us a deeper confidence in the super-human nature of His mission, and in the inspiration of His whole life-record. We may regard it as a demonstration, that if our Gospel were a merely human fabrication, this temptation had never been found in it. Not that it is not *naturally* there, but that man in his speculations upon divine things, and especially so at the time the Gospel was written, is forever *only speculation*, and therefore *unnatural*. The wilderness and the Jordan supplement each other. From highest heights and lowest depths—from Christ's whole being, divine and human, from heaven, earth, and hell, come one testimony—Christ is Emmanuel, a Son of Man, who is Son of God.

It must be observed, that this *temptation* stands at

the threshold of Christ's avowed work, of His official life, so to speak. Stress must also be laid upon the fact that it was a *temptation.* It is true, our words *temptation* and *trial* have a common origin, start from the same germinal thought. Together they express that which gives proof of our moral being, that which defines the amount of true moral being within us. But they are different things. They are rather the *two sides* of one thing. They act upon different elements. Temptation appeals to our weakness. Trial appeals to our strength. Temptation attempts to reduce us by surrender. Trial attempts to reduce us by storm. Temptation comes with a bribe. Trial comes with a threat. If we yield to a temptation, and accept its reward, we have gained nothing, for we have lost ourselves. If trial shall strip us, and at last crucify us, we are more than conquerors, for we are forever glorified. We may always distinguish between temptation and trial by observing the elements of which they are composed. We are in *temptation* when we are *inclined toward* a thing, which the moral sense within us tells us to be wrong. We are in trial when we are under providences, from which all that is carnal and earthly within us *prompts us to escape.* In temptation we are attracted. In trial we are repelled. They are the centrifugal and centripetal forces of moral being. They create what we call the antagonism between the flesh and the spirit. The spirit lusteth against the flesh, and the flesh against the spirit. What we would we ought not—what we ought we cannot, as much as we would. "But they that are after the flesh do mind the things of the flesh." They occupy two wholly different planes. Temptation moves upon our baser nature, upon all that is temporary and sensuous. Trial moves upon our diviner nature, upon all that is eternal and spiritual. The one leaves us stranded down with the husks and swine. "That which is born of the flesh is flesh." The other exalts us to communion with God in the abodes of the glorified. "That which is born of the spirit is spirit." *We have reached the plane of true trial only when we have crossed forever the plane of temptation.* We find God only when we have renounced the world, the flesh, and the devil. "They that are in the flesh cannot please God. He passes the temptation plane before he enters fully upon the trial plane. Hence it is only the sons of God, and pre-eminently *the Son of God*, on whom *trial* is laid, and the measure of service is the measure of trial, and because His service was to be transcendently greatest, both His temptation and His trial were transcendently severest.

Out of this, then, we evolve somewhat the *necessity* that the Son of God should be tempted. It was needful that He should be strong, not that He was hedged about by any power which no temptation could reach; not in that He was ignorant of the forces of darkness; but He must be strong in that He can resist every form of attack, strong positively and strong negatively. He must not be great because He sits merely at our end of the universe, but great because He covers all there is of the universe, because there is no part of it over which He is not supreme. The first Adam was innocent so long as he was ignorant. The second Adam is innocent, not merely because He touches eternal heights, but because He has sounded eternal depths; not because some force has left Him alone, but because He has forever subjected all forces. As such He is the representative of the human race in the higher life, as the first Adam was the representative of the human race in the lower life. Upon Him, too, all the laws of good and evil are to act, just as they act upon us. His temptation is but the condensed reality to which the human race was, has been, and is subjected; the reality beneath which the human race failed, which failure makes it a race fallen and lost, the reality against which the Son of Man triumphed—triumphed, that as death was in Adam so life might be in Him. *He is our forerunner.* Hence the value of the manhood of Christ. He trod the pathway alone, but treading it, He opened it, and marked it, *for us.* Yes, my friend, if you have not hold upon Christ in this dark world, or, better still, if Christ have not hold of you, I know not what life can be to you, or how you can live at all. Overcoming these, He showed the result of victory, escape from the devil, angels ministering to us; overcoming these, He goes out to a divine life, a divine service, to which He invites us, the success of which He assures us, the necessity of which He demonstrates, if we would be sons of God, *heirs* of God, and *joint heirs* with Him.

"He was led up of *the Spirit* into the wilderness." You will observe it is no part of God's plan that we should escape temptation. We sometimes say, how mysterious it is, God should have created us such beings in such a world. But from what has been said, you perceive the necessity of such a being if there would ever be any moral beings at all. It would have been much stranger if we had not been so created and in such a world. You perceive what a true moral being is, that from which the idea of all that is mechanical, or accidental, or without intrinsic or inherent merit, is excluded. You read of Heaven, of a Kingdom of God. You see it is not something which is arbitrarily created, but a Kingdom of pure soul, a Kingdom the arena of action for moral and spiritual glory. But for just that life of Jesus, that life of temptation and trial, you could have had no high conception of the truly divine, *so unless you partake of that life, you can have no part in the Kingdom of true Glory.* "You must be born from above." It is this life of temptation and trial which defines for us what man is, not an animal, not a devil, not merely for time. Through it you arrive at spirit, at moral being, at immortality. You perceive what it is to believe, what it is to believe in Christ, what faith is, how, as I once explained it to you, it is soul-vision.

We are in a wilderness. Take man and view him merely with reference to abundance of bread, with reference to time and the powers of earth—take him as the center of this strange economy upon which we are cast, and life is to our souls what a wilderness is to our bodies. Admit that all the faculties man has were intended merely to feed him sumptuously and cloth him in purple and fine linen—still what is he? Take those who have so lived, those who have been successful, those who have tried the experiment Christ declined. Take what we call the kings of the earth. How many kings, of all that have ever lived, challenge the admiration of their race? You might count them all upon your fingers, but even of those, what is it that challenges our admiration? It is not their palaces, nor their power, nor their abundance, nor their pomps. It is an element above that, an element of mind, of something we call humanity, a something which nothing earthly can buy and with which nothing earthly can compare. Take

Solomon, who thinks to-day of his ivory or his peacocks? The queen of Sheba did not see the true glory of Solomon; and if he is still a king is it in the abundance of the things he possessed? Nay, who are the kings of the earth? Lord Bacon is to-day more a king than any Plantagenet, and the only wonder about is that he was a lord. The great rejuvenating forces are forever springing up from the roots of humanity. Christ was described as a root out of a dry ground. What makes Britain? Is it her army, her navy, her commerce, her manufactories. Then what makes these? Is it her colleges, her science, her literature, her fine arts? Take out her brave *hearts* that have dared, and do dare, to stand up for right, for justice, for truth, for liberty, and where is Britain? Is any nation upon earth great without these? And yet here you reach an altitude altogether beyond all that is sensuous and earthly. You have attained to a height beyond all that is animal, something which alone is human, something too that is divine.

Beside all that, do the people destitute of the higher element, possess most of the lower? Do the Indians upon the Plains wring from nature a better subsistence than we have in our civilization? Do the tribes of Africa enjoy a better life than the people of Germany? Do you not see, that it is only in the possession of the higher that you can at the same time possess the lower? Do you not perceive that to have only the animal life, is of itself to fail? Do you not see written all over life the great thought, that the real forces are, after all, the moral forces? That man cannot even manage his civil, commercial, and social greatness without it—that if he undertake it, weakness, just at the very point where *strength* is essential, brings the whole fabric in confusion about his ears, how, in fact, anything that may be called a fabric is impossible? how, when you come to run the thought through life as it spreads out before you, you have in certain circles failure, collapse, disappointment, or what we call by other words dishonesty, fraud, self-seeking—how such beings are really not the friends of their race, and how at last for whatever degree of success they may have attained, for whatever time they may have been able to stand, they are indebted to the sons of God—how, for whatever we may have, we are dependent at last upon the higher life, the family, trade, art—dependent upon schools and morals and science, and the whole thing upon religion? I would give much for the power to impress that thought upon you. I would give more for the power to stimulate you toward all that thought to inspire.

Now, this is precisely what the devil is forever aiming at, to keep us in our dwarfed and animal being. He helps nothing so much as the accumulation of earthiness, in any of its forms, because it is the sure ruin of all heavenliness. The three elements of this Christ-temptation, are the three essentials of all temptation. When conscious life first dawns upon us, when aspiration first awakes, we gaze and behold we are in a wilderness, *i. e.*, where food for *man* is not spontaneous. The wants of these bodies, because our lowest wants, how natural that Satan should come there first. He says to us, "command that these stones be made bread." He sets up these bodies in one clamorous claim for recognition and gratification. He clothes us in a fear, lest some day should come in which there would not be enough to sustain life, without asking us whether such an empty life were worth the saving. He starts out the young with that idea, the idea of an establishment. He keeps them at that endless and impossible problem, *Turn earth into bread.* Mark the significance of the first command of God to Adam, "Thou shalt not eat." How simple! But how wonderful that it should be as needful to-day! Thou shalt not drink, thou shalt not drown all that is divine within thee, in that which is sensuous and carnal. Do that, and you of necessity go out to a being with every heavenly ray extinguished. You make earth a desert. You leave yourself a prey to all ills and woes. *In the day that thou doest it, thou diest.* Mind sleeps, and soul sleeps, and heart sleeps. In the slumber of these, man is dead. The absence of the higher is the absence of the lower as well. If man has a power over nature, it is only as he is man, only as he is not animal. If the five barley loaves and two small fishes are to be in this wilderness more than enough, it is only as we are sons of God, able to command and be obeyed. Sink him into the animal, and all that the earth can produce for him is thorns and briars. He must take his chances with other animals. His weapons of defence are defenceless. His level is low. Nature is his equal, and in the aggregate, more than his equal. All time attests this; yet, there is man still beating at the same old problem.

And indeed, Satan seldom needs to go beyond it. He is a hard worker, but he never does any unnecessary work. What we call wicked life is no temptation *to the wicked.* How natural it seems, they practice it greedily. You see, if you stop anywhere, at Satan's bidding, he is your master. You yield, and your life-struggle is done. Life to you is no struggle. You shrug your shoulders when you look upon real men and see the troubles they have to go through, and chuckle over yourselves that you are free. But, who is the gainer? I do not mean to say you have not to work, but your work is nowhere off your own level; just there you must grind. You have no agency in the grand things of God, no part or lot in the heritage of a son of God. The well being of others is no concern of yours. The safe-guards of society—all that gives you liberty and safety, you enjoy the very facilities by which your work is done, the offspring of toiling brains, results the costs of which are written in aching hearts, and sacrificed lives; they are eliminated from your thoughts. As the Psalmist said, they are not plagued like other men. They come in no misfortune like other folk. Their sensibilities slumber. They are not up on the life-plane of trial. With all your work the world is not indebted to you, but you to the world. You are its pensioner, not its benefactor. You are the borrower not the lender—not the force that carries, but the burden to be carried; not the feeders, but the eaters. Can you accept the position? I do not say you have nothing to do. You have a great deal to do. Your work is heavy—a wise man could not carry it. Ignorant of the high moral forces, living where high moral forces are not. You have to carry a weight of fear and vigilance, to keep what you have. Not that you exactly want it. You know before your shoes are cold, somebody will be after it. Your grandchildren will never touch it. Satan has cheated you. You have commanded stones to be made bread, but what of it? You cannot eat it. Death stands there at the end of your journey, and what a grim shadow death is! I cannot linger here, but I say there Satan hath prevailed with multitudes, and you can see them all along in life, stranded and ruined. The command is made to you. Shall you be cheated by it?

But some do not surrender at the first challenge. Perhaps the majority of men pass somewhat on to the workings of the second element. It must be, that all men think sometimes of their souls, and try to take some sort of a stand worthy of their immortality. "He carries him to the pinnacle of the temple."

I say mark the fact that Christ was the avowed Son of God. This tempation comes to those who stand out to be sons of God. He carries Him to the pinnacle of the temple. It is a strange place for Satan to take anybody. But all that is outward, all that is showy, no matter what we call it, all that is shadowy, even though it be symbolic of divinest relation, is approachable by Satan. He comes up to *worship even* with the sons of God. His object is to make us rest in ordinances, to turn religion into form and ceremony, to make us hypocritical and Pharisaic, to give us, instead of God's precious truth in Christ, the wretched theologies and creeds of men, to turn everything still *into* that which is outward and temporal. He stands beside us in the contemplation of our loftier being, brings before us, not God, but ourselves, not that which is above us, but that which is below us, plays upon the strings of our selfishness, our pride, paints before us the consoling messages, the smooth things, things intended beyond all doubt for the sons of God. But he says: "See how high you are, how safe you are." You are at once the companion and the care of angels. The whole power of omnipotence is pledged to sustain and guard you. If you trace religious developments, if you examine history you will find this delineated in every system that ever set up to be a religion. The Hindoo, the Moslem, the Romanist, every sect, upon earth, what a sense of security, what a disposition to seclude, what a practice of excommunication! what impious confidence in limiting salvation to itself! It all comes from the devil. You see, the proposition of Satan is true enough. *The Son of God is secure.* There is no doubt about that. The insinuating fallacy is, the taking for granted that we are the sons of God. You see this fallacy sometimes, when *we* select out all the sweet and precious passages from the Bible, and turn all the rest over to somebody else. You see this in that thing which clings sometimes to professors of religion, *spiritual pride,* the worst disease that ever affected a soul.

Upon that pinnacle of the temple, you are in a dangerous place. Hold on the faster in humility and reverence and godly fear. You have entered upon no child's play, your work is no holiday sport, God is not mocked. Take heed lest you fall. New relations involve new obligations, the higher the position and power the higher the responsibility—position is nothing but a snare, unless there be with it a corresponding moral power. It is in vain we have escaped the turning of stones into bread if in a delirium of spiritual pride we fall to tempting the Lord our God. God will not hold him guiltless that taketh His name in vain. If we contemplate the Church, does it not seem indeed as if we had forgotten that to have changed our places is not necessarily to have changed our natures. Do we realize that to have broken away from the old Egypt is not necessarily to have entered the promised land? Where are the graces and virtues, yes, the struggles and trials which ought to characterize the children of

God? Do we not seem to the world often to be the easiest and most self-complacent of mortals? Do we not ourselves often see men who, in a profession of religion, have not so much a new nature as a new degree of their old nature, men who have not put on the new Adam, but a new degree of the old Adam, men not so much dissatisfied with the world as they are satisfied with themselves, who have religion enough to make them pray, but not religion enough to make them honest and useful and meek and merciful; whom in short, the Church has to carry, and who are like the earthy a portion of that burden which the true children of God have at last to bear. Can you be one of them? Can I be one of them? The pinnacle of the temple? When we contemplate it in its great assumption, its pride of place, and name and appearance, doing its own petty will, we can feel it is a dangerous place. There is need of angels then, and that Scripture, the Saviour used, comes back to us, double-edged and keen. "Thou shalt not tempt the Lord thy God." Religion is no sham, no make believe, and, if the wicked cannot enter heaven, neither can they who are without holiness see the Lord.

But what shall we say of this third element? There is upon earth a line of action peculiarly and emphatically called worldliness. It is not a line of temperate, noble and holy purpose, but of action, begotten of whatever there is in us which is carnal and sensual. In its highest and best manifestations it is so close upon the line of nothing, we never ask respecting it, "where is the good of it?" but only, "where is the harm?" It never rises, in any of its degrees, into positive usefulness and wisdom. Every degree of it, is from the plane of nothing, downward into wrong and darkness. It is the unchallenged arena of what are technically called "high life" and "low life," for extremes often meet. Hence it is often the culmination of the other two temptations, one turning stone into bread, furnishes the means, and the other, the pinnacle of the temple, makes it respectable. But mark, how it is all yet upon the plane of the showy and the outward, the earth and the earthy. It is a stimulant of every evil *passion* in man, of every nerve of his darker and fallen being. It is the perversion of faculties which God gave for purposes noble and divine. It oils the wheels of trade, but it often makes trade itself a crime. It creates public place and public honor, but it often makes public place and public honor the very pillory of all degradation. It traffics in manliness and virtue. Glory, kingdom, power, glittering pomp are there, but they sit upon a throne built of ruined humanity; a hideous *self*, like a fiery moloch, feeding upon the children of men. It creates burdens for the fatherless and the widow. It mars every relation of society. Its very breath is insincerity, and also impurity. It creates and sustains whatever there is in life demoralizing, immoral, and dangerous. Its only reality is its disappointment and its wrong. Its promises are a shadow and a name. But all this will the devil give, if you will fall down and worship him. No *Christian* can possibly be in it. There is force here in the idea of a *mountain*, for if a Christian look upon it at all, he must look *down* upon it. But the Christian is tempted to go there. Yes, my friend, and when you are there, whirling in the giddy mazes of fashion, flattered, caressed, and applauded, when you ride upon the car of success or prosperity, Satan may be nearer to you than you would like to have him, if you only knew, but if you are a professing child of God, the more pressing is the temptation, for you read in your catechism that you renounce the world, the flesh, and the devil. You see you must do it, not because the Church says so, but the Church says so, because you *must do it*, if you would enter the the abodes of the blest. The *worldly Christian*, a contradiction in terms—but the *worldly Christian* is the best bait for Satan's trap. To be a Christian in deed and in truth, you must have set your face like a flint against the world, the flesh, and the devil, and your heart like a mirror toward the glory of the Kingdom of God.

Now, have I set before you to-day, any idea of a Christian life? Have I explained to you any of those expressions you often hear, like that of a Christian conflict, the idea of a struggle? Do you see the flesh on the one side, and the spirit on the other? Do you perceive that the idea of trial is not repulsive, for it is instantly the pledge of a regenerate nature, and the only road to the glory of God. I would like to give you, if I could, the idea of different planes of being. You would not like to be merely an animal. But how much above the animal would you like to be? I would like to give you this idea, that moral being means, that you are to choose what plane of being shall be yours. Temptation comes that you might decide, and trial comes to test your decision. I would like to say this, whatever plane you choose, you shall grow more and more into it. Think it not strange. You shall have your choice. God will not cheat you. No; you think that by and by, it will be time enough for you to decide. But why should you think that? You observe the poor man whose God is money—does he get the less miserly as he grows old? You take the man who has buried all his nobler faculties in self, does he find them more vivid as life ebbs away? All things beget after their kind. If you sow the wind, you will reap the whirlwind. You might get alarmed when you feel, by and by, that death is on your track—some men do, some are too insensible even for that; they have no bands in their death. They die as the brute dieth—but those who do, have lost, too often, all spiritual vision, life sinks down into one dark and dismal abyss. Never having been born from above, the things that would make for their peace are hidden from their eyes. But you *are* deciding whether you will or not, every day. That is one of the mysteries you need to look into. *Life is real.* Not to choose is still a choice. Did you ever reflect upon that expression of the Saviour, "the outer darkness?" You see God hath a kingdom, a *home.* It is heaven, the abode of pure soul. If you have not that you are simply left out. That is all. But what is that all? God grant none of us may ever know. No angels minister there. The devil never departs. The two spheres are *two*—a gulf lies between. Was it no mercy that Christ trod there to warn you? Do no revealings of God's love, no intimations that this Gospel is God's blessed scheme of rescue for you, strike through this temptation of Christ? Do you not see that the Gospel is so framed as to bring you an intimation of its divine intention? Does God not call you? When you reflect upon Satan, is he not himself a warning to you? What answer will you make to-day? What record shall be inscribed upon the books that are to be opened? In the world you shall have tribulation, do what you will. Christ alone overcame the world, and in Christ alone can you overcome.

But, brethern, before I close, just let me say this; some of us are in trial. I mean we are conscious of a great struggle, a struggle we voluntarily took up, being called of God. Well, from what has been said, where else would we be? You see you are upon the plane of trial. When you look back through the Bible and through all the centuries, who are they who alone are fit to live? Who are they who alone do live? Oh, I think it is a great blessing to have passed the border land of temptation. Do you not find as you get older, that you get better satisfied with what God gives you and less and less troubled about anything the earth has to give? Are there not many providences and many experiences which are ministering angels? If you had to go back and take up life again, would you not take up just the same kind of life, only more of it? Well, that is where this theme has a voice for us. Take up just as much of it as we can. The more single the eye, the more absolutely filled with light will the body be. The more truly we are the sons of God, the more truly shall we stand revealed in the last day with Jesus, in the far more exceeding and eternal weight of glory.

LOVE ACTING IN FAITH.

Luke 18: 8.—Nevertheless when the son of man cometh, shall he find faith on the earth?

The whole of this passage of which the text is a part, was occasioned by a question put to Christ by the Pharisees. They asked of Him, "when the Kingdom of God should come." The Lord's answer took its form from His knowledge of the Pharisaic conception or misconception of that kingdom. The Pharisees had an idea that the Kingdom of God was to be a visible, pompous, human kingdom. The Apostles had the same idea, because it was the prevailing idea. They stood upon the level of their times as all of us stand upon the level of ours, and notwithstanding the repeated attempts of the Saviour, it was not till after His resurrection He succeeded in giving them a realizing sense of the kingdom He would establish. The Lord's answer to these Pharisees was—"The Kingdom of God cometh not with outward show." It is not after the pattern of earthly kingdoms, nor responsive at all to the cravings of the gross, carnal heart. It is not outside of you, but inside of you. It is not *out*sight, but *in*sight. It is the *vision* of things divine, and a life harmonious with *them*. "*The kingdom of heaven is within you.*"

Turning to His disciples, whose faces doubtless were upturned to His in amazement and disappointment, with eager inquiry written upon every line, He endeavors to guard them against mistakes in eventful times soon to come. "Do not expect any such kingdom," He says, "as the Pharisees expect. Even this that you see around you is to be swept away. They will expose me to every woe and finally reject me. But I shall come notwithstanding, and fearful will be the day of my coming. It will not do for you to be half-hearted then. You will need the power of this spiritual kingdom. By you the new kingdom will have to be built, and by those after you." Thus, by a most delicate transition, he carries their mind onward to their great mission, onward through the struggling ages, to

His second coming, telling them in a parable, that the one instrumentality by which the Gospel kingdom was to grow, was this inner vision, this sight of God, this trust, this faith, that however long their hope was deferred, however desperate their cause might seem, it still could not fail. If a human judge, and he none of the best, could be touched by the desperate pleadings of a helpless widow, through motives to which his nature were alive, how much more would God, a righteous judge, never forget the pleadings of His bereaved Church, this deserted, widowed race, till its longings be met and its cause won! Your business is always to pray and never to faint, to see me and God and heaven, and know that because these are in your own heart and in proportion as they *are* there, my kingdom comes. There still gazing upon those mystified faces, seeing the fearful interval between that seed He was sowing, and the ultimate harvest He knew would come up, out of the depths of His yearning spirit bursts the ejaculation: "Nevertheless, when the son of man cometh, shall he find faith on the earth."

Of all things difficult to define, and therefore difficult to impress upon the human mind, is this thing, *faith.* The difficulty arises from our *carnality*, from the fact that we live, like the Pharisees, in our grosser, *outer*, animal nature, not in our intellectual, moral and spiritual nature. The thing most talked about in the world, is still the thing most difficult to understand, *religion.* It is a thing which each soul has to perceive for itself. It is *soul-vision.* The best that mortal language can do is to suggest it. It never can express it. It is like every other pure essence. The poet cannot tell us his experiences, whatever he tells us is only the shadow of what he sees. The painter, the sculptor, they make no legacy of their skill. The true riches must be acquired. Above all, the pearl of great price must be *sought*. Religion! Wisdom! In all thy gettings, get that. It is the Supreme good, and so we strive. We strive for each other, Jesus strove for us all.

It is constituted of three prime elements, "faith, hope and charity." Paul says, *charity* is the greatest; John says, *faith* is the victory that overcometh the world. Of essentials in any thing, it is very difficult to say which is the most important. Of essentials, we may have more room for its exercise, but even that cannot exist without the others.

This word faith is employed in several senses. Perhaps a better expression would be, this word faith has many methods of application. It is not a thing peculiar to religion. I mean by that, religion is not its only sphere. It is the one thing essential to human life. It is the perception of, and reliance upon, certain principles or laws, leading to certain results. The physician sees the laws of health, he makes his prescription in reliance upon those laws. The parent sees the laws of society, of well or ill-being, and he trains his child according to his vision. The merchant sees the laws of trade, of demand and supply, of public trust and mistrust. According to his sagacity he makes his ventures. All that is faith. Some of it is very low, to be sure, but still it is faith after its kind and in its degree, and yet we cannot say it is the *faith* that is *low*. The vision is good. It is only the application which is mean or noble. But faith is never a fixed quantity. It is not the same to you and me. It varies, and all the faith possible for you, in this world or any other, is *that* you possess, whatever its kind, or whatever its degree. It is so in everything. You cannot show some men even how to make money. But like every thing else, faith can grow, *i. e.*, your vision can extend. It does extend in whatever direction you give it, and hence the value of what we call experience. Faith, therefore, in any plane on which you put it, is simply vision. As such, it may be more or less. It may rise from the particular to the general, from the individual to the universal.

In religion it always does this, and hence you have the word *faith* applied to that exercise of the soul, by which, in its longings, out of the depths of its convictions, it looks up to Jesus and says, "Lord, I believe." At first even that may be very tremblingly said. There may be no clear conception of *how* Christ is the Saviour, of what salvation is. Faith may be, and is at first, as the smoking flax and the bruised reed. But it grows till the soul can rejoice in the "*full assurance*" of faith. But another soul may go beyond that, into a wider perception of law, or a wider application of the same law. One soul may see *it* is saved, another soul may see that the law which saved it, shall also inevitably work *till all are saved.* Hence we have different expressions for faith, sometimes subjectively, the exercise of the vision within us—sometimes objectively, that upon which the vision is fixed. Sometimes the principle itself, sometimes that in which the principle shall result. But always in one general formula, faith is the substance of a desirable thing, the evidence of a thing we yet cannot grasp.

We talk about faith, by and by growing into sight. Faith is always growing into sight, if it is growing at all. Faith will grow forever and ever. The archangels have more faith than we have, because they see more than we do. The visions in the heavens above, are not visions with these bodily eyes. The kingdom of heaven as I said just now, is *in*sight, not *out*sight, a thousand glories are every day spread before these physical eyes which we see not. You and I gaze upon the landscape, but we do not see the same thing, as Newton, or Walter Scott, or somebody who said about himself and his dog Diamond, they both gazed upon the stars, but they saw very different worlds. Yes, and there are more glories in all things than any of us see. The glories of God are not what any physical eye can report. All vision at least is soul-vision. Wonderful as all these *bodies* are, they are only a clod, and many a man has nothing more, and would you call him a man at all? All space and all time and all eternity can make you no more than that clod, except as you .open your spirit and receive space and time and eternity. That reception is faith. Faith is therefore a variable quantity. There are degrees of it so great that cherubim and seraphim, may be said to have faith, and degrees of it so feeble, we may question whether we have it all. Would the angels call *our* visions faith? If you look at the Apostles, you can distinctly trace the growth of their faith. At first, how dim it was! How blind they were! They saw nothing! The words of Christ awoke in them hardly the remotest response. The wonderfulness of His being seemed scarcely to have dawned upon them. How wonderful that they should be with Him, and be thinking all the time of a palace and a sceptre, of flimsy pomp, and never ask a word of the mysteries that were beating in all being about them, not a word about any scientific truth He might have told them, not a spiritual fact He might have revealed, of what the soul was, of where the spirit went, of how it could see God, only evermore paltry self, and poor, blind Israel. Even after the resurrection, "Lord, wilt thou at this time restore again the kingdom to Israel?" How was it possible for that Saviour to dwell there? What a hopeless task to make an impression upon a soul so dead! How absolutely hopeless, that work would have seemed to an angel or archangel to wake up spirit so dead, and yet from that point draw a contrast between Christ and them. What an interval was there! Do you catch no glimpses there of the *God incarnate!* God never despairs. All things are possible to perfect vision. Any but God would have left us alone. Do you see nothing of the wonderful condescension and sacrifice? Do you see that Christ was a revelation to us of *God*, of goodness, of love; that he who had seen Him had seen the Father. *He* seems to see not *earth* at all Amid all sorrow and sin, amid the conspirings of this very blindness of men, with the surgings of all providence beating against Him, *He stands like a rock.* He has vision. He knows even our blindness shall be overcome. He knows that a race shall be redeemed from darkness and that a world shall be saved from woe. Only to God are all things possible. Only God, never abandoned us.

But *how* should this race be saved? By His revealings. They were a revelation of *God.* By giving us the inner vision, the vision of divine things, do you see how His sacrifice saves, that if he had never come we could never have known God. Do you see that to believe in Christ is to believe upon that which was in Christ, to believe in the God-soul, the God-power, and that that power works in the man-soul and creates power that he who hath the Son of God hath life, and that to have life is to have the Son of God. Do you see that the incarnation is the explanation to us of this being, God *for* man, and man *for* God, God *in* man and man *in* God, that the incarnation is at once a prophesy and pledge of the destiny of the race, that the promise which Jesus otherwise made is involved in it, that the gates of hell should not prevail against us? Do you see how afterwards, when the scales had fallen from the Apostolic eyes, how they leaped themselves into that new life, *how they had faith?* Do you see the meaning of the scales that fell from Paul's eyes, how persecution and want and death had no influence over them at all, and how, for the first time, they were truly alive, how the Scribes and Pharisees and Elders were only so many ghosts before them; and what a power they were? Against the new life, Emperors and Herods and High Priests and all that the world called power, availed nothing. That faith really was the victory that overcame the world, and so it has always been. It is faith which has removed mountains, discovered continents, and revealed worlds. It is vision, and do you see, if the world were never to be wholly redeemed, Christ would never have undertaken it.

Well, you can see all that to-day, multitudes of us can see it. You can see the interval between the Apostles before Pentecost and those same Apostles after Pentecost. Had their faith not grown? You see the interval between our world to-day and our world that day. Has faith not grown? Are there no more Christians now than there were in the first century? Of us Christians all together, are there none of us that see into divine things further than those who first believed? And yet, as compared with the man Christ Jesus, and as compared with the vision that angels have, can we be said to have any faith? Would you call this *faith* that we have? What do we see?

And this is the point to which I wished to bring you. This passage of Scripture has been employed to convey the idea that Christ said, the world would grow worse and worse, to make Christ contradict Himself, and say the gates of hell should prevail. Multitudes there are to-day who believe that, and I want to ask you whether you can call that, faith in Christ, faith in God, faith in divine things? Multitudes there are to-day, who are looking upon the world in sourness and gloom, telling us that it has gone to destruction, when Jesus has died that it may never go to destruction—telling us it is the devil's world, when Jesus bought it with His own blood, and made it God's world—telling us all men are going away from Jesus, when Jesus said if He were lifted up He would draw all men unto Him. After all the marvellous things the ages have brought forth, and all the marvellous things our eyes have seen, telling us Jesus died in vain. Do you call that faith? When the angels see the purposes of God, when Jesus beholds our slowness of heart, are there no sighs in heaven. And through this, can you not see what Jesus means, in the text, When I come, be it soon or be it late, shall I find anything here I can truly call faith? anything truly becoming to my disciples? anything worthy the sons of God?

Now this, I say, brethren, is the one thing we are wanting to-day, we Christians. We have not the courage to go in and possess the land. I do not say the world has more faith than the Church, not at all. But I do say the Church has not half the faith she might have. The faith of the race, the soul-vision of mankind, is infinite as compared with what it was eighteen hundred years ago, and it has grown by means of the Church. Jesus Christ has been the light of the world. But it might have grown more, and would have grown more, had our faith all along been more. Look at the world. The leaves of the tree have been for the healing of the nations. Look at science. Is that no part of the Kingdom of God, and is it nothing to inherit that? Look at art. Is that no part of the divine legislation? Is it no part of God's great plan, that by the employment of intellect and soul, man can inherit the earth? Is that the work of the devil? If your boy were stretched dying in New York, anxious only to breathe his last accent in your parental ear, would telegraph and rail be no blessing to you both? Is a true civilization opposed to God? Is all our talk about a human fraternity, is a literature, teeming with high-born thought, with far-reaching truth, emanicipating man from bigotry and ignorance, and superstition; is philosophy, asking of every element of being the most urgent questions; is freedom from dogma, and from priestly dictation, and liberation of intellect, and schools for the masses, and libraries and lectures, and reforms, and homes for the blind, and the deaf and the indigent—is all that born of the will of the flesh, and of the inspiration of the devil? One would so imagine to hear us Christians talk sometimes. Why, my brethren, the Church is the parent of them, and they in their reflex influence are the feeders of the Church. Were the wells that were digged in Canaan, and the houses that were built, and the grapes that grew, and the vines and figtrees, all unreal and not worth having? Did God not intend them for His inheritance? Was not the only thing wanting to them a people worthy of them?

And is it not so to-day? *We are of little faith.* Down below all Christian life, there is a groundswell of fear that the people will get along without religion. You know the people of England cannot see how there could be any religion in the masses if the Church were cut loose from the State, just as if they thought the payment of Church rates could make religion, just as if we should think that to remove our water board and water tax, the people would never thirst. How in this country we keep up churches and have religion, is a mystery to the Europeans. When Pere Hyacinth was recently in New York, a prominent clergyman took him into his church, showed him the costly building, the Sunday school room, lecture room, reading room. How is it, says the father, you get these things with no government to help you? The people give their money, says the pastor. Do your laws compel them, asked the father. No; it is purely voluntary. What, gave all this of their own accord! he exclaimed—ah, I see it now, God and the people, God and the people. As I have walked your streets and seen your temples and cities, I have caught a new idea of your greatness. I see it all now—God and the people. Yes, my brethren, the very pledge of the incarnation is God in the people, and the people in God, humanity in Diety, and Deity in humanity. The Holy Ghost, the God-life, working and quickening the human spirit, the man-life. You cannot quench it or stop it, if you should try. You could not keep religion from man by all the powers of earth united. If you should pass a law to-morrow, to take religion from the people, that law would have but one effect, and that instantly to grind the blind legislators to powder. What an absence of faith there is, when we cannot see it! If you should pass a law imposing empty forms and ceremonies, any mere make believe, they would not have it. They demand *thought* and reality and the God-life. That they will have, and we ought to be thinking of how more and more they shall have it. Why, to-day, what is it that is uppermost in our world? What name is it that stands above all names? The cross and Jesus. Philosophers are asking about it. Historians are searching into it. The press is throwing off as many sermons as novels. You can read them even in your daily papers. Yes, brethren, one thing that makes me think the second coming is near, is, that Jesus said, we should see him seated upon the clouds in power and great glory. In all the clouds that are rolling around us, above them all, I see Jesus seated in power and great glory. He rides upon all the storms, and all the elements are his ministers. Infidelity, from the lips of a poor faithless Roman, says, yes, He was God. Philosophy says, yes, thou art the desired of all nations. History says, thou art King of kings, and Lord of lords. Faith says, thou art the Lamb of God that taketh away the sins of the world, the healing of the nations, the sum of all blessing.

I know there is darkness enough, and crime and wrong and sorrow enough. But where is it? Just where the world sees it must of necessity be, just where men make it. There is enough. But will you go through this great city and pass by its churches and its houses of comfort, its living citizens, and go to the pest house and the gutter and sewer and pick up its filth and stench and say, what a city of corruption! What a hot-bed of death! Is your next door neighbor a thief? Has the bosom on which you recline ever betrayed you? Can you find nothing lovely and nothing pure? If *you* find meanness everywhere, are you sure you do not carry some of it there yourself? You must remember that the paper in the morning which brings you the news of the crops and the decrees of Senators, brings also the accumulated crimes of the civilized world, and as if they were not great enough in themselves, they are not unfrequently embellished and multiplied. I know we have enough. The earth is travelling in agony and the groans of the race are still going up to God, but has nothing been done? Is there no light? And why is there as much darkness as there is, except that you and I have not been better and nobler ourselves; claiming to be sons of God, have not had the *faith* which pertains to the sons of God? While we complain of the crimes and vices and evils of life, does our *faith* lift us above the vanities and follies of the world, into the sunlight of the graces and virtues of the Son of God, into the breadth, and height of the Gospel glory? No, beloved, I believe that every Sunday when we say that "confession," we say the truth: We have erred and strayed like lost sheep. We have followed the devices and desires of our own hearts. We have offended against God's holy laws. "We have left undone the things we ought to have done, and done the things we ought not to have done, and there is no health in us." That is true, and that is the thing God wants in us, *health, faith,* vision of divine things; remembering the words of the Master, you are the salt, you are the light—remembering that one reason why the world is so wicked is partly because we ourselves are so little above it, we ourselves are not much better. We are still of little faith, and therefore not half the power we ought to be. The thing, of all things, which should walk the earth the most hopefully and yet the same time the most *humbly* is the Christian. It is no part of *faith* to be grumbling. You get rid of darkness only by creating light. One thing we want to get rid of, and that is the habit of tying God down to our little grooves and insisting that He shall be there alone. We have faith in dogmatic formula, and Church machinery, which instead of being *vision* are blinds over the vision we might have. That was the sin of the Jew, that is the sin of the Papacy, that is the sin of sect. God is broader than man and the Gospel comprehends the race. You cannot put either of them in your little ism, nor I in mine. Oh! what a light there had been upon earth if we had long ago learned to stretch all ism to the fulness of Christ.

Hear what a thoughtful Japanese said in our country the other day. He is a student in one of our colleges, a fact in itself full of hope. He says: "As I deliberate on the history of Christianity in Western nations, I find precedents which show, that if the Church, as an institution, is established in Japan *before the people are taught the Gospel*, then there will be no social improvement for my people, for the morality and prosperity of nations advance, according to their knowledge and practice of the *specific duties and virtues of the Christian religion as we find it in the New Testament.*" I tell you that man had not studied Christianity in vain. He preaches the Gospel to us. What we want is the power, the principle, the vision, the faith, not the form, or the mere creed, or the sect. If any of us choose to anchor there, the world will pass us by. Neither circumcision availeth anything, nor uncircumcism, but *a new creature*, neither circumcision availeth anything, nor uncircumcision, but *faith which worketh by love, love acting in faith.*

Beloved, believe in God, in Christ, in the Holy Ghost. Believe God is everywhere, and therefore goodness and love. Believe in that. You are going out to-day to the duties and conflicts, the trials and sorrows, the joys and hopes of another year. And how are you going? My dear brother, if you have no faith, if you are working like a mole for a mere existence, you had better never been born. If you see the kingdom of Christ, and are working for *that,* then there is a day of glory for you in the manifestation of the sons of God. I have brought these thoughts to you this morning, that you might go as in the very presence of God, believing this to be God's world, believing yourself to be under His hand, endeavoring to see Him in all that is around you, putting Him in all your work, with a nobler faith, with a manlier trust, consecrating soul and body, intellect and business, pleasure and pain, and all life, to the glory of Him who hath called you, and yearns for you to be near to Him in all holiness. So you will fulfil your mission, so life will give you the best, life can give you a home with God. I know our bark is in the midst of the sea, tossed by the waves; darkness is around us, and we have been toiling all the night. But what of it all! Jesus is on board. His very presence is the pledge that we cannot sink. Presently, He can arise and say "*peace,*" and the waves shall be still, and the storm shall be laid, and we shall be at the haven where we would be. The knowledge of God's perfect and everlasting love, the fullness of the eternal kingdom. Let us have faith.

CONSECRATION TO GOD.

EPHESIANS 5: 1, 2.—Be ye therefore followers of God, as dear children, and walk in love as Christ also hath loved us, and hath given Himself for us, an offering and a sacrifice to God for a sweet-smelling savor.

THE verse before this in the last chapter, reads, "Be ye kind one to another, tender-hearted, forgiving one another, even as God for Christ's sake hath forgiven you," and so this verse follows. Though we gain in the aggregate by having our Scriptures divided into chapters and verses, we sometimes lose somewhat, by cutting a paticular topic in two. Such a loss we in a measure sustain here. The subject of the Apostle in this immediate place, embraces a view of the various relations we sustain to each other, and the spirit we are to exhibit in these relations. He is looking squarely at the fact that we are social beings, which is as emphatically a fact as that we are individuals. We have faculties and properties *by means of* society, and *for* society. We are like the figures which express an arithmetical number. Our values increase or diminish by reason of our place. We have inherent forces of our own, but combination, or society, is the vitality of individual force. "We are members of one another." One coal of fire in a grate goes out. Five hundred coals make a fire. Moral being is so constituted as to demand of us a *conscious recognition* of the moral forces. It has made the cultivation of wise moral forces imperative. Rather, all moral forces are wise, good, holy, and moral being demands of us their recognition and cultivation. When we see facts which indicate immoral forces, we misunderstand the cause of the facts. They actually result from *the absence of a true moral force.* The action of the true moral forces would prevent such results, and place others in their stead. Neglect the moral forces, and you get immorality. Extinguish your light, and you are in the dark. Blot out the sun, and all the earth would freeze. Leave the sun blotted out, and it would appear as if frost itself were positive—when it would only be heat more and more departing. All malice, unkindness, hard-heartedness, are but the want of mercy, sympathy, and love. The world is so bad, because so many of us are no better. One man truly rich is a well-spring of life to his fellow men. All ought to be rich. Christ was infinitely rich. He was the universal Redeemer. *The Christian is rich.* All moral forces are active in him. He is salt. He is light. That is his mission, to build up and keep the moral forces alive. He who does not do it is not a Christian. Any number of Christians, uniting in a given combination, is a Church. But a Church which has lost its moral potency, is a dead Church, no Church at all.

The highest of all moral forces is *love. God is love.* It is impossible to tell *all* that love is. There have been many attempts at defining it. It is not simply "friendship without wings," as I think the French call it. It is not merely *passionate instinct,* as the sensualist conceives. It is not the combination of these two, as some have pronounced it. It appears to be the resultant of a tribute levied upon every faculty and attribute of true moral being. If there is anything of strength, anything of truth, of wisdom, of purity, of unself, it is in love. If there is anything of service, of help, of endurance, it is found in love. If there is anything that *seeks* in restless, untiring sympathy, it is love. If we can take another's place, love can do it. If a desired end is to be accomplished, all things are possible to love. It is that to possess which is to enrich another. It is that which, in proportion as it enriches another, is itself rich. All things depend on God. God alone is perfect love. He loves irrespective of our action—loves *in spite* of our action. "He is kind to the evil and to the good." He so loved the world as to give His only begotten Son to save it. Herein is love, that while we were yet sinners Christ died for us. He forgives us our sins every day whether we ask Him or not, whether we know we are sinners or not. He pities us all the more that we feel not we are sinners, do not seek a knowledge of forgiveness, are not therefore weaned by forgiveness from our sin. This it is to grieve God, that we remain insensible, indifferent to all His love. This it is to disinherit ourselves, to be lost, *not to have the Spirit of God.* This it is to be poor and naked, an object of pity, "*dead* in trespasses and sins." The difference between the righteous and the wicked is not so much in God's feelings toward them as in their feeling toward Him. God cannot hate anybody, or anything. I know the Bible says, "God is angry with the wicked every day." But it cannot be anger as we are angry. That is a weakness, weakness is not in God. Nature is cruel against the man who impiously resists her. Whoever resists her, resists to hi sown costs. Whoever resists God, will find it were better God were angry and would blot him out forever. But *grief* is divine. It is only a rich nature that can pity. It is only the richest nature that can pity most. The glory of our salvation is, our *merit* has nothing to do with it. It is God's free gift in His Son. The best of us are so far from God we have literally nothing to commend us to Him. He has to pity us all, and bears with us from day to day more on account of our desires, than our attainments. He *grieves* over our leanness. We only cease to be pitiable, or an object of grief, as we cease to be sordid selves, as we become like Him, as we have that which is love, as we are above *weakness*, such as anger, envy, unsympathy, pride, selfishness, as we are strong in bearing all things, like a fountain of pure water pouring out health and purity whether the hand that receives it be soiled or clean, as we are a tower of support to the weak and erring, as we prevent what the wicked create, as we neutralize the envy, hatred and malice the unrighteous beget. *Hence, love is the whole duty of man.* Our business upon earth is to cultivate it as a spirit within us, an animus, the presiding force of our being. That is what salvation is, forming our desires in that direction and conforming our lives to those desires. We have nothing to do with other people's actions toward us, except to see that our love is equal to the tests God applies, *through* what we call "providence" *in* this thing we call "society."

When anger begins to rise in a wise man, he does not say the other man is hateful. He says to his own soul, thou art weak. Thou hast something to learn. Hence, "love worketh no ill to his neighbor," however deserving of ill that neighbor may be. It is ill enough that he does deserve it. The visiting of ill is not the work of a holy agent. His work is to prevent ill. Like God, his mission is to roll back evil, to overcome evil with good, that if the wicked will go on in their wickedness they must do it, not by means of us, but in spite of us. We are co-workers with God. Hence, "all the law is fulfilled" in one word, even in this, "Thou shalt love thy neighbor as thyself." So that amid all the combinations of life, and the vexations of society, the wise man asks, not what action his neighbor's conduct *merits*, but what action is worthy of himself. What does his own rule of life prescribe? What would the Saviour have done? It will not do to say this is placing too high a standard for human action. What does the life of Christ mean? What else is a *Christian* life? If Christ's example were nothing, how are we better off with it than we would have been without it? You see noble independence, freedom, soul-strength, looming up there. You see heaven of necessity there. Heaven is the aggregation of the pure, the meek, the strong. This is one of the glories of the incarnation. *It manifests God in action*, HEAVENLINESS. It brings the divine being here to our apprehension, defines the divine nature for us, marks the road to its attainment, does it *here*, not only amid elements which would to all appearance make it impossible, but does it by means of these elements. This is to be a Christian, *to be like Christ;* nothing else. "In this the children of God are manifested and the children of the devil. Whosoever *doeth not righteousness* is not of God, *neither he that loveth not his brother*, for this is the message that we have heard from the beginning, that we love one another." "A new commandment give I unto you that ye love one another *as I have loved you*." "Love ye your enemies, that ye may be the children of your Father which is in heaven."

It can be done by nothing in the world, but by faith in Christ, by strength which God supplies through Christ.

Now, St. Paul says, "Be ye therefore followers of God, as dear children;" more literally, "Be ye imitators of God, or like God, as children beloved. In the family, the child like the father, the child worthy of its parentage, is the true child. "God for Christ's sake hath forgiven you. *Therefore,* be ye followers of God, as dear children, and walk in love, as Christ also hath loved us and *given Himself* for us, *an offering and a sacrifice* for a sweet-swelling savor." To love those only who love us, is not necessarily *to love* at all; we cannot help it, and there is no virtue in it. The publicans do even the same. A child loves its mother, but it would be even below nature if it did not. True love is not only not without our consent, it is a culture. Love that the Apostle speaks of, godly love, religious love, is not the mere parental bond, nor the action of that law of affinities which binds heart to heart in mysterious attachment. It is not mere social respect and worldly politeness, making feasts for those who make feasts for us. "These things are divided unto all people under heaven." It is not *patronizing* those even who cannot make a feast for us, as Simon did toward Christ. All such love is only another form of self-love. When a man makes a great feast and displays all his riches and invites you, it is not the measure of respect he has for you, but the measure of respect he wants you to have for him. Christian love is the spirit, the character, the condition of soul, known more as benevolence and beneficence, aiming at the good of others through that action called *self-sacrifice.* Christian love is curative. It finds employment for our faculties, our skill, any and every talent God has given us. The ills in society, the perverseness of men, the crosses they erect for us, the burdens they impose, are the measure of *unself* there is in us. He only is rich who has something to give. Who can give most is richest of all. There is great force in that idea of which the Romanists retain the perversion, the idea of absolute consecration. With them it is consecration to *the Church*, "to a *religious life*" as they call it—*i. e.*, to a life, not merely of separation, but of seclusion, a life that buries soul and body, that neutralizes every faculty, a paralysis of all spirit. No mortal can pray all the time, or keep his mind constantly fixed upon any topic, especially such as are considered religious, except as he ceases to have a mind. But there is force in the idea of *religious consecration.* The world wants something beside prayers, something more than *technical* religion. It does not want much money nor much machinery. It wants that which is above all price and which never can become mechanical. *It wants manhood, womanhood, moral force, love power,* that which can lift burdens, and kindle thought and love, and give other souls time to breathe, and it wants it not in monasteries and nunneries, but right out in the very press and throng of crippled, needy, suffering men and women. Vicarious sacrifice is the one law of all life. We look with despair upon our fruitless expenditures, upon our complex machineries. Well we may. Soul is the only force that hath life in itself. Christ-life is the only life that quickens. Our churches are magazines of *Christian sentiment.* Our Christian homes are the burial places of soul-force which, if alive, would quicken the world.

I know of a woman to-night, in a damp basement,

struggling with poverty and all the woes of a widow. She has three helpless children. She is fighting with a heroic desperation to keep her children together. I can get money to keep a shelter over her head, but the woman will soon die, die of foul air and poor food, and scanty clothes, and overwork, and above all, of a dreary, aching sense of loneliness. Three orphans will be left for some friendly home-for-friendlessness. And three such orphans! They have not known the comfort of cleanliness. They eat, when they can, not as human beings should, and though that woman would tear out her heart to save them, they know not what love is. There is no *time there* for love. Of all the Christians in this city, there is not one to be a guardian angel to that family, one to sit with that woman as a sister, and sew—one to send a thrill of encouragement through her soul—one to keep her back from the grave, or, by instruction and training, to place her little ones, by and by, above the temptation of vice, and prepare them for a dwelling place with God. An hour's sewing or cleaning there, every day, would be the best prayer that could be offered for her. It would go to her heart. And how many cases are just like hers, and that in a world where so many of us have given ourselves to God, with nothing to do; have taken up the cross, and are called by the name of Christian. Talk of sending women to the women of India. That is all very well, but some of the women of Baltimore need women sent to them. Are not *Christians* the supreme want of our world to-day? Why are there so many ills in society, so much perverseness in men, but that so few of us have love to that degree which can make a sacrifice, love which can give ourselves to prevent wrong and evil, to create wisdom and peace? Do you see the force of what I said, that vicarious sacrifice is the law of life? What erects more crosses and imposes more burdens than ignorance? Go into the slums and dens of any city, and there you see only the resultants of neglect. It is easy enough to censure, and say it is all good enough for them. So said not Christ, respecting ourselves. The love of the Gospel is that love which considers men unfortunate, rather than faulty, which causes us to take the place of the offender, and feel that *we* were there, except that God's love had kept us back, except that some mercy, springing in the sacrifice of a father or mother, or friend, some merciful providence of God, had fallen to our lot. Rowland Hill once stood beside a gallows when an unhappy criminal was launched into eternity. His throbbing ejaculation was, "There swings Rowland Hill, but for the grace of God." What he said was true, and it was the grace of God that taught him to feel it. Down in the sinks of life, are wretches, not there because they want to be there, there because some dark, crushing calamity sent them there; there because no hand was reached down in time to save them; there, as we would have been there, had not some blessing rescued us. They are ourselves, had not God's grace taught us better. What the world wants is rescuing, saving, blessing, Christian personality, real men and women-life. God meant the Christian to be that, somebody to stop the woe, somebody to give life. *Christ did that.* We are content to look down upon men, and not always with pity. We are content to treat them as they deserve. So was not Christ. Evil, sin, wrong, when it assailed Him, just simply exhausted itself. The shaft buried itself in His heart forever. There was an end of it. The anger even of the world's anger, was that it could not anger Him. Oh, the blessing of that God-life then! Make Jesus fall to simple human level, and you blot out Jesus, and all light goes out with Him. Take Him away as our forerunner, and how dark is our prospect! Think that you cannot attain to such a life, or that there is no such life, and you blot out heaven. No device the world had was capable of measuring the love of Christ. He ended all strife by simply letting it exhaust itself. Then, turning *toward* us, He not only exerted His miraculous powers in healing us, He went to *great pains* to do us good. For aught we know, He might have stood in the Great Temple and cured, at a word, every malady in Israel. But He did not do that. He undertook long journeys. He hungered often. He slept on the ground, all to come in direct personal contact with men—all to impart *Himself*. For all that matter, He need not have come at all. He might have set upon a star, and have amazed us by some marvellous act, but then we would have been as far removed from God as ever, for God does that every day. He gave just what we wanted, that which God left us, but that which was to Him sacrifice, that which cost, that which alone to us expresses love. We, in our dealings toward each other, go as far as benevolence is pleasant, go till it begins to cost, till we reach the point where sacrifice is needful. There we stop. We strike ingratitude, and say it is no use. We strike meanness, and say the man is not worth caring for. The very depth of his need we make the very reason for deserting him. Oh, the fathomless riches of the love of God! How the law of life in Christ Jesus sets us free from the law of sin and death! How it is the only law that can do it! How Christianity is the only religion that promises a millenium! How to any other a millenium is impossible! How our world must groan and suffer till we so learn this law, that it shall beat in all our hearts and nerve all our exertions! Do you not see that, one reason why He gave Himself a sacrifice, was, that we might give ourselves a sacrifice, and that *only* in proportion as we do that, is blessing possible for our world?

But this line of life, this law of action is not to be viewed merely in the light of a duty. It is not something *imposed* as a trial. I look upon it as the natural craving of love, that, through which the soul finds relief. It is a great deal better men should do well from fear, than that they should go on doing ill, but whoever carries duty with him everywhere, carries a burden he would do well to roll off, carries that with him which he will never want in heaven. It is true, if every man on earth were up to duty this world would be brighter than it is, but if every Christian were only no higher, it would be vastly darker. This love is not to be worked out of mere conscience, conscience is a good thing but it does not range over the upper stories, the love-chambers of our being. It is very limited, and very thin, and whoever is clothed only in that will feel cold. I cannot imagine that conscience sent Paul in a blaze of light over a known world. Conscience could have staid at Rome or Ephesus, could have made him tolerably comfortable in Athens, nor was it anything like the mere hope of reward. That in itself is but another form of selfishness, and is itself to lose the reward. *The reward of love is the soul itself which love creates, or transforms into her own image.* The child that greets you in the morning with a kiss *because* it *must be* respectful, or that would purchase thereby some little indulgence, would not be the child that would most please you. But the child who, all unconscious of self, found itself happy in your embraces, and flew there because it was relief to get there, that is the child that loves you. The charm of love is its unconsciousness of itself. Whenever you find an individual, or an institution, or a church spreading itself in long reports like a business advertisement, you have evidence of disease rather than of health; you have not that spirit which uttered itself so constantly in Christ, "see thou tell no man." Nothing but love can fill up and overflow even the measure of duty. Nothing but love made Christ upon the roadside in Israel, at Gethsemene, and upon Calvary, a possibility. To such love only all things are possible. It is the one invincible force. It can remove mountains. Oh, the mountains it has removed! Knowing nothing itself of sacrifice, its action is spontaneous. Its yoke is easy. Its burden is light. God's love! No man can tell it. Jesus Christ is its only perfect expression.

Walk in love, as Christ also hath loved us and given Himself for us—an offering and a sacrifice to God for a "sweet-smelling savor." How such a life would go up as an evening sacrifice! It seems strange the Apostle should set before us, so frail, a model so high. And yet how strange it would be if he did not. How it is we treat all such Scriptures as figurative, and *therefore unmeaning*. What said Christ Himself? "Be *ye perfect as* your Father in Heaven is perfect." Not perfect *up to* your Father's perfection, but perfect *as*—not perfect as the Pharisee was perfect—as the Mahomedan is perfect, as any self-righteousness is perfect, but perfect *as* God is perfect, *as* Christ was perfect, perfect in love. "Be ye holy, for I am holy." Love your enemies. Do good, and lend, *hoping* for nothing again, and your reward shall be great." Read the sixth chapter of Luke. Read the Sermon on the Mount. Contemplate Christ Himself. Contemplate Heaven—the archangels, the cherubim, and seraphim—the beings that have been developing there through ages before our world was built; how can we ever dwell with them? "Your reward shall be great." Can we then make any sacrifice? What are the sacrifices of God? That which crucifies all we do not need. That which develops all in which a soul can be rich. You have knowledge, and impart it. The simple act brightens the knowledge you have, and magnifies it. You have time. You give it to some poor soul that hath no helper. One hour buys for you more enjoyment than a life-time of idleness. You have money. You take the burden from some poor heart, and you find it the best investment you ever made. The Apostles gave their lives, and more than any men they have gained immortality. *They have saved their lives.* Such are God's sacrifices—the multiplication of all good. Such is the mystery of goodness—such the alchemy of love. You read of the day which shall manifest the Sons of God. Christ often spoke of it. You read of rewards. As sure as we live at all, the day will come which shall divide us as a shepherd divideth his sheep from the goats. Salvation is not a fixed quantity. One star differeth from another star in glory.

It is this line of thought, I think, the Apostle wants to bring out for us, this higher life, this life of unself, of *consecration* to God. I do not know what to say to those of you who have never entered it, not perhaps *thought* much about it. I do not know what life can mean to you. The most expressive words of the language, love, eternity, God—the most wonderful facts of time, religion, Christ, the cross—what do they mean? Life, death, immortality, do they mean bread and clothes and indulgence, and three-score years and ten? Is that all? Think of these things. Herein is part of the love of Jesus. It comes to seek you, to rouse you, to make you sensible of your opportunity. "Awake, thou that sleepest, and Christ will give thee light." But none of us are as sensible as we ought to be. Every day is laying great golden chances at our feet and we are trampling over them. We are praying every day for a higher life, but *God will give us Himself, only as we give ourselves to Him.* That is the law of religion. The measure of the divine life *in* you, is exactly the measure you have of this divine life. "Who hath the Son of God hath life. Who hath not the Son of God hath not life." The measure of the Son of God we have is the measure of life we have. "Call me not Lord, if you do not the things I say. He that heareth these sayings of mine and *doeth them* builds a house that shall never fall." Therefore let us take heed to our alms, to our charities, our duties, our labors of love, our time, our whole life. Let us be sure that in our giving we reach the giving point, the point where we *feel* we are giving. Let us be sure that every day somebody in this world is better off for our being in it. Let us not forget it is *ourselves,* a divine personality this world most wants. That is what Christ gave. "*He gave Himself.*" That is faith to do as He did. That is part of God's love too that He gave us such a blessing, a being around whom our comprehension can fasten, toward whom our affections can go out, in whom our hopes can center, whom the more we know Him, the more we love Him, and with respect to whom, if we have anything to deplore, it is that we are so far from Him. May we have grace to do as Paul bids us. Be followers of God as *dear children,* not as hired servants. Then so far our prayer will be answered. God's Kingdom will come. His will be done on earth as it is in heaven.

THE LONG HEREAFTER.

JOB 3: 17.—There the wicked cease from troubling, and there the weary are at rest.

IT has been conjectured by some that since the composition of the book of Job is poetry, no such man as Job ever really existed. But whether any man called Job ever lived or not, certain it is some man lived who had the experiences ascribed to Job, or else such a book were impossible. Though it is a book of poetry it is very far from being a book of picture, and though we may not be in the habit of considering truth generally poetic, it is very certain that all real poetry is truth.

To an unskillful reader, this third chapter of Job presents much to shock, perhaps much to offend. Job curses the day in which he was born and reproaches every agency which lent its aid to give him being. To a sensitive mind it all reflects upon the Great Creator, and our first wonder is how any man, reputed a good man, could ever have fallen into such a sin. He envies those who had passed into oblivion, and it is of the grave, with a longing to be there, he utters the words of the text: "There the wicked cease from troubling, and there the weary are at rest."

He whose life has presented no crisis which sends him down to the depths of his being, cannot in any proper sense be called a man. He who in the presence of the great struggle, with every faculty of his being under tribute to sustain him, has not had thoughts of the vanity of life similar to those of Job, must have been something more, or something less than mortal. The very gist of this life is to define to man moral existence, to define man to himself, and he knows not himself or any man who does not know the darkness and helplessness inherent in our creature being, who does not know God to be the strength and fullness of being, and the service of God the sum of all blessing. To *know* this every height and every depth of our whole nature must be laid open, and while it is true, the wise shall inherit glory, it is also true we can be made perfect only through suffering, and so, in the life of all the wise as in that of Job, whom the Lord loveth, He chasteneth, and because He loves us all, He chastens all.

This life, thus being to us nothing more than a school, or process of preparation for life, our circumstances, position and belongings, are no certain indication of what *we really are.* They cannot define a man any more than tools can define a workman. Books do not make a *wise* man. An army cannot make a general. At best our circumstances, position and belongings only define what kind of man we are. It is only *character* vitalizes life, and the man is written upon his actions just as the skill of the painter stands above the colors upon the canvas, or the genius of the architect above the pile he rears. To know him you must see him in combination. For him to know himself he must be placed where passion, interest and motive, grapple in conflict. There you discover him a selfish man, a crafty man, a worldly man, a bad man, or you know him, a useful man, an honest man, a benevolent man, a holy man. A reference to one side or the other, whether we are conscious of it or not, works in all our actions and in all our estimates of action. In the vigils of the night, it is the goodness or badness of a man which presses itself upon our ruminating souls. Over our grave every friend and every foe, if they have really known us, pronounce in the silent convictions of their soul our real character. More especially is it the case, as years recede, as passions die, as material and deceptive belongings disappear, history, human conviction, writes our names upon the page of life, or upon the page of death. What did he for his race? Did he stand upon the side of wisdom? Was he a tower of strength or only a snare? Was he a son of God, or a son of the devil? All the vocations, all the pretences, all the achievements of man, dwindle him down, or lift him up to one or other of these. So, I say, this life is a school, a preparation, a probation.

Its benevolent design in God, was to make us conscious of moral being, to fit us for a higher and a better life. It is to take us out of darkness into light, out of weakness into strength. At first sight, all nature seems to be against us. Every step of our life confronts us with some real or imaginary danger. But over and above the hostility of simple nature, the prevailing conduct of men makes moral existence seem to be based upon a series of contradictions, and thus to render moral virtues impossible. How can a man be unselfish where every man is eager only after his own? Who can be humble, where humility is only another name for being trodden under foot? Who can be temperate, where every element within us or without us, lures us to indulgence? Who can be charitable, where all around us is envy, hatred and malice, and all uncharitableness? To lie down, and drift with nature and this world, is easy. Men will flatter us when we do as they do. They will make that enviable which they consider so desirable, and it seems as though the human race had conspired to banish real wisdom and holiness from the earth. They apply God-given names to things of human creation. They admit the existence of virtue, and then define what virtue is, and you know that even religion itself is a very good thing, provided it is only a name. But, let it assume a real shape, let it attempt to pull down the vail of sin which hangs as a covering over the face of this mortality, and you array against you every faculty and passion of man. To all human appearance, to be wise is certainly to be very foolish, for the wisdom of God is foolishness with man; and hence it is, all the wise have had to contend at every step against all the missiles of contempt and ridicule, or at least, if the world does not despise and laugh at them, it assumes every attitude of composure and self-importance the more condescendingly to pity them. The wicked have never ceased from troubling, and this side of absolute glory, they never will.

But these means of grace, otherwise these apparent

hostilities to glorified being, do not stop here. Our dangers are not only from without, they are also from within. When all our faculties unite in what we might call self-possession, when our surroundings present a fixed and reliable platform, we are to a great extent delighted with action. By some means man delights in achieving, and we can undertake as readily on God's side as any other, provided also the doing will exalt us. A great many men never stop to define their action, whether it be truly for God's glory, or only another phase of their selfishness. Hence, so many works are consecrated to God, with which God has nothing to do. They are wrought in our pride, and for our glory, and the sacred name of God is only a covering to conceal a secret selfishness. How many battles are fought and very generally applauded, when the truth would have more generally prevailed, had there been no battle at all. How easy it is to fight, when a crowd of spectators urge us on! How easy to long for a great fortune and a great position with which to serve God. But the greatness we want, and which this world wants, is not that of great fortune or great position, nothing after the pattern of our vain plans or hopes. So God causes to come in other agencies, realities contingent upon our creature nature. They make our plans to fail. Hope after hope is laid in the dust. The pride of our eyes and lusts of our hearts are removed far away. Disease touches these bodies. Paralysis creeps over our faculties, and so weary is the flesh, life itself becomes a burden. The very trial we would be spared is the very trial sent to us. The very element in life which is bitter, is the very element pressed home to our lips. Then, like Job, we begin to think life is a vanity, evil is the day in which we were born. Then, like Job, we take to another delusion, and wish very ardently to die. You know how common this is, in affliction, in weakness, to wish very piously to depart. But what of our service to God! Suppose this is God's will—suppose He wishes us truly to know whether we love Him for His own sake—suppose there be one more speck of selfishness not yet extracted—suppose He has some virtue to reveal, the power of His grace, which only our helplessness can bring out. Are we willing, and while we wait, realize that he who waits still serves. While nature asks that the cup shall pass away, shall grace exclaim, "Not my will but thine be done." So, that while the wicked cease not to trouble, here the weary cannot rest.

This is the design of this life to take us out of darkness into light—out of weakness into strength—out of selfishness wholly into God. He is blessed who is tried. Job, in his time, was probably the only man to whom his trials could be sent. God, in mercy, sometimes does not disturb us. The chastening would only crush us, and not bless us. We ought to thank God. He does not leave us to ourselves. We ought to pray to Him that our life-action be not the resultant of mere habit, or position, or restraint; that our neighbor's life be not the measure of ours; that we may not seek our own, but only the things of Christ. Then our lives would not be ill-defined; our notions of being would not be confused—our hopes of the future would not be dim, nor in their nature unreal. It is to be feared when we enter the circles of disembodied spirits our whole thoughts will undergo revolution, and very much of disappointment will greet us. Of course no vicious being can enter Heaven. But neither can we conceive of a useless or selfish being there. Heaven is not the abode of those who would never have gone there if they could have helped it, nor of those who would only go there to escape a service elsewhere; nor of those who want to go there only in the name of Heaven to narrow Heaven down to themselves. Heaven is a place of universal service—service transcendently high and solemn and important—service, the very doing of which is reward, and for which only a holy soul is fitted. "Then the wicked cease from troubling," that is true; "Then the weary are at rest," that is true; but, oh, it is going home, and home, you know, is not where nothing is to be done. It is not inertia, but rest, which admits of much action. It is wholly the service of love—a service never of restraint or expediency, only of the conviction that what serves not God can be no exaltation to the creature. It is service only of the great and noble, who, out of all the trials and battles of life, have proved themselves the sons of God.

You read in the Bible of Heaven, it is true; but what of Heaven? Does it not sometimes seem strange Christ Jesus did not reveal to us more of that land of rest? But does it not, also, occur to you at the same time He did reveal all that by any possibility could be revealed? You know no words of ours can portray anything beyond our experience. If you speak of love, I understand you according to my idea of love. When a man tells you there is no love in the world, he only tells you he never had any. You will observe certain symbols are used to illustrate, but only to illustrate; knawing worms, and fires, and stripes represent loathsomeness and pains beyond which our conceptions cannot go. Thrones, and songs of triumph, and festal joys represent powers and emotions in a degree beyond which this sphere furnishes no illustration.

So, on the other hand, Heaven is oftener spoken of with reference to what it is not, than with reference to what it is. "There the wicked shall cease from troubling." "All tears shall be wiped away." "Sorrow and sighing flee away." "There is no night there, nothing to deceive or make a lie." Beyond all doubt God's moral government is one. All moral being is one. We shall have the same universe around us, and the same faculties within us. When these bodies are renovated and spiritualized there will be joys for us through every avenue it furnishes to our souls. Borne upon the wings of our volition, other worlds will present beauties transcending those of our own, if that were possible. There can be no prison-house for the redeemed. God's great nature will outspread in combinations to charm and electrify the eye. Every element, animate or inanimate, will be vocal with a music to delight the ear. Every presentation of every world will be the starting point of thought, and mind will dwell in all mysteries, because every mystery solved will reveal God—highest joy of all the exercise of all holy affection. Love will be the one essence of all essences, the nectar drop which will sweeten the cup of all being, chiefest of all, the love of God. What that means I cannot tell. I sometimes wonder whether all prayer will cease in Heaven. It seems to me no soul can possibly comprehend God, and till it does, no soul can cease its longings, and the sweetness of longing seems to me the sweetest a soul can know. It will not be a longing which will know no gratification. So far from it, we shall know more and more of God, but the more we know, the more to me it seems impossible we should cease to long. Longing will be alleviated by doing and acquiring. Hence I say we shall have our work, every work with its object and every object combining also in it our co-workers. Our love there for the saints is not to be a miscellaneous, unmeaning sentiment. It is to be general and universal, true—*i. e.*, there will be no unlove, no envy, no malice. There will be none we cannot love, but it is while general to be also particular, *e. g.*, our Saviour was a heavenly being. He loved all men. He especially loved His Apostles. He emphatically loved John, chose him for a closer intercourse and a sweeter communion.

We, too, shall have our kindred and more congenial spirits bound to us in every sympathy. I think we shall differ there as we differ here. Not all souls will possess every characteristic in the same degree. Just as we know each other here better than words can express, better than our visible features betray, just as we select souls here, because of their responsiveness to our own, so there we shall have home-spots in our inner being for kindred and chosen loves. That home-spot will always be theirs. We will never betray them. They will never desert us. Think of that! They wlll understand us. Affection will entwine with affection, hope with hope, and purpose with purpose, till revolving cycles shall find us almost one. I sometimes think our circles there are to be something of our circles here, which may be added to but never taken from. The thought that we are to know each other in that world, admits of no question. Mutual recognition is a necessity. Every relation we have sustained here is to have its fruition there. All this is not conjecture. You remember when Christ had risen, He had His same body, the print of the nails was in His hands, the rent of the spear was in His side. When John, in a glorified vision, saw the glories of that heavenly world, he saw one "like to the Son of Man." That Son of Man to John was none other than that crucified Jesus—that meek and lowly Saviour. To His people, I believe He will always be He who tabernacled with men, who was crowned with thorns; that look of compassion, that yearning tenderness, that furrowed brow, they will always be radiant with a love which only God could know, when He stood transfigured upon the Mount, when He assumed a heavenly aspect to commune with heavenly beings—He was the same Jesus, only clothed in light. Moreover, there met Him, Moses and Elias, not persons looking *like* Moses and Elias simply, but Moses and Elias looking as they had looked in their mortality. Yes, we shall know each other. Jesus said He was going to prepare a place for us, that where He was there we might be, and if we are all with Him, then we must all be together. Next to the joy of laying our crowns at that Saviour's feet and joining in the song of the blessed, will be the joy of seeing all, and being with our loved ones gone before. Yes, contemplate the blessed remains—those sainted mothers, those angel babes, those cherished friends; oh, joys transporting, to be with thee, to know no more languishing, no more parting, no more shadows to fall across our lives, no wicked there to sow discord or trouble, no weary bodies to betray us into impatience. We shall be joined to ours and they to theirs, generation to generation, circle to circle. The saints of all ages will be there, the glorious company of the Apostles, the goodly fellowship of the Prophets, the noble army of martyrs, in peace and good will; sorrows all past, wicked all gone, no purposes thwarted, nobody to offend—Christ Jesus forever King, rewards only begun, our works following us, reminiscences from this earth will float to us there, kind words and holy deeds will live once more. All whom we have blessed in the name and for the sake of Christ, all who have blessed us, whether we have known them or not—mysteries will be cleared up, and this poor world will be a poor world no longer. It will have given us treasure in heaven. I believe we shall love it, love to think of it. It shall be God's world, Christ will have been upon it. We shall have been upon it. Here we were redeemed, and have learned to call God our Father and Christ our Saviour.

One thing, however, gives us pause. Shall we miss none we have loved, over whom we have prayed? Shall we search with no anxiety among all the blessed, for one more soul not yet found? Possibly not. If that name be not written upon the Lamb's Book of Life, we shall know God knew best. We shall not simply submit, but acquiesce in His will. We shall know that we ourselves could not love what loved not God. But this is what will trouble us. Suppose, with respect to that soul we have been delinquent. Suppose, in our earth relations, we knew not our privileges as children of God. Suppose my worldliness has misled that soul, or my neglect has caused it to wander out of the way, though saved myself, will there be no regrets? Will no pensive hour creep upon me—no shadow ever rest upon my spirit? Or, when I see the very faithful far up in glory, radiant with a light and joy unknown to me, light and joy of a devotion here in which I did not share; when I look back and realize how good was God in putting blessing in my path, from which I turned away, because it looked like trial—when I think of the poor, and struggling, and careworn, I forgot, just as Dives forgot Lazarus, of the children of ignorance I might have instructed, of the heathen I might have helped to enlighten, of the hours I might have cheered and the homes I might have blessed, of a benedicite here and a cup of cold water there. Shall no sigh escape me, when I think the opportunities are gone, all gone forever? I know the Scriptures say, sorrow and sighing shall flee away, but that means the agencies or causes of sorrow and sighing are to flee away. I cannot conceive how all regrets are to pass away, for nothing dies from the human mind. All memory will live. I cannot imagine that Eli can forget his children, or that Peter can ever cease to remember how he deceived his Lord, or ever recall it with anything but grief. I know that no soul in heaven will ever tell me of my fault. Oh, no; there will be charity there to cover all my faults, and Jesus will forgive—but oh, can I ever forget? Oh, brethren, our little animosities and strifes, our bickerings and judgings, our hard thoughts and little selfishnesses, are they to live there? When we sit down to count over our earth pilgrimage will these too come up? Are we even there, among the blessed, to be sometimes ashamed, and looking each other in the face, mindful of our formalities, insincerity and heartlessness, are we to be mantled in humiliation? I say this troubles me. But do not such thoughts as these explain to us much of Scripture, much our dear Master told us, much which we so often forget? Do you not perceive how it is, we are to reap as we sow—how it is, in that world one star differeth from another star in glory, how heaven grows out of, and is consequent upon this earth, and how there will be most heaven there, when there has been most heaven here? Do you not understand what Christ means, when He says, Lay up for yourselves treasure in heaven, when He tells us to watch, to strive, to love even our enemies, to govern even our secret thoughts, because there is nothing secret which shall not be manifested, and nothing hid which shall not be revealed? Do you not see how all deception, of every sort or degree, is cheating nobody at last, but ourselves? Can you not understand blessed are the pure in heart, the meek, the merciful, the hungering and thirsting after righteousness? Can you not see how it is, this life of trial, this life of sorrow and sickness, where the wicked trouble and the weary cannot rest, is to prove that blessed record, "He that now goeth forth *sorrowing*, bearing *precious* seed, shall doubtless come again *with joy, bringing* his *sheaves* with him? Can you not see how this life is a strange and solemn existence, how every event, or incident, or belonging, is a special providence for *us*, and every providence a golden opportunity? What need there is of diligence, vigilance and prayer, to walk so that we too may be meet and fit for the enjoyment of the saints in light.

You perceive, then, brethren, the force of what I tell you; this life is a probation—a crucible to test your real being. You see how nature and Providence are to act upon us; but, above all, how, as moral agents, we are to act upon nature and Providence, and out of the elements of every-day life here to build up a true life for the long hereafter. You see that when God asks us to serve and glorify Him, He asks us to lay up blessedness for ourselves. You see to whom and to whom alone that other world is a world of releasement—a world of rest. You see the thing for us is not to wish to die so much as to be prepared·for Heaven.

Now, these thoughts are peculiarly appropriate to us to-day. In the providence of God we are brought to the last Sunday of our expiring year, with all its record is nearly gone to be registered upon the Book of God *for* us or *against* us. To review it is a duty; for, to sum it up, is to sum up our whole life. It is only the resultant of all that have gone before. I do not ask you what your vocation or position in life is. Now, is it a wrong thing if, in that vocation and position, you have been diligent? The economy of this life is something. It is unjust, and the man who has not been faithful in that which is less, will never have opportunity to be faithful in that which is much. I ask only in your vocation and position what are you? What is the spirit which pervades your life and gives you character as a man, as a member of society, as a Christian? Have the precepts and example—have the incarnation and the passion of the Saviour—has Christ's blessed Gospel made you a child of God. In the allotments of Providence, have joy and prosperity made you more thankless and selfish—more worldly and thoughtless? Have the losses and adversities, the sorrows and bereavements, made you more humble, more submissive, more trustful. Pressed at every step by cares, and trials, and responsibilities, do you realize they are sent of God--that He alone is your strength. Or, left in loneliness and helplessness, do you feel that Christ is tenfold your friend? Does one holy hope nestle in your heart to-day which nestled not there a year ago? Has there been over your life this year a halo of sweetness and blessedness unknown to other years. In your houses have you brought your children nearer to God? Do they feel to-day that you realize how you are only a pilgrim and sojourner here—that you are seeking the golden city with a longing to be there, and one other longing that they, too, in God's time, may come to be with you. In our social and civil circles for the young, and ignorant, and helpless, does there, by our exertion, prevail one beneficent influence which last year did not give? Are our means, our talents, our lives, consecrated to God and His glory? And, if men do not know, does God know; are our prayers registered in Heaven? Have we been upon God's side, or upon the side of ourselves only and the world? I think sometimes, when we enter the abodes of the blest, the first thing they will ask us is: "Where was our post in the great struggle of earth? how speeds the great fight?" They are waiting till this world is wholly redeemed. They are waiting for that hour. All that enter there have been soldiers of the cross. They have had their battles; they have fallen in the fight, and now they have their story to tell—a story of interest to every saint—because it has helped to swell the great victory of the Son of God. Our story will soon have to be told. My brother, where is thy post? How speeds the fight so far as your conflict goes? You see how short the time is; as you judge to-day upon the end of a year, so you will soon judge upon the end of this life. In your business you can only stand a little longer. In your pleasures and estates your name will soon cease to mingle. Christian, at your post, whether of doing or suffering, you shall soon be relieved. This very year how many have gone from us—some leaving us rich memories and blessed hopes—memories that lighten our steps along the road, and hopes that beckon us on to the bosom of peace and of God. It is meet we should remember them, for I do not believe they cease to be mindful of us. It is meet we should thank God for their good examples, and to pray Him that with them we may be partakers of His heavenly Kingdom. Let us, then, brethren, with such thoughts as these, let us realize what life is, that God is over it all; that our good is designed in it all. Let us, brethren, so fill up all our years in all holiness, that in our time we go not like one "who wraps the drapery of his couch about him, and lies down to pleasant dreams;" but who shakes off the shadows of night and wakes to the joys and privileges of the eternal day—like him who casts off all dreams and wakes to the bright and eternal reality. Our home is where the wicked cease from troubling and the weary are at rest; our abode is no longer a tabernacle, but a mansion in the golden city, where the saints of all ages are—where the throne of the Saviour is—where love and peace, and rest, shall reign forever and ever.

www.ingramcontent.com/pod-product-compliance
Lightning Source LLC
LaVergne TN
LVHW020219110826
845151LV00003B/761

* 9 7 8 1 4 2 5 5 3 3 0 5 2 *